Patrick Leigh Fermor

Patrick Leigh Fermor is of English and Irish descent. After his stormy schooldays, followed by his walk across Europe to Constantinople, he lived and travelled in the Balkans and the Greek Archipelago acquiring a deep interest in languages and remote places.

He joined the Irish Guards, became a liaison officer in Albania, fought in Greece and Crete where, during the German occupation, he returned three times (once by parachute). Disguised as a shepherd he lived for over two years in the mountains, organising the resistance, and led the party that captured and evacuated the German Commander, General Kreipe. He was awarded the DSO and OBE, was made Honorary Citizen of Heraklion, and later of Kardamyli and Gytheion. He is a Corresponding Member of the Athens Academy.

He now lives partly in Greece in the house he designed with his wife Joan in an olive grove in the Mani, and partly in Worcestershire.

Artemis Cooper

Artemis Cooper is the author of *Cairo in the War 1939–1945* and other highly acclaimed books.

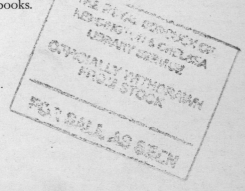

Also by Patrick Leigh Fermor

The Traveller's Tree (1950)
The Violins of Saint-Jacques (1953)
A Time to Keep Silence (1957)
Mani (1958)
Roumeli (1966)
A Time of Gifts (1977)
Between the Woods and the Water (1986) ✓
Three Letters from the Andes (1991)

Words of Mercury

Patrick Leigh Fermor

Edited by Artemis Cooper

JOHN MURRAY

Text © Patrick Leigh Fermor
Introduction and editorial matter © Artemis Cooper 2003

First published in 2003 by John Murray (Publishers)
A division of Hodder Headline

Paperback edition 2004

1 3 5 7 9 10 8 6 4 2

The moral right of the author has been asserted

A CIP catalogue record for this title is available from the British Library

ISBN 0 7195 6106 X

Typeset in Garamond by Servis Filmsetting Ltd, Manchester

Printed and bound in Great Britain by Clays Ltd, St Ives plc

Hodder Headline's policy is to use papers that are natural, renewable and recyclable
products and made from wood grown in sustainable forests. The logging and
manufacturing processes are expected to conform to the environmental regulations of
the country of origin.

John Murray (Publishers)
338 Euston Road
London
NW1 3BH

The young Patrick Leigh Fermor on the island of Ithaca in 1946.

Photo Joan Leigh Fermor

FOR JOAN

'The words of Mercury are harsh
after the songs of Apollo'
Love's Labour's Lost

Contents

Contents

PEOPLE

Contents

Introduction

Soon the delighted cry of '*Delphinia!*' went up: a school of dolphins was gambolling about half a mile further out to sea. They seemed to have spotted us at the same moment, for in a second half a dozen of them were tearing their way towards us, all surfacing in the same parabola and plunging together as if they were in some invisible harness. Soon they were careering alongside and round the bows and under the bowsprit, glittering mussel-blue on top, fading at the sides through gun-metal dune-like markings to pure white, streamlined and gleaming from their elegant beaks to the clean-cut flukes of their tails. They were beautiful abstractions of speed, energy, power and ecstasy leaping out of the water and plunging and spiralling and vanishing like swift shadows, each soon to materialize again and sail into the air in another great loop so fast that they seemed to draw the sea after them and shake it off in mid air . . .

These are the opening lines of a passage from *Mani* on dolphins which readers of Patrick Leigh Fermor come back to again and again, for the sheer joy of it. There are other favourite passages too: the discovery of Byron's slippers at Missolonghi, the description of the Munich Hofbräuhaus, the crowning of the last Emperor of Byzantium – each one displaying the breadth of his learning, his extraordinary memory, and the dazzling quality of his prose.

The purpose of this volume is to put these passages alongside introductions, reviews, memoirs and articles that Paddy* has written over the years. The book covers the whole range of his writing. It will be welcomed by his legions of admirers, and forms a perfect introduction for those who are not yet familiar with his work.

Paddy's irrepressible exuberance made him a noisy and unruly schoolboy, yet he did not dislike learning – in fact (with the exception of

---

* At the risk of sounding over-familiar, 'Paddy' – the name by which he is known to friends and fans alike – will be used rather than the over-formal 'Leigh Fermor'.

mathematics) he devoured it. An avid reader from an early age, he developed a passion for history, poetry, and languages both living and dead in the course of his rather disjointed school life.

His last school was King's, Canterbury, from which he was sacked for holding hands with the greengrocer's daughter. After this he was sent to a crammer in London, with the idea of preparing him for Sandhurst and a career in the army. This plan did not last long, for Paddy decided instead to walk from the Hook of Holland to Constantinople. It proved to be a turning point in his life, and the best education he could ever have had.

Starting in December 1933, at the age of eighteen, Paddy walked through the snowbound Netherlands, and spent his nineteenth birthday in Austria. Travelling as rough as possible, he slept in barns and hostels, with shepherds, bargemen or pedlars for company. However, a friend's letter in Munich brought him into contact with the landed gentry and country-house owners of central Europe. He must have been a popular guest, for those he stayed with never failed to send him on his way with letters of introduction to friends and relatives further along his route.

The aristocracy of Europe were still living the life that they had lived a hundred years before, sitting squarely in the middle of their estates which were still farmed by oxen and peasants. It was a pleasant life, but monotonous. The appearance of a charming young tramp in travel-stained clothes was a welcome distraction – all the more so when he appeared so delighted and intrigued with everything around him. One can imagine the pleasure of these kind grandees as Paddy listened eagerly to their stories, immersed himself in their family histories, quizzed them on the local dialects and customs of the region, and spent hours in their libraries reading everything he could lay his hands on. Yet one must not imagine that his journey was spent simply swanning from one schloss to another. There were still plenty of nights spent in barns and monasteries, in inns and hostels, in caves and sheepfolds, on people's sofas and under the stars.

Although Paddy kept notebooks of his travels, he did not publish an account of his first journey until many years later. So when *A Time of Gifts* appeared in 1977 and *Between the Woods and the Water* in 1986, the life of the mid-thirties that he describes had been utterly destroyed, and much of the land he had walked over had been in the grip of communism for years. Yet his memory recreates this world with an astonishing freshness and immediacy, and recaptures the young man he was then: full of curiosity, optimism and joy in the vibrant diversity of the world.

Paddy finally reached Constantinople on New Year's Day, 1935, and then moved south into Greece. He spent his twentieth birthday in a monastery on Mount Athos. In Macedonia, a few months later, he took part in a royalist campaign against rebellious republican troops which ended in a dashing cavalry charge across a bridge over the river Struma. By now, Paddy had fallen in love with Greece. He learnt the language and, over the next few years, roamed the country.

It was in Athens that he met the first great love of his life, the Rumanian Balasha Cantacuzène. They both wanted to get away from the city – he to write, she to paint; and for many months they lived in an old water mill surrounded by lemon groves, looking out towards the island of Poros. They could not live at the mill for ever; and when the time came to go, Balasha suggested that they move to the house she shared with her sister Hélène in Moldavia, the north-ernmost province of Rumania, and the home of this branch of the Cantacuzène princes for generations.

The house was called Baleni, and it is lovingly described in this volume. Here Paddy spent the last years before the war, interspersed with visits to England and France. He was at Baleni when war was declared, and he immediately went back to London to join up. Paddy and Balasha did not meet again till long after the war.

Prompted by his dash of Irish blood, Paddy enlisted in the Irish Guards; but the War Office had marked him out as a fluent Greek speaker, and he was commissioned into the Intelligence Corps. In the winter of 1940 he served as British liaison officer to the Greek army fighting the Italians in Albania. After the fall of Greece his unit moved to the island of Crete, where Paddy took part in the battle against the German airborne invasion. After the Germans captured Crete, Paddy became one of the handful of SOE officers whose job it was to coordinate the various resistance units on the island.

Paddy spent a year and a half in Crete, dressed as a mountain shepherd. He returned to Cairo at the time of the Italian surrender, bringing the Italian divisional commander with him. A few months later he was parachuted back into the island, in command of the Anglo-Cretan team which planned and carried out the abduction of General Kreipe in April 1944. This meticulously planned operation, carried out under the noses of the Germans, earned Paddy the DSO. *Ill Met by Moonlight*, written by Paddy's friend and second in command Bill Stanley Moss and published in 1950, describes the abduction; it was later made into a film starring Dirk Bogarde. Paddy has never published his account of that time, but this volume contains an extract of a report he wrote many years later, which has not appeared before.

That same year, 1950, saw the publication of Paddy's first book *The Traveller's Tree*, about the travels he had made in the Caribbean in 1947–8. *The Traveller's Tree* won the Heinemann Foundation Prize for Literature, and established Paddy as a writer of remarkable talent. At the same time, *Ill Met by Moonlight* confirmed him as a war hero, at a time when men were very much judged by what sort of a war they had had. He embodied the Renaissance idea of a man of action who is also a scholar. It was a romantic image that his looks, charm and natural buoyancy made all the more engaging.

Paddy makes friends easily; and one of the joys of his company is that he talks just as he writes. Around a convivial table, he would at first be no more than one voice among many. Then, sparked by a single idea, sometimes even a single word, he would be off, in pursuit of a trail only he could follow. Leaping up to find a reference in Shakespeare or Sir Thomas Browne he would plunge across, say, sixteenth-century Europe, raising the shades of princes and cardinals, creating fantastic castles in the air, pausing to admire a bend in the Danube before diving into a maze of linguistic analogies, which might end with a chunk of Browning recited from memory or his own translation of 'Widdecombe Fair' into Italian. These extraordinary monologues, verbal roller-coasters that leave his audience dazzled and exhilarated, are completely spontaneous and unrehearsed. He has what the Cretans call *leventeiá* – a charm and zest for life that other, duller folk can only envy.

To hear him talk one might think that his writing must come easily, but it does not. Writing for Paddy has always been a laborious process, every draft being rewritten and corrected over and over until it reaches his own high standard. In his youth he wrote in cheap hostelries, the houses of friends, ruined castles, anywhere where there was a room with a table and not too many distractions. It was the urge to find a quiet place to write that led him to stay in a number of monasteries, including the beautiful Benedictine monastery of Saint-Wandrille in Normandy. His experience of the monastic life was the subject of his next book *A Time to Keep Silence*. And four years later, in 1956, he published his only novel *The Violins of Saint-Jacques*, which was made into an opera by Malcolm Williamson.

His travels in Greece, begun when he was twenty-one, continued through the late 1940s and 50s. Often accompanied by the photographer Joan Rayner (née Eyres Monsell) whom he first met in Cairo during the war and was later to marry, Paddy explored the remotest parts of Greece: by bus, or mule, or on foot. Between journeys they lived in Greece for months at a time, usually on the island of Euboea, or on Hydra, in the house of the painter Nico Ghika.

Paddy's very personal view of Greece is described in two books which have become classics: *Mani*, published in 1958, and *Roumeli* in 1966. Mani is the southernmost part of Greece. When Paddy explored it, it was known as an inhospitable wilderness of parched rock and blinding sun where only the most back-breaking toil permitted a few hardy peasants to eke out a living. Through Paddy's eyes, the Mani comes vividly to life. The Maniots with their towered villages, their deadly vendettas (sons of the family were called 'guns'), their ancient customs and long history, their struggles against the Turks and their piratical past, become heroic figures in a landscape that, for all its harshness, is also wonderfully beautiful.

Paddy and Joan decided to settle in the Mani. After a long search they found the perfect place, on a little promontory overlooking a bay near Kardamyli. When they bought the land in 1964, there was no water or electricity in that part of Greece. The house, designed by Paddy and Joan who supervised every stage of its construction, was built with stone quarried by the local stonemason from the rock on which it stood. Not a single power tool was used to build it. On one level it is a simple, unpretentious house, its doors and windows usually open to the sea air; but every detail has been thought out, and every proportion is right.

It was here, in a study overlooking the olive trees and cypresses in their garden with the sea beyond, that Paddy wrote *A Time of Gifts* and *Between the Woods and the Water*, and where he is now working on the third volume which will take him through Rumania and Bulgaria to Constantinople and beyond. From Kardamyli he and Joan have set off on many of the travels described in this book, and it is here that their friends, many of whom he has portrayed with such affection, came to visit them year after year.

The present book is divided into five sections. *Travels* describes journeys to (among other places) India, Italy, Germany, Rumania and the Caribbean, while some of the more curious stories and customs he has encountered in his adopted country appear in *Greece*. The section called *People* includes portraits of friends, heroes and eccentrics; *Books* contains an account of his early reading, as well as reviews and critical essays. The last section, *Flotsam*, shows Paddy at his most playful, and displays the never-ending delight that he takes in words.

ARTEMIS COOPER

Travels

The Munich Hofbräuhaus

from *A Time of Gifts*

As he travelled up the Rhine in the winter of 1933–4, Paddy was uncomfortably aware of the Nazi presence; but he was more impressed by the warmth and generosity of ordinary Germans. Trudging through Munich in swirling snow, however, the huge boulevards contained alarming numbers of men in Storm Trooper and SS uniform, and 'everything struck chill to the heart'. He was in a strange and uneasy mood as he approached the Hofbräuhaus which was, and still is, one of the chief landmarks of the town.

I caught a glimpse down a lane of Gothic masonry and lancets and buttresses and further on copper domes hung in convolutions of baroque. A Virgin on a column presided over a slanting piazza, one side of which was formed by a tall, Victorian-Gothic building whose great arched undercroft led to a confusion of lesser streets. In the heart of them stood a massive building; my objective, the Hofbräuhaus. A heavy arched door was pouring a raucous and lurching party of Brownshirts on to the trampled snow.

I was back in beer-territory. Half-way up the vaulted stairs a groaning Brownshirt, propped against the wall on a swastika'd arm, was unloosing, in a staunchless gush down the steps, the intake of hours. Love's labour lost. Each new storey radiated great halls given over to ingestion. In one chamber a table of SA men were grinding out *Lore, Lore, Lore*, scanning the slow beat with the butts of their mugs, then running the syllables in double time, like the carriages of an express: '*UND – KOMMT – DER – FRÜHLingindastal! GRÜSS – MIR – DIE – LORenocheinmal*'. But it was certain civilian figures seated at meat that drew the glance and held it.

One must travel east for a hundred and eighty miles from the Upper Rhine and seventy north from the Alpine watershed to form an idea of the transformation that beer, in collusion with almost nonstop eating – meals within meals dovetailing so closely during the hours of waking that there is hardly an interprandial moment – can wreak on the human frame. Intestinal strife and the truceless clash of intake and digestion wrecks many German tempers, twists brows into scowls and breaks out in harsh words and deeds.

The trunks of these feasting burghers were as wide as casks. The spread of their buttocks over the oak benches was not far short of a yard. They branched at the loins into thighs as thick as the torsos of ten-year-olds and arms on the same scale strained like bolsters at the confining serge. Chin and chest formed a single column, and each close-packed nape was creased with its three deceptive smiles. Every bristle had been cropped and shaven from their knobbly scalps. Except when five o'clock veiled them with shadow, surfaces as polished as ostriches' eggs reflected the lamplight. The frizzy hair of their wives was wrenched up from scarlet necks and pinned under slides and then hatted with green Bavarian trilbies and round one pair of elephantine shoulders a little fox stole was clasped. The youngest of this group, resembling a matinée idol under some cruel spell, was the bulkiest. Under tumbling blond curls his china blue eyes protruded from cheeks that might have been blown up with a bicycle pump, and cherry lips laid bare the sort of teeth that make children squeal. There was nothing bleary or stunned about their eyes. The setting may have reduced their size, but it keyed their glances to a sharper focus. Hands like bundles of sausages flew nimbly, packing in forkload on forkload of ham, salami, frankfurter, krenwurst and blutwurst and stone tankards were lifted for long swallows of liquid which sprang out again instantaneously on cheek and brow. They might have been competing with stop-watches, and their voices, only partly gagged by the cheekfuls of good things they were grinding down, grew louder while their unmodulated laughter jarred the air in frequent claps. Pumpernickel and aniseed rolls and pretzels bridged all the slack moments but supplies always came through before a true lull threatened. Huge oval dishes, laden with schweinebraten, potatoes, sauerkraut, red cabbage and dumplings, were laid in front of each diner. They were followed by colossal joints of meat – unclassifiable helpings which, when they were picked clean, shone on the scoured chargers like calves' pelvises or the bones of elephants. Waitresses with the build of weight-lifters and all-in wrestlers whirled this provender along and features dripped and glittered like faces at an ogre's banquet. But all too soon the table was an empty bone-yard once more, sound faltered, a look of bereavement clouded those small eyes and there was a brief hint of sorrow in the air. But succour was always at hand; beldames barged to the rescue at full gallop with new clutches of mugs and fresh plate-loads of consumer goods and the damp Laestrygonian brows unpuckered again in a happy renewal of clamour and intake.

I strayed by mistake into a room full of SS officers, Gruppen- and Sturmbannführers, black from their lightning-flash collars to the forest of tall boots underneath the table. The window embrasure was piled high with their skull-and-crossbones caps. I still hadn't found the part of this Bastille I was seeking, but at last a noise like the rush of a river guided me downstairs again to my journey's end.

The vaults of the great chamber faded into infinity through blue strata of smoke. Hobnails grated, mugs clashed and the combined smell of beer and bodies and old clothes and farmyards sprang at the newcomer. I squeezed in at a table full of peasants, and was soon lifting one of those masskrugs to my lips. It was heavier than a brace of iron dumb-bells, but the blond beer inside was cool and marvellous, a brooding, cylindrical litre of Teutonic myth. This was the fuel that had turned the berserk feeders upstairs into Zeppelins and floated them so far from heart's desire. The gunmetal-coloured cylinders were stamped with a blue HB conjoined under the Bavarian crown, like the foundry-mark on cannon. The tables, in my mind's eye, were becoming batteries where each gunner served a silent and recoil-less piece of ordnance which, trained on himself, pounded away in steady siege. *Mass*-gunfire! Here and there on the tables, with their heads in puddles of beer, isolated bombardiers had been mown down in their emplacements. The vaults reverberated with the thunder of a creeping barrage. There must have been over a thousand pieces engaged! – Big Berthas, Krupp's pale brood, battery on battery crashing at random or in salvoes as hands adjusted the elevation and traverse and then tightened on the stone trigger-guard. Supported by comrades, the walking wounded reeled through the battle smoke and a fresh gunner leaped into each place as it fell empty.

My own gun had fired its last shot, and I wanted to change to a darker-hued explosive. A new *Mass* was soon banged down on the board. In harmony with its colour, it struck a darker note at once, a long Wagnerian chord of black-letter semibreves: *Nacht und Nebel!* Rolling Bavarian acres formed in the inscape of the mind, fanning out in vistas of poles planted pyramidally with the hops gadding over them heavy with poppy-sombre flowers.

The peasants and farmers and the Munich artisans that filled the tables were much nicer than the civic swallowers overhead. Compared to the trim, drilled figures of the few soldiers there, the Storm Troopers looked like brown-paper parcels badly tied with string. There was even a sailor with two black silk streamers falling over his collar from the back of his cap, round the front of which, in gold letters, was written *Unterseeboot*. What was this Hanseatic submariner doing here, so far inland from Kiel and the Baltic? My tablemates were from the country, big, horny-handed men, with a wife or two among them. Some of the older men wore green and grey loden jackets with bone buttons and badgers' brushes or blackcocks' feathers in the back of their hatbands. The bone mouthpieces of long cherry-wood pipes were lost in their whiskers and on their glazed china bowls, painted castles and pine-glades and chamois glowed cheerfully while shag-smoke poured through the perforations of their metal lids. Some of them, gnarled and mummified, puffed at cheroots through which straws were threaded to make them draw better. They gave me one and I added a choking tribute to the enveloping cloud. The accent had changed again, and I could only grasp the meaning of the simplest sentences. Many words were docked of their final consonants; '*Bursch*' – 'a chap' – for instance, became 'bua'; 'A' was rolled over into 'O', 'Ö' became 'E', and every O and U seemed to have a final A appended, turning it into a disyllable. All this set up a universal moo-ing note, wildly distorted by resonance and echo, for these millions of vowels, prolonged and bent into boomerangs, sailed rico-chetting up through the fog to swell the tidal thunder. This echoing and fluid feeling, the bouncing of sounds and syllables and the hogs-heads of pungent liquid that sloshed about the tables and blotted the sawdust underfoot, must have been responsible for the name of this enormous hall. It was called the *Schwemme*, or horse-pond. The hollowness of those tall mugs augmented the volume of noise like the amphorae which the Greeks embedded in masonry to add resonance to their chants. My own note, as the mug emptied, was sliding down to middle C.

Mammoth columns were rooted in the flagstones and the sawdust. Arches flew in broad hoops from capital to capital; crossing in diagonals, they groined the barrel-vaults that hung dimly above the smoke. The place should have been lit by pine-torches in stanchions. It was beginning to change, turning now, under my clouding glance, into the scenery for some terrible Germanic saga, where snow vanished under the breath of dragons whose red-hot blood thawed sword-blades like icicles. It was a place for battleaxes and bloodshed and the last pages of the *Nibelungenlied* when the capital of Hunland is in flames and everybody in the castle is hacked to bits. Things grew quickly darker and more fluid; the echo, the splash, the boom and the roar of fast currents sank this beer-hall under the Rhine-bed; it became a cavern full of more dragons, misshapen guardians of gross treasure; or the fearful abode, perhaps, where Beowulf, after tearing the Grendel's arm out of its socket, tracked him over the snow by the bloodstains and, reaching the mere's edge, dived in to swim many fathoms down and slay his loathsome water-hag of a mother in darkening spirals of gore.

Or so it seemed, when the third mug arrived.

Surely I had never seen that oleograph before? Haloed with stars, the Blessed Virgin was sailing skywards through hoops of pink cloud and cherubim, and at the bottom, in gold lettering, ran the words: *Mariä Himmelfahrt*. And those trusses of chair-legs, the tabby cat in a nest of shavings and the bench fitted with clamps? Planes, mallets, chisels and braces-and-bits littered the room. There was a smell of glue, and sawdust lay thick on the cobwebs in the mid-morning light. A tall man was sand-papering chair-spokes and a woman was tiptoeing through the shavings with bread and butter and a coffee pot and, as she placed them beside the sofa where I lay blanketed, she asked me with a smile how my Katzenjammer was. Both were utter strangers.

A *Katzenjammer* is a hangover. I had learnt the word from those girls in Stuttgart.

As I drank the coffee and listened, their features slowly came back to me. At some point, unwillingly emulous of the casualties I had noticed with scorn, I had slumped forward over the Hofbräuhaus table in unwakeable stupor. There had been no vomiting, thank God; nothing worse than total insensibility; and the hefty Samaritan on the bench beside me had simply scooped me up and put me in his hand-cart, which was full of turned chair legs, and then, wrapping me in my greatcoat against the snow, wheeled it clean across Munich and laid me out mute as a flounder. The calamity must have been brought on by the mixture of the beer with the schnapps I had drunk in Schwabing; I had forgotten to eat anything but an apple since break-fast. Don't worry, the carpenter said: why, in Prague, the beer-halls kept horses that they harnessed to wickerwork coffins on wheels, just to carry the casualties home at the brewery's expense . . . What I needed, he said, opening a cupboard, was a 'schluck' of schnapps to put me on my feet. I made a dash for the yard and stuck my head under the pump. Then, combed and outwardly respectable, I thanked my saviours and was soon striding guiltily and at high speed through these outlying streets.

I felt terrible. I had often been drunk, and high spirits had led to rash doings; but never to this hoggish catalepsy.

Bicycle Polo

from *Between the Woods and the Water*

When in Budapest in the spring of 1934, Paddy had been invited to stay with Count and Countess Józsi Wenckheim at their house, O'Kygos, near the city of Békéscsaba on the Great Hungarian Plain.

I was halted next day by the Körös. There was no bridge in sight, so I followed a bank teeming with rabbits until an old fisherman, pale as a ghost and dressed all in white, sculled me to the other side. The people in the inn looked different and I pricked my ears at the sound of a Slav language. They were Slovaks who had come here centuries ago, hundreds of miles from their old abode, to settle in the empty region when the Turks were driven out, devout Lutherans of the Augsburg Confession, unlike the Protestants of Debrecen who were Calvinists to a man.

The distance was getting longer than I had reckoned. For once, I sighed for a lift; I didn't want to be late, and just as the wish took shape, a cloud of dust appeared on the path and then a governess-cart with a fleece-capped driver and two nuns. One of the sisters made room with a smile and a clatter of beads. We drove several miles and the town of Békéscsaba hovered far away to the right, with the twin steeples of the Catholic cathedral and the great tea-cosy of the Protestants' green copper dome glimmering beyond the tall maize-stalks. Both had vanished again when they put me down at my turning. The nuns were rather impressed when I told them my destination, and so was I.

László's elder brother Józsi (Joseph), head of that numerous family, and his wife Denise were the only two of all my benefactors on the Great Plain I had met before. It had been at a large, rather grand luncheon at their house on the slopes of Buda and when they had heard I was heading for the south-east, they had asked me to stay. Another brother, Pál, a diplomatist with the urbane and polished air of a Hungarian Norpois, said, 'Do go! Józsi's a great swell in those parts. It's a strange house, but we're very fond of it.'

Once through the great gates, I was lost for a moment. A forest of huge exotic trees mingled with the oaks and the limes and the chestnuts. Magnolias and tulip trees were on the point of breaking open, the branches of biblical cedars swept in low fans, all of them ringing with the songs of thrushes and blackbirds and positively slumbrous with the cooing of a thousand doves, and the house in the middle, when the trees fell back, looked more extraordinary with every step. It was a vast ochre-coloured pile, built, on the site of an older building perhaps, in the last decades of the nineteenth century. Blois, Amboise and Azay-le-Rideau (which I only knew from photographs) immediately floated into mind. There were pinnacles, pediments, baroque gables, ogees, lancets, mullions, steep slate roofs, towers with flags flying and flights of covered stairs ending in colonnades of flattened arches.

Great wings formed a courtyard and, from a terrace leading to a ceremonial door, branching and balustraded steps descended in a sweep. As I was crossing this *place d'armes*, several people were coming down the steps, and one of them was Count Józsi. Forewarned by Lászlo, he spotted me at once. He waved a greeting and cried, 'You are just what we need! Come along!' I followed him and the others across the yard to a shed. 'Have you ever played bike-polo?' he asked, catching me by the elbow. I had played a version of it at school with walking sticks and a tennis-ball on the hard tennis-courts; it was thought rather disreputable. But here they had real polo-sticks cut down to the right size and a proper polo ball and the shed was full of battered but sturdy machines. Józsi was my captain, and a famous player of the real game called Bethlen had the rival team; two other guests and two footmen and a groom were the rest of the players. The game was quick, reckless and full of collisions, but there was nothing to match the joy of hitting the ball properly: it made a loud smack and gave one a tempting glimmer of what the real thing might be like. I couldn't make out why all shins weren't barked to the bone; nor why, as one of the goals backed on the house, none of the windows were broken. The other side won but we scored four goals, and when the iron Maltese Cats were back in their stands, we limped back to the steps, where Countess Denise and her sister Cecile and some others had been leaning on the balustrade like ladies gazing down into the lists.

What luck those nuns turning up, I thought a bit later, lapping down whisky and soda out of a heavy glass! Someone took me along a tall passage to my room and I found one of the young polo-playing footmen there, spick and span once more, but looking puzzled as he tried in vain to lay out the stuff from my rucksack in a convincing array. We were reciprocally tongue-tied, but I laughed and so did he: knocking one another off bicycles breaks down barriers. I got into a huge bath.

Countess Denise and Count Józsi were first cousins and earlier generations had been similarly related. 'We are more intermarried than the Ptolemies,' she told me at dinner. 'We all ought to be insane.' She and Cecile had dark hair and beautiful features and shared the rather sad expression of the rest of the family; but it likewise dissolved in friendly warmth when they smiled. Her husband's distinguished face, under brushed-back greying hair, had the same characteristic. (In a fit of melancholy when he was very young he had fired a bullet through his breast, just missing his heart.) He looked very handsome in an old claret-coloured smoking jacket. Dürer's family came from the neighbouring town of Gyula, the Countess said; the Hungarian Ajtós – 'doorkeeper' – was translated into the old German Thürer – then into Dürer when the family migrated and set up as gold- and silversmiths in Nuremberg. Afterwards in the drawing room, my footman friend approached Count Józsi carrying an amazing pipe with a cherry-wood stem over a yard long and an amber mouthpiece. The meerschaum bowl at the end was already alight, and, resting this comfortably on the crook of his ankle, the Count was soon embowered in smoke. Seeing that another guest and I were fascinated by it, he called for two more of these calumets and a few minutes later in they came, already glowing; before they were offered, the mouthpieces were dipped in water. The delicious smoke seemed the acme of oriental luxury, for these pipes were the direct and unique descendants of those long chibooks that all Levant travellers describe and all the old prints depict; the Turks of the Ottoman Empire used them as an alternative to the narghileh. (That sinuous affair, the Turkish hookah, still survived all over the Balkans and before summer was out I was puffing away at them, half-pasha and half-caterpillar, in many a Bulgarian khan. But Hungary was the only country in the world where the chibook still lingered. In Turkey itself, as I discovered that winter, it had vanished completely, like the khanjar and the yataghan.)

Ybl, the architect of the castle, had given himself free rein with armorial detail. Heraldic beasts abounded, casques, crowns and mantelling ran riot and the family's emblazoned swords and eagles' wings were echoed on flags and bed-curtains and counterpanes. The spirits of Sir Walter Scott and Dante Gabriel Rossetti seemed to preside over the place and as I had been steeped in both of them from my earliest years, anything to do with castles, sieges, scutcheons, tournaments and crusades still quickened the pulse, so the corroborative detail of the castle was close to heart's desire.

Wheatfields scattered with poppies enclosed the wooded gardens and the castle, and when we got back from a ride through them next morning, my hostess's sister Cecile looked at her watch and cried out, 'I'll be late for Budapest!' We accompanied her to a field where a small aeroplane was waiting; she climbed in and waved, the pilot swung the propeller, the grass flattened like hair under a drier and they were gone. Then Szigi, the son of the house, took me up the tower and we looked out over an infinity of crops with shadows of clouds floating serenely across them. He was going to Ampleforth in a few terms, he said: what was it like? I told him I thought it was a very good school and that the monks umpired matches with white coats over their habits, and he seemed satisfied with these scant items. Exploring the library, I was fascinated by a remote shelf full of volumes of early nineteenth-century debates in the Hungarian Diet; not by the contents – humdrum stuff about land-tenure, irrigation, the extension or limitation of the franchise and so on – but because they were all in Latin, and I was amazed to learn that in Parliament until 1839, and even in the county courts, no other language was either spoken or written.

The bicycle polo after tea was even rougher than the day before. One chukka ended in a complete pile-up and as we were extricating ourselves, our hostess called from the balustrade.

A carriage with two horses and a coachman in a feathered and ribboned hat was drawing up at the foot of the steps. Dropping his stick, our host went over to help the single passenger out, and when he had alighted, bowed. This tall, slightly stooping newcomer, with white hair and beard of an Elizabethan or Edwardian cut, a green Alpine hat and a loden cape, was Archduke Joseph. Living on a nearby estate, he belonged to a branch of the Habsburgs which had become Hungarian and during the troubled period after Hungary's defeat and revolution, he had briefly been Palatine of the kingdom – a sort of regent, that is – until the victorious Allies dislodged him. Our hostess had been coming down the stairs as the Archduke was slowly climbing them, calling in a quavering voice, 'Kezeit csókólóm kedves Denise grófnö!' – 'I kiss your hand, dear Countess Denise'; – and when he stooped to do so, she curtseyed, and, diagonally and simultaneously, they both sank about nine inches on the wide steps and recovered again as though in slow motion. When we had been led up steaming and dishevelled and presented, we leaped back into the saddle and pedalled and slashed away till it was too dark to see.

I was lent something more presentable than my canvas trousers and gym shoes for dinner. The Archduke joined in the chibook smoking afterwards and the memory of those aromatic fumes still enclouds the last night and the last house on the Great Plain.

Carpathian Uplands

from Between the Woods and the Water

I got to Tomeşti at nightfall, where I found another pre-arranged haven under the roof of Herr Robert v. Winckler; he was a tall, thin, scholarly man, living alone with his books and his guns on the steep edge of the forest. He and his library were a treasure-house of relevant knowledge, and the stairs, on the way to bed, were forested with horns, antlers, fowling-pieces and wolf-traps. There were the skins of two enormous wolves on the landing, a stuffed lynx on the wall, a row of boars' tushes and a bear's skin on my bedroom floor; and the last thing I remember before blowing out the candle is the double reflection of the wick in its glass eyes. The depth of the flared embrasures showed the thickness of the walls, and the logs stacked to the ceiling beside the massive tiled stove told how cold it must have been in winter. It was hard, in the summer moonlight, to imagine the onslaught of the wind along the canyons, the icicle-portcullises and the silent obliterating flakes that would place all these buildings under siege.

Transylvania, the Banat of Temesvár, the Great Plain, the Tatra mountains, Bukovina, Galicia, Podolia, Lodomeria, Moravia, Bohemia, Wallachia, Moldavia, Bessarabia and, above all, the Carpathians themselves – how closely the geography of Austria-Hungary and its neighbours approximated to the fictional world of earlier generations! Graustark, Ruritania, Borduria, Syldavia and a score of imaginary kingdoms, usurped by tyrants and sundered by fights for the throne, leap into mind: plots, treachery, imprisoned heirs and palace factions abound and, along with them, fiendish monocled swordsmen, queens in lonely towers, toppling ranges, deep forests, plains full of half-wild horses, wandering tribes of gypsies who steal children out of castles and dye them with walnut-juice or lurk under the battlements and melt the chatelaines' hearts with their strings. There are mad noblemen and rioting jacqueries; robbers too, half-marauder and half-Robin Hood, straddling quite across the way with their grievous crab-tree cudgels. I had read about betyárs on the Alföld; now haidouks and pandours had begun to impinge. Fur-hatted and looped with pearls, the great boyars of the Rumanian principalities surged up the other side of the watershed, ghostly hospodars with their nearly mythical princesses trooped in tall branched crowns round the walls of fortress-monasteries in frescoed processions; and beyond them to the north stretched icebound rivers and steppes and bogs where herds of elk moved at a shambling trot, and, once upon a time, the great aurochs, extinct now except on heraldic shields; wastes unfolded north-east to which unstable troops of Cossacks laid claim, or destructive settlements of Tatars; further still, a kingdom of sledded Polacks retreated into the shadows, and then a region of snowfalls where the Teutonic Knights cut the pagans of Lithuania to bits on the frozen Baltic, surviving still in the East Prussian world of scars and spikes; and beyond them, all the Russias . . . But to the south, closer than these and getting closer with every step, the valleys and woods of the Danube had been the theatre for momentous battles between Christendom and Islam: the armies of the Sultan moving upstream under green banners and preposterous turbans, while kings, voivodes and cardinals (the contusion of whose maces absolved them from bloodshed) and all the paladins of the West – their greyhounds curvetting beside them, sunbeams catching gold-inlay under their ostrich-plumes and spirals and stripes on their lances like Uccello's in the *Battle of San Romano* – cantered light-heartedly downstream to their doom.

An old addict, I had been re-reading Saki just before setting out. Many pages are haunted by 'those mysterious regions between Vienna Woods and the Black Sea', and here I was, as deep in that maze of forests and canyons as it was possible to get. The timbered slopes outside the windows, and thoughts of the snow and the winter solstice, brought these stories to mind, especially the ones about wolves, the villains and the presiding daemons of East European winter. The terrible arrival of *The Interlopers*, in the last monosyllabic paragraph of the story, might have taken place a few miles away; and another, *The Wolves of Czernogratz*, with the howling crescendo of the same dread monsters, conjured up a thousand castles to the north and the west; and I had always been struck by the broken traveller in *The Unbearable Bassington*, 'a man whom wolves had sniffed at'. István was one, my host another, Gróf K a third; Transylvania was full of them. All the castles were haunted, and earthly packs of wolves were reinforced after dark by solitary werewolves; vampires were on the move; witches stirred and soared; the legends and fairy stories of a dozen nations piled up and the region teemed with everything that Goethe told the New World it was better without: 'Useless memories and vain strifes . . . knights, robbers and ghost stories . . . Ritter und Räuber und Gespenstergeschichten . . .' In the end, I stayed three nights, listening to stories of wolves and forests and reading in the library, and some of it must have found its way into the bloodstream. M. Herriot has left a consoling message for cases like this: 'La culture, c'est ce qui reste quand on a tout oublié.'

A scramble through valleys and foothills, bearing south-west to avoid the Lugoj road, and a night's sleep under an oak tree, brought me dog-tired and long after dark on the second day to a brick-kiln on the Caransebeş road, where I curled up and fell asleep just as the moon was coming up.

Ada Kaleh

from *Between the Woods and the Water*

Paddy reached the island of Ada Kaleh, which lay in a bend in the Danube near the Hungarian, Rumanian and Yugoslav borders a few miles downstream from Orşova, in August 1934. The island no longer exists. It was flooded by the building of the Iron Gates dam in 1971, and now lies fathoms deep below the waters of an artificial lake.

After the bridge at Turnu-Severin, the doctor travelled on to Craiova and I caught a bus back to Orşova, picked up my stuff, bought a ticket for the next day's boat, then walked a couple of miles downstream again and found a fisherman to scull me out to the little wooded island I had had my eye on ever since rejoining the Danube.

I had heard much talk of Ada Kaleh in recent weeks, and read all I could find. The name means 'island fortress' in Turkish. It was about a mile long, shaped like a shuttle, bending slightly with the curve of the current and lying a little closer to the Carpathian than the Balkan shore. It has been called Erythia, Rushafa and then Continusa, and, according to Apollonius Rhodius, the Argonauts dropped anchor here on their way back from Colchis. How did Jason steer the *Argo* through the Iron Gates? And then the Kazan? Medea probably lifted the vessel clear of the spikes by magic. Some say the *Argo* reached the Adriatic by overland portage, others that she crossed it and continued up the Po, mysteriously ending in North Africa. Writers have tentatively suggested that the first wild olive to be planted in Attica might have come from here. But it was later history that had invested the little island with fame.

The inhabitants were Turkish, probably descendants of the soldiers of one of the earlier Sultans who invaded the Balkans, Murad I, or Bayazid I, perhaps. Left behind by the retreating Turks, the island lingered on as an outlying fragment of the Ottoman Empire until the Treaty of Berlin in 1878. The Austrians held some vague suzerainty over it, but the island seems to have been forgotten until it was granted to Rumania at the Treaty of Versailles; and the Rumanians had left the inhabitants undisturbed. The first thing I saw after landing was a rustic coffee-shop under a vine-trellis where old men sat cross-legged in a circle with sickles and adzes and pruning hooks scattered about them. I was as elated when bidden to join them as if I had suddenly been seated on a magic carpet. Bulky scarlet sashes a foot wide gathered in the many pleats of their black and dark blue baggy trousers. Some wore ordinary jackets, others navy-blue boleros with convoluted black embroidery and faded plum-coloured fezzes with ragged turbans loosely knotted about them; all except the hodja's. Here, snow-white folds were neatly arranged round a lower and less tapering fez with a short stalk in the middle. Something about the line of brow, the swoop of nose and the jut of the ears made them indefinably different from any of the people I had seen on my journey so far. The four or five hundred islanders belonged to a few families which had intermarried for centuries, and one or two had the vague and absent look, the wandering glance and the erratic levity that sometimes come with ancient and inbred stock. In spite of their patched and threadbare clothes, their style and their manners were full of dignity. On encountering a stranger, they touched heart, lips and brow with the right hand, then laid it on their breast with an inclination of the head and a murmured formula of welcome. It was a gesture of extreme grace, like the punctilio of broken-down grandees. An atmosphere of prehistoric survival hung in the air as though the island were the refuge of an otherwise extinct species long ago swept away.

Several of my neighbours fingered strings of beads, but not in prayer; they spilt them between their fingers at random intervals, as though to scan their boundless leisure; and to my delight, one old man, embowered in a private cloud, was smoking a narghileh. Six feet of red tubing were cunningly coiled, and when he pulled on the amber mouthpiece, charcoal glowed on a damped wad of tobacco leaves from Isfahan and the bubbles, fighting their way through the water with the sound of a mating bull-frog, filled the glass vessel with smoke. A boy with small tongs arranged fresh charcoal. While he did so, the old man pointed towards me and whispered; and the boy came back in a few minutes with a laden tray on a circular table six inches from the ground. Seeing my quandary, a neighbour told me how to begin: first, to drink the small glass of raki; then eat the mouthful of delicious rose-petal jam lying ready spooned on a glass saucer, followed by half a tumbler of water; finally to sip at a dense and scalding thimbleful of coffee slotted in a filigree holder. The ritual should be completed by emptying the tumbler and accepting tobacco, in this case, an aromatic cigarette made by hand on the island. Meanwhile the old men sat in smiling silence, sighing occasionally, with a friendly word to me now and then in what sounded like very broken Rumanian; the doctor had said that their accent and style caused amusement on the shore. Among themselves they spoke Turkish, which I had never heard: astonishing strings of agglutinated syllables with a follow-through of identical vowels and dimly reminiscent of Magyar; all the words are different, but the two tongues are Ugro-Finnic cousins in the Ural-Altaic group of languages. According to the doctor it had either drifted far from the metropolitan vernacular of Constantinople or remained immovably lodged in its ancient mould, like a long-marooned English community still talking the language of Chaucer.

I didn't know what to do when leaving; an attempt at payment was stopped by a smile and an enigmatic backward tilt of the head. Like everything else, this was the first time I came across the universal negative of the Levant; and, once more, there was that charming inclination, hand on breast.

So these were the last descendants of those victorious nomads from the borders of China! They had conquered most of Asia, and North Africa to the Pillars of Hercules, enslaved half Christendom and battered on the gates of Vienna; victories long eclipsed, but commemorated here and there by a minaret left in their lost possessions like a spear stuck in the ground.

Balconied houses gathered about the mosque and small workshops for Turkish delight and cigarettes, and all round these crumbled the remains of a massive fortress. Vine-trellises or an occasional awning shaded the cobbled lanes. There were hollyhocks and climbing roses and carnations in whitewashed petrol tins, and the heads and shoulders of the wives who flickered about among them were hidden by a dark *feredjé* – a veil pinned in a straight line above the brow and joining under the nose; and they wore tapering white trousers, an outfit which gave them the look of black-and-white ninepins. Children were identically clad miniatures of the grown-ups and, except for their unveiled faces, the little girls might each have been the innermost of a set of Russian dolls. Tobacco leaves were hung to dry in the sun like strings of small kippers. Women carried bundles of sticks on their heads, scattered grain to poultry and returned from the shore with their sickles and armfuls of rushes. Lop-eared rabbits basked or hopped sluggishly about the little gardens and nibbled the leaves of ripening melons. Flotillas of ducks cruised among the nets and the canoes, and multitudes of frogs had summoned all the storks from the roofs.

Hunyadi had put up the first defensive walls, but the ramparts all round belonged to the interregnum after Prince Eugene had taken Belgrade and driven the Turks downstream, and the eastern end of the island looked as though it might sink under the weight of his fortifications. The vaults of the gun-galleries and the dank tremendous magazines had fallen in. Fissures split the ramparts and great blocks of masonry, tufted with grass, had broken away and goats tore at the leaves among the debris. A pathway among pear trees and mulberries led to a little cemetery where turbaned headstones leant askew and in one corner lay the tomb of a dervish prince from Bokhara who had ended his life here after wandering the world, 'poor as a mouse', in search of the most beautiful place on earth and the one most sheltered from harm and mishap.

It was getting late. The sun left the minaret, and then the new moon, a little less wraith-like than the night before, appeared on cue in a turquoise sky with a star next to it that might have been pinned there by an Ottoman herald. With equal promptitude, the hodja's torso emerged on the balcony under the cone of the minaret. Craning into the dusk, he lifted his hands and the high and long-drawn-out summons of the *izan* floated across the air, each clause wavering and spreading like the rings of sound from pebbles dropped at intervals into a pool of air. I found myself still listening and holding my breath when the message had ended and the hodja must have been half-way down his dark spiral.

Surrounded by pigeons, men were unhasteningly busy at the

lustral fountain by the mosque and the row of slippers left by the door was soon lengthened by my gym shoes. Once inside, the Turks spread in a line on a vast carpet, with lowered eyes. There was no decoration except for the mihrab and the mimbar and the black calligraphy of a Koranic verse across the wall. The ritual gestures of preparation were performed in careful and unhurried unison, until, gathering momentum, the row of devotees sank like a wave; then tilted over until their foreheads touched the pile of the carpet, the soles of their feet all suddenly and disarmingly revealed; rocking back, they sat with their hands open in their laps, palms upward; all in dead silence. Every few minutes, the hodja sitting in front of them murmured 'Allah akbar!' in a quiet voice, and another long silence followed. In the unornate and hushed concavity, the four isolated syllables sounded indescribably dignified and austere.

A Cave on the Black Sea

First published as 'A Balkan Welcome', *Holiday Magazine*,
May 1965

*In December 1934, Paddy was travelling down the Black Sea coast of Bulgaria.
The goal of his journey, Constantinople, was less than 150 miles away to the south;
but somewhere between Varna and Burgas, the path petered out just as night was
coming on.*

This was Europe's easternmost rim; but it was hard to remember
that the ocean-like sweep that flashed from the cliffs of Bulgaria
to the bare horizon was inland water: Tcherno Moré, Kara Su, Mareă
Neagră, the Euxine, the Black Sea . . . Constantza, Odessa, Batum,
Trebizond, Constantinople . . . The names were intoxicating. Due
east, the Caucasus lay; Asia Minor to the south; north, the Danube
and Rumania, and north-east, the Ukraine and all the Russias. The
chill that crackled in the December air was a hint to a traveller of
those limitless impending snows.

Inland, to the north-west, rose the Great Balkan range. At the
other end of this brilliant morning I could just see the ice-bright and
blue-shadowed snows and, to the south-west, a faint gleam of the
Rhodope mountains. Perhaps it was just about here that the migrat-
ing storks I had seen pouring over the Stara Planina four months
before had struck the Black Sea coast on their way to Africa. The tiers
that rolled inland, so arid then underfoot, were feathered now with
young grass. The Bulgarian winter had not yet begun and the emerald and moss-bright froth across the russet soil spread a fiction of
early spring. The hills were empty. Glimpses of villages soared
inland, their chimneys balancing above them veils as thin and blue as
un-inhaled tobacco smoke. Slow threads rose swaying and expanding from distant bonfires, as though Mohicans were signalling. The
hillsides uncoiled red scrolls of plough; beehives, muffled for the
coming winter, stood in cataleptic kraals; and only the far-sounding
bells told that the flocks were grazing their way across Bulgaria at a

glacier's pace. Magpies fidgeted about the landscape and an unstable confetti of gulls whitened the grass and the furrows.

When the track dipped steeply into a coomb, streams curled to the sea over a crescent of sand and the ravines that twisted inland were filled with bare, silver walnut trees and the spidery winter distaffs of poplars. Hundreds of hooded crows were settled along the boughs and a clap of the hands would shed them deafeningly into the sky as the branches sprang free, sending them up the valley in a drift of soot for a league or two; then back they swung to plunge the spinneys into raucous mourning again. Some people say that these birds – suddenly ominous by their numbers – live for more than a hundred years; a number of these might have pecked at the dead in the Crimean War; a few Methuselahs could even have flown south across the Ukraine after following the Grande Armée from Moscow.

In an inlet, close to the sand's edge, an old man was smoking a narghileh on the doorstep of a hut beside a little boat beached among the rushes. His high-cheeked face was a benign skeleton leaf of wrinkles. In faulty Bulgarian on both sides, we talked of the coldness of the day and the brightness of the sun. He was an old Tartar fisherman, the only human being I saw all day.

For, as the miles mounted up, the scene grew emptier until rising woods concealed the interior. Trees sank to the sea's edge and the path curled across tilted glades full of white and red anemones. The smell of herbs filled the air. Myrtle, bay and arbutus – dark green leaves crowded with berries as big and scarlet as strawberries – sank seaward. Blueblack ilexes jutted among them, their roots looped in plaited arches like the roots of trees in Japanese paintings.

Downhill, at the end of plunging tunnels of evergreen, the European continent disintegrated in tufted spikes and islets standing in green water as translucent as glass, darkened, as it receded, to the blue of a peacock's neck as it fled away to the skyline. Creases slight as a breath on silk stirred the almost still water just enough to ring these spikes with a bracelet of white. Headlands followed each other in a south-westerly recession of plumed capes dwindling at last to dim threads that could belong equally to the sea or the sky.

In the late afternoon, sunbeams filled the tilted clearings and struck the tree boles and the leaves with layers of wintry gold. Rafts of light hung in the leaves, fell through the woods in spokes and broke up the loop of shadow over the water with windows of radiance. The solitude and the hush were complete. A promise of the Aegean and the Greek islands roved the cold Bulgarian air, sending a hint of their spell across the Propontis and the Bosporus to the shores of this huge barbarian sea.

A trio of cormorants had flown across the Tartar's cove and I had seen their craned necks, beaks swivelling like periscopes, sticking out of the water farther south. On the rocks a dozen were standing now with wings heraldically half-open, as though hung out to dry. I followed a path downhill towards them, but they took flight in an urgent wedge over the water, which was now patterned with streaks of zinc and lilac. The track grew thinner; by dusk all trace of it had vanished and I found myself climbing through undergrowth and rocks: leaping from slab to slab, dodging pools, bestriding fissures and ledges, hoping for a gap that might lead uphill again. When it was dark I went on by torchlight, negotiating the water and the steeper confusion of boulders, determined to turn back if it grew worse.

Then I lost my footing on a ledge and skidded, with a screech of hobnails, down a slant like a barn roof. A drop and a jolt threw me waist-deep into a pool. Jarred and shaken, with a gash on my forehead and a torn thumb, I climbed out, shuddering with cold. At the bottom of the other end of the pool, about two fathoms down, the torch was sending a yellow shaft through sea anemones and weed and a flickering concourse of fish. I wondered what would have happened if in my rucksack and overcoat and heavy boots, I had followed the torch into the depths. Should I take off my heavy stuff and dive for the drowned light? I was shaking and my teeth were chattering. The sun had only just set: waiting till dawn meant twelve or thirteen hours in the freezing dark.

In case there were someone on this empty-seeming coast, I decided to shout. But what? I had forgotten, if I ever knew it, the Bulgarian for *Help*. All I could think of was the formal cry of 'Good evening' – '*Dobar vecher!*' I shouted for a few minutes but with no reply. My stick was floating on the shallower part of the pool, so I retrieved it. With a reluctant look at the lost torch and the glittering mob of fish now going mad round that fallen portent, I began to fumble my way forward, tapping and feeling a way along the rocks: sliding, crawling on all fours, climbing ledges slippery with bladder-wrack, wading up to my armpits and sounding ahead with the stick for fear of a sudden drop. Now and again I sent up my cry of inappropriate affability. Stars dimly indicated distant masses in silhouette. After a long slithering advance, a few constellations, appearing in front where all had been black before, indicated that I was reaching the cape.

I crept on, preferring to wade now; the water was less cold than the night air. When I crawled on the rocks, the air embedded me in icy plate-armour. Within a few minutes of each other, as though by collusion, both my bootlaces broke; the boots became loose, dragging anchors under water and heavy fetters up and down the blades of rock. Breathless and exhausted, I lay on a ledge until spurred on by the cold. At last, lowering my half-shod foot on to what I thought was the surface of a pool, I felt the solidity of sand and the grate of pebbles. Another pace confirmed it; I was on the shore of an inlet. Round a buttress of cliff a little way up the beach, a faint rectangle of light, surrounded by scattered chinks, leaked astonishingly into the darkness. I crossed the pebbles and I pulled open an improvised door, uttering a last *dobar vecher* into the measureless cavern beyond. A dozen firelit faces looked up in surprise and consternation from their cross-legged supper, as though a sea monster or a drowned man's ghost had come in.

Ten minutes later, in gym shoes, canvas trousers, two shirts, several layers of jersey and a shepherd's hirsute cloak, with three or four slugs of *slivovitz* burning inside me, sipping a second glass of tea brewed from mountain herbs and two inches deep in sugar, I was crouched in front of a blaze of thorns stacked as high as a bonfire. I was still shuddering. One of the inhabitants of the place had washed the blood off my face and feet, another had plied a towel. Recovered from their surprise at the apparition of this sodden and bleeding spectre, they had leaped to my help like Bernardine monks.

It took some time to focus and segregate the figures moving about in the firelight and the smoky shadows. They were wild-looking men. Six were dressed in the customary earth-brown or dark blue homespun; patched, tattered, cross-gartered with thongs over their felt-swaddled shanks and shod in canoe-tipped cowhide moccasins. Knives were stuck in their wide red sashes and, like me, they were hatted in flat-topped sheepskin kalpaks that had moulted most of their fur. An old man with a tangled white beard seemed to be the leader of this group. Four others, equally torn and tattered, wore blue jerseys and seamen's peaked caps set askew. Shepherds and seamen, in fact. The oldest of the sailors had only one hand, with a star tattooed on the back of it.

Gradually the surrounding firelit hollow resolved itself into a long cave, arching high overhead but not burrowing very deep. Blades of rock formed much of the outer wall, unmortared masonry filled the gaps, and branches and planks and flattened petrol tins stamped with *Sokony-Vacuum* in Cyrillic characters, completed it. The flames picked out fans of shrub springing from the rock and a high cluster of stalactites; they also summoned from the shadows a scattering of gear which told of the cave's double function: a boat tilted on its side, oars, rudders, huge carbide lamps, long-shafted fishing spears, tall multi-pronged tridents with barbed spikes like eight-toothed combs, anchors, geometric fishing traps, creels, bait baskets, corks, gourd floats, wedges, coils, drooping russet festoons of net and links of rusty chain. A small anvil topped an embedded tree stump.

The other side of the fire displayed a set of conflicting clues: wicker cheese baskets on planks, a leaning sheaf of crooks and a grove of white, hanging globes – cheese that had been poured liquid into dripping goatskin bags, hairy side innermost. A cauldron of whey simmered over a second fire, and the stooping Cyclopean grey-beard stirred and skimmed. Across the dark reaches at the far end ran a breast-high wall of bleached stones and furze, and the mystery of an abrupt and derisive cachinnation beyond.

The old man took a brand from beneath the cauldron and flourished it with a possessive smile. The lasso of radiance that his flame looped into the murk lit up a thicket of spiralling and bladed horns and the imperial beards and matted black-and-white pelts of fifty goats; a wave of the torch kindled a hundred oblong-pupilled eyes, provoking another falsetto jeer, a click of horns and the notes of a few heavy bells. A patina of smoke and soot polished the walls of the cave. Jags of mineral were tables or sideboards for these troglodytes. Half a dozen dogs slept or foraged around; a reclining white mongrel with hanging tongue and forepaws crossed observed the scene through close-set eyes, the left one of which was surrounded by a black ring. The sand and the pebbles underlay a trodden crust of goats' pellets and fish scales, and the cavern reeked of fish, goats, curds, cheese, tar, brine, sweat and wood-smoke. It was an abode harmoniously shared by Polyphemus and Sinbad.

Supper was finished but they ladled me out the last of the lentils while one of the fishermen poured oil in the frying pan, laid a couple of mackerel across it and, in due course, whisked them out sizzling by their tails and put them in the tin plate the lentils had that instant vacated. I must have been coming to; these delicious fish were demolished at speed. What were they called? *Skoumbri*, one fisherman said; no, no, cried the others: *skumria*. There was some friendly teasing about this, for the shepherds were Bulgars and the fishermen were Greeks, members of the Greek community scattered all over southern Bulgaria. I was surprised to see these irreconcilables in each other's company. One of them apologized, saying they had finished the *slivo* and wine. I dug a contribution out of my rucksack: two bottles of raki from Tirnovo, one safe in a wooden flask, the other mercifully intact. In spite of an occasional shudder and a rattle of teeth, my spirits, as the food and drink piled up, began to rise. The circulating raki ignited a mood of nautico-pastoral wassail and by the time the second bottle was broached the wind-battered and weather-chipped faces were wide-mouthed in song.

A goatskin, which I had taken to be a vessel for milking the ewes, turned out to be a bagpipe. But when the old man puffed it full, the drone through the horn trumpet died in a wail that called forth an answering howl from the white dog, briskly silenced by a back-handed cuff. A crease in the cracked parchment had split. I patched it up, to everyone's applause, with a criss-cross of adhesive tape. As the sound swelled again one of the fishermen began a burlesque Turkish belly dance, called the *kütchek*. He had learned it, he said, in Tzarigrad, the Bulgarian for Constantinople, the town of the Emperors. It was very convincing, even to the loud crack that accompanied each spasmodic wrench of the haunch and the midriff, produced by the abrupt parting of the stiff interlocked forefingers of both hands as they were held, palms joined, above his head.

The comic effect was enhanced by the fierce and piratical looks of Dimitri the dancer. 'He needs a *charchaff*,' one of the shepherds cried. He wrapped a cheesecloth round the lower part of Dimitri's face. The rolling of his smoke-reddened eyes above this yashmak turned him into a mixture of houri and virago. Meanwhile Costa, another sailor, advanced into the firelight with the same rotating motion as Dimitri. Uninhibited laughter broke out. A third fisherman tied a two-foot length of rope into a ring, made Costa step into it, then lifted it to the level of his thighs and made him stretch his legs apart. When the rope was taut he inserted a heavy log which he turned over several times, till the log in the twisted rope could be made to lift or drop like the beam of a siege engine. The comic impropriety of this vision brought the house down. (I wonder whether Aristophanes knew of this device? It would have been handy for the Lysistrata . . .) A mock pursuit of the veiled Dimitri began, with Costa moving by leaps: the ithyphallic gait of a pasha-like grasshopper bent on rape. To drive this fierce aspect home, he pulled out one of the shepherds' knives and held it between his teeth.

The bagpipe howled with growing stridency and the spectators jovially clapped out the time. Dimitri oscillated with lumbering skittishness; the uncouth chase brought the sweat to Costa's brow, while monstrously enlarged shadows of their evolutions loomed about the cave. Finally a long scream of the pipe propelled him, with his legs splayed and knees bent, round and round his partner in mock-lecherous leaps. Cheerfully goaded by the onlookers the bagpiper blew faster and faster until the panting pibroch mercifully ended at last with the diminishing wail of an ox under the knife: my running repair had come unstuck. Laughing and out of breath, Costa collapsed with mock melodrama. The raki travelled round the cave in a hubbub of laughter, and the flames threw a beltane chiaroscuro over hilarious masks.

Another bottle was miraculously discovered. Panayi, the fourth of the fishermen, lifted a long object from the boat. When he rejoined us on the floor, the unwinding of the cloth revealed an instrument halfway between a lute and a mandolin. Ivory and mother-of-pearl inlaid the sounding board, and ivory and ebony ribbed its gleaming bowl; but the great length and slenderness of the neck which slanted from his cross-legged lap, while he screwed the pegs into tune and plucked the eight wires with a hen's quill, gave it the air of a court minstrel's instrument from a Persian painting: an incongruously delicate and skilfully wrought thing for this rough den.

When it was in tune, the player showered an intricate pattern of minims and crotchets into the falling hush of the grotto and then plaited a flowering wreath of chords in different keys which cohered, after a short halt, in a tune whose slow, heavily stressed and almost lurching beat fell between metallic cascades of short notes and defined a rhythm that slid insidiously into the bloodstream until even the musician himself, stooping over the strings or gazing into the flames with large grey eyes, seemed to be mesmerized by his own music.

Panayi the lutenist was a tall and muscular man and the slender *bouzouki* looked frail in his great hands. He and the older man began a song that sounded like a lament. It was full of repeated phrases and Oriental modulations, and at moments it was designedly strained and grating. Oddly placed pauses syncopated the run of the words. The older man marked the beat by slapping the side of a gourd with his star-backed hand, steadying it with the stump of the other.

The night moved into a different gear. Linked at arm's length by a hand on each other's shoulder, Costa and Dimitri were standing side by side; their feet were together and each unsmiling face hung, chin on breast, like that of a gallows-bird. This initial immobility thawed into movement as slight as the bending and straightening of the knee; the feet, flat on the ground with heels together, opened at an angle, then closed and opened once more. Both right feet were then lifted and slowly swung backward and forward. A left-foot jump brought their torsos seesawing forward in a right angle to balance a simultaneous kick on the ground behind them with their right. Then the dancers swept forward for an accelerated pace or two, braked and halted with their right bent legs, from the knee down, lifted parallel to the ground and sweeping in slow scything movements and falling again. An unhurried flick sent both right feet soaring, and their hands

smote together under their knees in a sudden clap; then they were
almost on their knees, hands on each other's shoulders again, gliding
sideways, then rolling forward in a gait resembling a sleepwalking
hornpipe.

Nothing could have been less carefree or orgiastic than the perverse mood of their evolutions: the subtle and complex beauty of
this peculiar dancing, coming, as it did, hotfoot on the straightfor-
ward bumpkin commotion of the first performance, was as much of
a surprise as would be the discovery, in a collection of folk verse, of
a contorted metaphysical jungle of conceits, tropes, assonances,
internal rhymes, abstruse allusions and concealed acrostics. At the
end of the dance, Dimitri joined us by the fire and swelled the
accompaniment with his own voice and another gourd. The next
dance, on which Costa now embarked solo, was, though akin to its
forerunner, odder still. There was the same delay and deliberation,
the same hanging head with a cigarette in the centre of his lips as he
gazed at the ground with eyes nearly closed and rotated on the spot
with his hands crossed in the small of his back. Soon his arms lifted
above his head and slowly soared in alternate sweeps before his lowered face, like a vulture rocking on a slow breeze, with an occasional
carefully placed crack of thumb and forefinger as the steps evolved.
The downward gaze, the precise placing of the feet, the sudden twirl
of the body, the sinking on alternate knees, the sweep of an out-
stretched leg in three quarters of a circle with the arms outflung in
two radii for balance – these steps and passes and, above all, the
downward scrutiny were as though the dancer were proving, on the
trodden fish scales and the goats' droppings, a lost theorem about
tangents and circles, or retracing the conclusions of Pythagoras
about the square of the hypotenuse.

But more striking still was the tragic and doomed aura that
invested this dance, the flaunting so quickly muffled and the intro-
vert and cerebral aloofness of the dancer. Absorption lifted him so
far from the others in the cave that he might have been alone in a distant room, raptly applying ritual and undeviating devices to abstruse
and nearly insoluble conundrums or exorcizing a private and incom-
municable pain. The loneliness was absolute. The voices and hands
had fallen silent, isolating the wiry jangle of the strings.

On a rock, lifted there to clear the floor, the round, low, heavy table was perched. Revolving past it, Costa leaned forward: suddenly the table levitated itself into the air, sailed past us, and pivoted at right angles to Costa's head in a series of wide loops, the edge clamped firmly in his mouth and held here only by his teeth buried in the wood. It rotated like a magic carpet, slicing crescents out of the haze of smoke and soon travelling so fast that the four glasses on it, the chapfallen bagpipe with its perforated cow's horn dangling, the raki flask, the knives and spoons, the earthenware saucepan that had held the lentils and the backbones of the two mackerels with their heads and tails hanging over the edge of the tin plate, all dissolved, for a few swift revolutions, into a circular blur; then it redefined itself, when the pace dwindled into a slowly revolving still life.

As the dancer sank gyrating to floor level, firelight lit the table-top; when he soared into the dark, only the underside glowed. He quickened his pace and reduced the circumference of the circles by spinning faster and faster in the same place, his revolutions striking sparks of astonished applause through the grotto: cries which rose to an uproar. His head was flung back; muscles and veins corrugated his streaming features and his balancing arms were outflung like those of a dervish until the flying table itself melted into a vast disc twice its own diameter and spinning at such a speed in the cave's centre that it should by rights have scattered the still life that it bore into the nether shadows.

Slowly the speed slackened. The table was looping through the smoke five feet from the floor. Soon it was sliding from its orbit and rotating back to its launching rock, unhurriedly alighting there at last with all its impedimenta undisturbed. Not once had the dancer's hands touched it; but, the moment before it resettled in its place, he retrieved the cigarette he had left burning on the edge of a plate. Dancing slowly back to the centre with no hint of haste or vertigo, he tapped away the long ash and replaced the cigarette in his mouth. Gyrating, sinking and rising again, he unwound the dance to its sober initial steps; then, straight as a wand and poised on tiptoe at his motionless starting point, he broke off and sauntered with lowered lids to the re-established table. Picking up his raki glass he took a meditative sip and, poker-faced in the clamour, slowly subsided.

I could catch a loose word here and there in the flow of Romaic as they talked among themselves. How was I to find out, with my clumsy rudiments of Bulgarian, the origin of these dances, the roots of their unique and absolute oddity? Panayi was swaddling his instrument for the night: its incendiary work was done but its message still twanged and hovered in our veins. Dimitri had dropped asleep for a moment, lying with his head on his arm. The one-handed elder clapped the raki bottle to his eye, as an admiral would a spyglass, to see if any was left. Costa the dancer smoked and smiled with the easy air of a geometrician who has proved what had to be proved; *Quod erat demonstrandum,* the silent smile seemed to say under the peak of the old cap tilted rakishly forward to shield his eyes from the flames.

The cave dwellers, after a final gulp of raki, began to settle for the night. I was to sleep at the sailors' end of the cave. Costa and Dimitri hospitably spread new leaves close to the fire, rolled up a coat as a pillow, piled blanket on blanket and laid the old shepherd's cloak on top of me. '*Kryo?*' they asked. '*Studeno?*' 'Cold?' – they had learned four or five words of English on their travels. Only an occasional tremor at wide intervals reminded me of my earlier mishaps; later impressions had snowed them under. There was nothing guarded or apathetic about these particular Greeks; the trance-like melancholy of their steps had evaporated with the last fumes of the dances and the music; their identical grey eyes were filled with humour, alertness and friendly warmth. I thought I had divined an extra feeling in their welcome and in their horny handshakes earlier on, and I had interpreted it as a late symptom of Greek feelings towards Lord Byron's countrymen. I was right. Dimitri said as much. Uttering the words '*Lordos Veeron!*' he raised his bunched fingers in a gesture of approval.

Sleep was long in coming. There was much to think about, especially Greece and the Greeks, which were drawing nearer every day. An occasional clank from the fifty goats at the farther end broke the deepening silence. A few yards off, beyond the twelve adjacent snores, I could hear the gasp of the Black Sea. The light ebbed from the walls and from the stalactites as the fire shrank to a feathery glow. Through a gap in the wall, three quarters of Orion blazed an icy slanting lozenge.

A slight clatter roused me as I was on the brink of sleep. It was the spectral, tiptoe figure, confident that everyone was asleep (ah! but they weren't!), of the dog with the black monocle, tidily licking the last of the lentils and fish gills out of the saucepan.

Rumania – Travels in a Land before Darkness Fell

Daily Telegraph Weekend Magazine, 12 May 1990

The passage is set in Rumania in the mid to late 1930s. It was written after Paddy revisited Rumania in 1990, following the fall of the Ceauşescus. In it he recalls pre-war life at Baleni, the estate in Moldavia belonging to his friend Balasha Cantacuzène, and Hélène ('Pomme') and Constantin Donici, Balasha's sister and brother-in-law. This is where Paddy lived during the months leading up to the declaration of war.

Seen through the windows of the night plane, Bucharest glimmered into being as dimly as a candlelit city under siege. The Revolution which had astonished the world was only a month old, and I wondered, as we landed, how much these amazing events had changed it; and for private reasons, I wondered too how different the whole country would be from the Rumania I had lived in for a couple of years before the war. We must go back a bit. In fact, more than half a century.

In spring 1934, I was on my way on foot to Constantinople, living on £1 a week and sleeping rough, but soon after my nineteenth birthday a letter of introduction in Hungary changed all this; I was lent a horse to cross the great plain: cowsheds and barns gave way to country houses and castles, and by the time I got to Transylvania – across the Rumanian border, that is, and entering the country, from a Rumanian point of view, through the back door – the Spartan trudge had turned into a stroll from one schloss to another.

The people I stayed with there were Hungarians still. After the First World War, Transylvania, formerly part of Hungary, had been granted to Rumania; but for Hungarians both sides of the border, the loss seemed mortal. (During these travels, I think I was absorbed in everything but politics. My reason for liking the Hungarians was their welcoming kindness, their dash and their spirit, and similar subjective grounds, later on, inspired an equal fondness for the Rumanians.)

Most of the Transylvanian Hungarians – two million of them –

were concentrated far to the east, whereas my new friends belonged to the scattered Hungarian landowners who had lived for many generations in the western and densely Rumanian parts. But, different in race and religion from the folk who surrounded them, too attached to their old homes or too poor now to uproot and start again in Hungary, they were akin to the Anglo-Irish ascendancy and their houses had a touch of their sadness and much of their charm. Blessedly, life was a hundred years behind the times.

My first stopping place, north of Arad, was the house of Baron Tibor Solymosy, a jolly bachelor and ex-horse-gunner, and it stood pillared and Palladian like the Haymarket Theatre in a sea of vineyards. The stay turned into a sort of initiation and it ended, with gypsy musicians and a party of neighbours, on the crest of a vine-clad hill in a party that lasted till dawn. After that, I was passed on from house to house like a bad penny. The next was a sort of hacienda among huge trees, the home of an eccentric Pole and his Hungarian wife, Klara Zay, an unkempt but brilliant horsewoman. (Horses played a great role. The roads destroyed cars, so short journeys were all in battered victorias, or on horseback.) Ötvenes, the next, was the scene of woodland paper chases and fireworks after dinner. Lilac was ending, but there were wild hollyhocks and red and white peonies and fledgling storks nesting on many of the chimneys.

South of the river Mureş, many days sped by at Capalnas, where Count Jenö Teleki lived with his famous collection of oriental moths. The last and longest sojourn was with Elemér v. Klobusicky – 'István' in earlier writings – an original and high-spirited ex-hussar just old enough to have fought in the war: weeks strewn with strange adventures which ended in a rackety midsummer jaunt with a wild and enterprising girl re-named Angéla, all over Transylvania. In a vast borrowed car, the three of us explored the old cities of Alba Iulia and Cluj and the important Magyar town of Tîrgu Mureş, the centre of the land of the Szeklers, who had settled there in the tenth century. Careering on, we struck south to Sighişoara, the castellated and tapering stronghold of Vlad the Impaler. Next day we all parted, and, very sadly, I was on my own again.

It was August by now. Slogging south along the flanks of the Retezat mountains, I stayed with some Rumanian shepherds in a high shieling; hardy, self-reliant men who lived in a world of steep woods, vast flocks and wolves and bears. After a halt with some learned Hasidic Jews who were running a logging business on the lower slopes, I crossed the Danube into Bulgaria, sleeping in barns and ditches once again; and I got to Constantinople on New Year's Day, 1935.

But before that year was out, I was back in Rumania at a place called Baleni, and for a long time. It belonged to two Rumanian sisters a few years older than I; we had met in Athens where one of them was a painter, and a light-hearted affinity sprang up. I wanted to start writing, we pooled forces, and after a summer and autumn painting and writing in a Peloponnesian watermill, the question arose: where now? An answer soon surfaced: 'We've got this tumble-down house in Moldavia. Why not there?' After a journey by sea to Constantza and north from Galatz by train, we got out at a small station where a carriage with an old Polish coachman was waiting: an hour's drive brought us to Baleni. It was a large, rambling, one-storeyed white house with a village and trees and a courtyard full of friendly dogs, with the wintry dales of Moldavia rolling away all round. To the east, beyond the Prut and the Dniestr, Russia began.

In those days Rumania sounded remote, and Moldavia, the northern of the two old principalities which in the nineteenth century were united in the eventual kingdom of Rumania, remoter still. Bucharest, in Wallachia, had become the booming centre of the young kingdom, and the charming Moldavian capital of Jassy, the town dwelling-place of the great boyars of the north, lapsed into elegant decay.

Deep in history, Moldavia was by far the stranger. Wooded and undulating, it steepened to the pine-clad Carpathians in the west and north – towards Hungary, Transylvania, Slovakia, Poland and the Bukovina – with the Wallachian plains to the south, and, south-east, the thousand bird-haunted square miles of the Danube delta. Then came the Black Sea; and in the east, the steppe flowed away towards Bessarabia and the Ukraine. The low regions were hot and dusty in summer, and dotted with flocks, rustling with wheat and maize and flickering with mirages; it was deep in snow in winter, and filled with the rumour of wolves. Here and there, at long carriage- and sleigh-drives from each other, shaded by tall trees and rookeries and backed by coach houses, stables, smithies and barns and cottages, the long Moldavian manor houses, close to their counterparts in the novels of Turgenev, were scattered like a dispersed fleet of white ships.

Plaster flaked from the columns and pediments, and indoors, room opened into room in vistas of Louis Philippe and Second Empire furniture. Benevolent or wicked voivodes gazed from the walls in half-Byzantine, half-Slavonic panoplies of fur hats, aigrettes, furred robes and pearls. There would be a western relation or two with powdered hair, boyar descendants with epaulettes and sabres, some touching girls in crinolines holding flowers and pigeons and, in this particular house, a handsome great-grandfather called Prince George Cantacuzène, in a Byronic Greek general's costume and scimitar, taking the surrender of the Pasha of Monemvasia.

At nightfall, as Niculina, spill in hand, lit the wicks of a succession of shaded kerosene lamps, the light caught the chipped gold of an ikon's halo, a samovar and cups and tea-time raisin-bread called *cozonac*, glass cases with the lumpy seals of parchments, the family's two-headed eagle, tall china stoves, the prisms of chandeliers, stags' antlers, the glass eye of a huge bear's pelt from the Carpathians, and thousands of books in several languages. The voices would be talking French rather than Rumanian. The results of this foible (the legacy, as in Russia and Poland, of several generations) were like the conversations on the first page of *War and Peace*, but less silly. Their themes were country ones, crops, timber to be felled, horses to be bought, sold or shod, and impending shoots: pheasant, waterfowl, bustard, deer, wolves, wild boar and bears. Although most of these country-dwellers were half-ruined, life was rich in tales of past extravagance, eccentricity, comedy and intrigue, with a duel here and there; but literature was the presiding theme; in spite of hard times, books still arrived from Paris and London.

It would be impossible to fit these two sisters into any category. Sent to school in France and England and finished and brought out all over the place, they were good, beautiful, courageous, gifted, imaginative, immersed in literature and the arts, kind, funny and unconventional; everybody loved them, and so did I. The husband of one ran the estate and their daughter looked like Millais' Ophelia. An indefinable charm pervaded the house, its inhabitants and all connected with it.

Most of a large estate had been lopped away in the agrarian reform. There was little cash about, people were paid in kind by a sort of sharing system; so, in a way, were the owners; and, on the spot, there was enough to go round. Elderly pensioners hovered in the middle distance and an ancient staff would come into being at moments of need.

I can see them all: Ionitza, the lantern-jawed cook; Ifrim Podubniak, the rather threadbare butler, never quite sober; white-coiffed Niculina, called *la femme électrique*, whose speed and alacrity made up for the non-existent current; she was in love with Mihai Pintili; he and Mihai Caval chopped logs and did odd jobs; and 'Saxon' Fifi, who was bedridden, slowly dwindled in a distant wing; there was Mustafa from the Dobrudja; Ivan, the Russian plumber who had taken part in the Potemkin mutiny, and Pan Stanislas the coachman, once a groom on a Tarnowski estate near Crakow, who had done his military service in the 2nd Schwarzenberg Dragoons, when Galicia was still Austrian. A shepherd called Petre played a long wooden flute, Ifrim's father carved me a three-stringed rebeck out of a walnut tree blown down in a storm; Anton, an accomplished violinist with a kicked-in face, played and sang when called upon, backed by half a dozen fellow gypsies settled in the village. There was one crone there who knew how to cast spells and break them by incantations; another, by magic, could deliver whole villages from rats. After sheep-shearing a *claca*, fifty girls and crones, bristling with distaffs would gather in a barn to spin; hilarious days with a lot of food, drink, singing and story-telling.

Snow reached the windowsills and lasted till spring. There were cloudy rides under a sky full of rooks; otherwise, it was an indoor life of painting, writing, reading, talk, and lamp-lit evenings with Mallarmé, Apollinaire, Proust and Gide handy; there was *Les Enfants terribles* and *Le Grand Meaulnes* and *L'Aiglon* read aloud; all these were early debarbarizing steps in beguiling and unknown territory.

Melting snows were the signal for wider explorations, while hay was reaped and ricks went up; the wheat harvest followed, and threshing and winnowing, then the vintage. The country people were tough, hardy and very likeable men in sheepskin jerkins and conical fleece hats, the women in coifs. I got to know everyone for miles. I felt half-Moldavian by adoption and tried to pick up their dialect and turns of phrase and their songs.

During the next year or two, this was my sheet anchor. There were journeys all over Rumania: a leisurely expedition with horses across north Bessarabia was particularly romantic (now it is entirely annexed by Russia and confusingly renamed 'Republic of Moldavia') – and I can still see the long trestle-tables spread under the oak branches, all set about with jugs of wine and *kvass*; and there were journeys by canoe in the vast whispering labyrinth where the Danube falls to pieces.

The summer days of 1939, while the peace of Europe disintegrated, were without a flaw. Two of the English guests staying there – Henry Nevile, who had just left school, and I – tore ourselves away in early September to join the army. As we all waved goodbye in the Gara de Nord in Bucharest ('Back in a few months!') we none of us realized how great and how lasting the break would be.

Back in England – at the Guards Depot and Aldershot and Matlock – reading between the lines of letters, I got an idea of the anguish they must have been feeling, especially when Paris fell and England was under siege. My friends were deeply averse to many recent trends in Rumania and all their sympathy was with the Western Allies.

After half a millennium of disasters, most of them due to the suzerainty of the Ottoman Empire, Rumania for the last half-century had seemed to be on a hopeful path. Hard lessons had been learnt and, with constitutional progress, many of the blemishes, which the Rumanians themselves were always pointing out, would have dropped away. Seen from today, the life I have touched on, especially in Moldavia, sounds like a golden age. Wrongly, of course: graft throve in the capital, King Carol's opportunist rule and the threats and violence of the Iron Guard were clouding the scene: and, before the year 1941 was out, the country, unbelievably, was allied to Germany. Soon her armies were advancing into Russia (which had just annexed Bessarabia and half of the Bukovina), and Hitler had handed the north of Transylvania over to Hungary. Letters had stopped; silence and darkness followed.

After a final retreat, with appalling losses, Rumania switched to the advancing Russians and soon, at the end of the war, like the rest of Eastern Europe – with fewer than 1,000 Communists out of a population of 18,000,000 – a mixture of coercion and fraud turned her into a Communist state. Meanwhile, the pre-war company I had kept had put me on a blacklist; for good, it seemed. But, with the coming of peace, letters crept guardedly to and fro and the blanks were gradually filled in.

The sisters had been nurses during the war; the land was confiscated; and on a grim morning in the late 1940s, a truck drove up with police and a commissar. They were allowed a suitcase each, and a quarter of an hour to pack. (The Cantacuzènes had been there for many generations.) Villagers in tears filled their arms with loaves, cheeses, eggs and poultry; then the truck drove them away for ever. The painter-sister and a male cousin tried to escape down to the Black Sea to Constantinople in a rowing boat, but they were betrayed and imprisoned. (Her cousin was lucky not to have been sent, like several of their relations, to die in the Danube–Black Sea canal. Never completed, this horrible trench was a dustbin for 'elements of putrid background' – this was the official term; it is said to have killed off 100,000 undesirables.) After their eviction, their family were taken 200 kilometres from where they belonged and put in a garret in a Carpathian foothill-town.

The moment the veto was lifted I went back to Rumania in 1965, with a short-term visa. Mixing with foreigners incurred severe punishment, but harbouring them indoors was much worse; so the visit had to be made by stealth, at night, and on the back of a motorbike borrowed by the Ophelia niece, who was working as a draughts-woman in Bucharest. We found them in their attic. In spite of the interval, the fine looks of my friends, the thoughtful clear glance and the humour were all intact; it was as though we had parted a few months ago, instead of twenty-six years. Their horrible vicissitudes were narrated with detachment and speed: time was short and there were only brief pauses for sleep on a couple of chairs. The rest of our forty-eight hours – we dared risk no more – were filled with pre-war memories, the lives of all our friends, and a great deal of laughter. It was a miraculous reunion. The sisters now eked out their state pittance by teaching French, English and painting.

Other Rumanian meetings came later, when they were eventually allowed abroad for two or three weeks now and then. There were joyful visits to friends in England and France and Greece. Early thoughts of leaving Rumania lapsed in the end, they resisted the idea partly from feeling it was too late in the day; also, they said that Rumania, after all, was where they belonged; secretly, perhaps, they shrank from being a burden to anyone. One by one the same dread illness carried them away. Nobility of character marked them all. They wrote many and brilliant letters and contact was unbroken. For some people under alien regimes, life is lived vicariously, pen in hand.

It took until the 1960s to find out what happened to my old Hungarian friends in Transylvania. They had all been evicted with special ruthlessness, 'István'-Elemér told me by letter: they had left for Hungary. (I found him at last in a workman's flat in Budapest, grinding away at the translation of engineering manuals from English to Magyar.)

A few years ago, I retraced my 1934 Transylvanian route, and the first halt was Ineu, where Tibor, my old horse-gunner friend, had lived. A new road had sliced off half of the park, there was a cheerless office and a noticeboard at the gate, so I left the car out of sight, and with some misgiving, shinned over the wall and dropped in. The place had a forlorn and unkempt look, and after all these years the house with its Palladian pillars seemed much smaller. But who were the figures drifting to and fro? People were wandering aimlessly about, standing inactive or sitting on the grass, all of them alone.

I spoke to one and I saw by the blank response that he was a lunatic; indeed, they all were. So with no one among these poor souls to stop me, I went indoors. The rooms had all been divided up; it was impossible to get one's bearings. Upstairs, things were clearer, and I found my old room. Eight beds filled it now, three of them occupied by vaguely smiling patients, so I sat down on an empty one for a think. A rosy-cheeked woman with a broom came in and asked who I was looking for. She brightened at Tibor's name: her people had all been in service with the family since her great-grandfather's time and she had stayed on as a cleaning woman. 'Yes, they all left – Tibor, Gabor, Iris, all of them, but they are all dead now. They were good people.' We talked about them for about an hour, and I stole away.

When I got to my old Teleki haven the other side of the river, it too seemed to have shrunk; an exactly similar, mad scarecrow population was adrift there too. I longed to know what had happened to Count Teleki's study and his books and his huge collection of moths. I drove on, feeling intensely depressed.

Further up the Mureş I went to see what had happened at 'István'-Elemér's. The house, Gurasada, was inhabited by an engaging Rumanian married couple running an experimental bamboo plantation. Their eyes lit up when they heard Elemér's name. They had never met him, but his fame lingered in the valley like a myth. 'We never asked to live in his house,' they observed sadly. Everyone else in the area had vanished. They gave me a bottle of *tzvica* for him, distilled from his own plums.

I had only driven a few miles in my hired Dacia car when a harvester asked for a lift. My slipshod vestiges of Rumanian at once gave me away as a foreigner and he looked bewildered and alarmed. He was about sixty, with hazel eyes in a bony face. Eventually I said, 'How are things here now?' He looked at me searchingly once or twice and then, after a long pause, said, 'You don't know who I am and I don't know who you are. Well, they are very bad! *Foarte rău!* We haven't got enough to eat, it's getting worse, we're worked to death, we live like slaves and it's all for nothing. We're done for.' When I said it might get better, he answered: 'It gets worse every year, every day, and *it will never end!* What do *they* care? We don't own anything, nothing's ours, no land, nothing, not even the ploughs or the tools we work with.' He lifted the sickle in his lap. 'Do you think *this* belongs to me? Nothing does.'

A fierce diatribe of resentment and hatred came pouring out. 'And nobody dares to say a word! If we do –' He left the phrase unfinished but lifted his arms and smacked his wrists together, indicating handcuffs. '*Inside!* There are thousands locked up! Thousands and thousands!' We said goodbye outside his village. The next passengers were two workmen. When I asked the same question, automatically by now, there was a long and embarrassed pause. One of them said hesitantly:

'Things are very good.' The other agreed on similar note. '*Da! da! Foarte bine!*', and that was that . . . I gave about fifteen lifts a day and when solitary passengers knew it was safe, they couldn't wait to blow off steam; if there were two or more, they were correspondingly evasive.

All that is, except for two well-fed young men with trilbies and briefcases who waved me down rather masterfully and, without a word, settled in the back and started talking to each other. I addressed them and when nationalities were cleared up, they answered my questions with fulsome praise of the country's prosperity. We were driving through a village where two queues stretched half-way down the street. 'What about all that?' I asked, 'I never saw them before the war.' One of them answered: 'Rumania's a poor country.' I said that it used to be very rich and they fell silent for the rest of the trip. Later, in my hotel in Deva, a plain-clothes policeman asked me long and maladroitly what my business was and when had I last been in Rumania? Where had I picked up the language? Then he riffled through my passport for half an hour and went away.

'*It will never end . . .*' The harvester's words kept coming to mind during the next few years. Everything confirmed them and they never sounded truer than this winter for, excepting Rumania, the whole of Eastern Europe, from the Berlin Wall to the first tremors in inert Bulgaria, was casting loose. There were isolated symptoms – the suppressed but unprecedented demonstrations in Braşov and the solitary voice of Doina Cornea – then suddenly came the stiffening protest and the outbreak in Timişoara, the gunfire, the tanks and the punitive slaughter; the flare-up of the revolution in Bucharest, followed by the end of the Ceauşescus with the whole world looking on, and the Securitate still firing from the roofs and regrouping in newly engineered catacombs.

It came clean out of the blue, and it was a fiercer and longer struggle than the revolts in all the rest of Europe put together and nothing more astonishing had happened there for forty years. Rumania's slowness to revolt had recently been attributed, by one or two writers, to lack of courage, which I knew to be wrong.

Everything, from the deeds of the late and post-medieval princes to the subsequent peasant revolts and the stubborn opposition, at

Mărăşeşti, to Mackensen's advance in the First World War, pointed the other way; and during 1944 it was confirmed from an odd source. I was part of an Anglo-Cretan commando hiding in the mountains with a captive German general who had commanded a division on the Kuban front; we were talking of Germany's allies, and he said the Italians weren't such poor soldiers as we and the Greeks seemed to think. We listed Germany's other European allies, and he dismissed them one after the other as useless. 'Which ones then, General?' 'Why, the Rumanians, of course! They were totally fearless in attack, and if they had to hold a point in defence, they were *like gun-dogs!* Sometimes till they were all killed.'

I remembered this, too, on the flight to Rumania.

Rumania – The Last Day of Peace

from Introduction to Matila Ghyka, *The World Mine Oyster*
(Heinemann, 1961)

Here Paddy describes an expedition in 1939 from Baleni made on the last day of peace.

The summer months [of 1939] succeeded each other all too fast and the evil omens multiplied; the storks that gathered from every roof and chimney to join the ragged south-bound armada were leaving a doomed Europe. To forget and to exorcize for a day the growing assembly of trouble, we set off, on the second day of September, for a mushroom-gathering picnic in a wood about ten miles away, some in an old open carriage, some on horseback; through the sunlit vineyards where the grapes were almost ready to be harvested and pressed, and out into the open country. The clearings in the wood, when we arrived, were studded with our quarry. Alighting and dismounting, we scattered in a competitive frenzy, reassembling soon with our baskets full to the brim. In the glade of this mysterious wood, with the tethered horses grazing and swishing their tails under the oak branches, the picnic spun itself out. Soon it was late in the afternoon and the great demijohn was empty and the old Polish coachman was fidgeting the horses back into the shafts and fastening the traces. The ones on horseback set off by a different way, racing each other across the mown slopes of the vast hayfields and galloping in noisy and wine-sprung zigzags through the ricks and down a wide valley and up again through another oak-spinney to the road where the carriage, trailing a long plume of dust, was trotting more sedately home. We reined in and fell into a walk alongside.

The track followed the crest of a high ridge with the dales of Moldavia flowing away on either hand. We were moving through illimitable sweeps of still air. Touched with pink on their under sides by the declining sun, which also combed the tall stubble with gold, one or two thin shoals of mackerel cloud hung motionless in the enormous sky. Whale-shaped shadows expanded along the valleys below, and the spinneys were sending long loops of shade downhill. The air was so still that the smoke from Matila Ghyka's cigar hung in a riband in the wake of our cavalcade; and how clearly the bells of the flocks, which were streaming down in haloes of golden dust to the wells and the brushwood folds a few ravines away, floated to our ears. Homing peasants waved their hats in greeting, and someone out of sight was singing one of those beautiful and rather forlorn country songs they call a *doina*. A blurred line along the sky a league away marked the itinerary of the deserting storks. Those in the carriage below were snowed under by picnic things, mushroom baskets and bunches of anemones picked in the wood. It was a moment of peace and tranquillity and we rode on in silence towards the still far-off samovar and the oil lamps and heaven knew what bad news. The silence was suddenly broken by an eager exclamation from Matila.

'Oh, look!' he cried. One hand steadied the basket of mushrooms on his lap, the other pointed at the sky into which he was peering. High overhead some water-birds, astray from the delta, perhaps, or from some near-by fen, were flying in a phalanx. (I shall have to improvise names and details here, for precise memory and ornithological knowledge both fail me. But the gist and the spirit are exact.)

'Yes,' he said, 'it's rather rare; the *xiphorhyncus paludinensis minor*, the *glaivionette*, or Lesser Swamp Swordbill – *Wendischer Schwertvogel* in German, *glodnic* in Moldavian dialect; I believe the Wallachians call it *spadună de baltă*. Varieties are dotted about all over the world but always in very small numbers. They live in floating nests and have a very shrill ascending note in the mating season.' He whistled softly once or twice. 'Their eggs are a ravishing colour, a lovely lapis lazuli with little primrose speckles. They have been identified with the Stymphalian birds that Hercules killed, and there's a mention of them in Lucian's *Dialogues* and in Pliny the Elder, and, I think in Oppian . . . The ancient Nubians revered them as minor gods and there's *supposed* to be one on a bas-relief at Cyrene; there's certainly a flight of them in the background of a *Journey of the Magi* by Sassetta – he probably saw them in the reeds of Lake Trasimene, where they still breed; and the chiefs of two tribes on the Zambezi wear robes of their tail feathers for the new moon ceremonies. Some people,' he continued, with a slight change of key, 'find them too fishy. It's not true, as I learnt years ago near Bordeaux. On a spit, over a very slow fire – of hornbeam twigs, if possible – with frequent basting and plenty of saffron, *glaivionette à la landaise* can be delicious . . . Alas: I've only eaten it once . . .'

His dark eyes, a-kindle with memory, watched the birds out of sight across the dying sky, and we all burst out laughing. The cosmic approach . . . It had been a happy day, as we had hoped, and it had to last us for a long time, for the next day's news scattered this little society for ever.

A *Brûler Zin*

from *The Traveller's Tree*

This passage comes from Paddy's first book The Traveller's Tree. It describes a journey round the islands of the Caribbean in 1947, which Paddy undertook with Costa, the Greek photographer, whose photographs illustrate the book, and his future wife Joan. The 'Brûler Zin' is a voodoo ceremony which took place on the island of Haiti, where Voodoo first emerged and where it is still a potent force.

A *Brûler Zin*, the most important ceremony in Voodoo, was being solemnized to celebrate the initiation as Hounci-Canzos of two neophytes from Curaçao. In order to attend the rite, they had crossed the Caribbean Sea in one of the schooners plying between the Greater Antilles and the Spanish Main: a journey which suggests that there is more connection between the secret Negro sects in the islands than is generally supposed.

The *tonnelle* lay behind a large bread-fruit tree in the heart of a pop-ulous quarter near the tramlines and rum shops. The drummers were plainly virtuosi, and the twenty white-clad houncis danced with the cohesion of a *corps de ballet*. Everything was disciplined and organized to the smallest detail. The ceremony had been going some time when we arrived, but, though there were about a hundred people in the *ton-nelle*, the mud floor was only occupied by the Houngan, the mambo, the houncis and the various postulants and acolytes of the peristyle.

The candidates, meanwhile, for whom the impending *Brûler Zin* was the last act of initiation, were invisible inside the Rada houmfor. Their six rigorous days of preparation were nearly ended. The first step of this preparation is confession and absolution in a church, fol-lowed by a second plenary confession to the Houngan, who repeats it aloud to his personal Lwa. Two days are then spent in rest and medi-tation and certain specific ablutions, and then there is another com-pulsory period in church. Next, as all this week is aimed at making the candidate a fitting vessel for the visitation of the Lwas, the Houngan and the mambo conduct a ceremony in honour of Aizan-Véléquété, the Lwa of purification and exorcism. After further ritual lustrations, the candidates are enveloped in sheets so that only their faces are exposed, and then stretched out on mats in the houmfor with their heads resting on pillows of stone. Here, living on a liquid mixture of maize and mushrooms and herbs, they remain in the darkness for four days of silence and prayer. Sacrifices and unctions and a kind of baptism punctuate this symbolic death, and the Houngan removes their souls and places them in a head pot. The vigil was about to finish.

The swordsman and his two standard-bearers were engaged in a prolonged dance of salutation. The swordsman, the Laplace, wove a path among the houncis, leaping and turning, and twisting a cutlass in the air, while two girls, slowly waving their red and blue silk banners on which eagles were embroidered in sequins, danced on his left and right. They remained together throughout the evening, moving and turning perfectly in line, rhythmically prostrating themselves and recovering in unison, and making the elegant pirouette-salute to all the staff and to the congregation.

At one moment the houncis were dancing in two lines, at another round the pillar, falling rhythmically to the ground in a circle and kissing the ground, so that the radiation of their white figures formed a white corolla; rising again with the dust grey on their lips and foreheads, chanting, all the time, to the clatter of the drums. The mambo appeared laden with their long necklaces of coloured beads, which they knelt in turn to receive. She arranged them so that they crossed in saltire on their breasts and backs. Libations were spilt, and a magic ring of white maize-flour drawn round the pillar, encompassed, in a circle about a yard in diameter, by the white cognizances of each great Lwa. The drums fell silent, and the initiates sank to their knees in a compact group and bowed their heads. In the universal hush the Houngan softly intoned a long series of prayers in French. [. . .]

Next, beginning with Legba, comes the invocation of the Lwas, a prolonged rubaiyat that grows more cabalistic in suggestion, until the names of the Lwas cease, to be replaced by a monody of pure sound from which all apparent significance has been purged: '*Lade immennou daguinin soilade aguignaminsou . . . Oh! Oh! Oh! . . . Pingolo Pingolo roi montré nous la prié qui minnin africain . . . Wanguinan Wannimé . . . En hen mandioment en hen . . .'* It seems that only a minimum of these words are of African origin, and their meaning is totally obscure. Nobody knows where or how they originated; whether they evolved in Haiti, or whether they are a memory of some hermetic language of the priests in Africa. Softly towards the end of these orisons the drums began to throb, first a tentative tap, then another, then half a dozen, until, after a pause, all the voices and drums had struck up again louder than ever, and the houncis were shuffling and revolving their way through a yanvalou. They danced slowly into the temple and the doors were closed. The peristyle was bare for a while of all but the drummers.

After half an hour of this emptiness, the door was thrown open and the swordsman and standard-bearers, waving their emblems, sprang down the steps in a single flying arc. The others streamed after them, howling, rather than singing, at the top of their voices. The procession, ceremoniously carrying little cauldrons, bottles, iron pegs, bundles of firewood and sheaves of green branches, began to revolve round the pillar at breakneck speed. The mambo danced at the rear of this saraband, waving flurried trusses of live white chickens above her head. Some of the dancers continued their round, while the others drove sets of iron pegs into the ground, sloping inwards to form primitive tripods, at three points round the pillar. Fires were kindled and flames were soon leaping up. The green branches were spread out all round them in a rustic carpet. Pouring liquids into the flames, the mambo flourished the clucking fowls along the proffered limbs of the houncis, and ceremoniously waved them to the four cardinal points: *'A table,' 'Dabord,' 'Olandé,'* and *'Adonai'* – east, west, north, and south. When the birds had pecked at the scattered maize in token of their willingness to be offered up – an omen which was greeted by jubilant shouts of 'Ah! Bobo! Ah! Bobo!' – they were consigned to the various officers of the *tonnelle,* who crouched with them beside the fires, over which the earthenware cauldrons – the *zins* – had now been placed on the tripods.

The method of sacrifice is swift and inhumane. Simultaneously all the chickens' tongues were torn out, and their legs and their wings were broken; then, with a dexterous and violent movement, their heads were wrenched off. The sacrificers were soon up to their elbows in blood as the chickens, with savage expertness, were pulled to pieces. Blood was poured into the cauldrons. Tufts of the neck feathers and the gutted and dismembered carcases soon followed them. The battery of tom-toms continued without a break, the drummers leaning forward at each roll with their long heckling snarl. The cauldrons and the flames, the flying feathers, the blood, the ring of serious black faces in the firelight above the carpet of green leaves, were a wild and disquieting sight. If a goat, a dog or a bull is to be sacrificed, scent is first poured all over the victim, and it is dressed in ritual trappings. It is suspended in the air by its four out-stretched legs; the priest castrates it and severs its windpipe with two deft cutlass-blows. It was impossible not to wonder what the sacrificial technique had been in the obsolete Mondongo human offerings. The modern observances of the Zobops and the Vlinbindingues were an even more irresistible theme for conjecture.

The door of the temple had again opened, and the gyrating swords and flags were leading into the open a procession which advanced with unnatural slowness. Surrounded by an escort of houncis, an object like an enormous white slug with an immense hump was crawling out of the shadows of the houmfor. As it worked its way towards us, guided by the houncis, it still remained problematical. It was, one finally realized, a white cloth with a man inside it. But how could he be twisted into that extraordinary shape? The houncis, crawling along beside it on all fours, were holding the edge of the sheet to the ground, so that not an inch of the person inside it could be seen. It drew level with the fires and stopped. The mambo fumbled with one corner of the cloth, the edge was slipped up a couple of inches, and two clasped hands were revealed, one black, the other dark brown, and both, I noticed, left hands. One man must have been crawling on his hands and knees, while a second, kneeling behind him with his body hunched over his arched back, stretched down across his shoulders to clasp the hands of his mount for support. The mambo pushed the black hand back under the cloth and rubbed the pink palm of the other with oil. She reached into a cauldron and scooped out a handful of hot maize-flour, and, working it with grimaces of pain into a paste, she moulded it to a cylinder and pressed it into the pink palm, forcibly closing the fingers over it and thrusting it back under the sheet. The boiling maize on the oil must have been almost unendurable. A tremor, accompanied by a long gasp, ran along the white shape, which slowly resumed its circuit. When it came round again, the other hand was subjected to the same ordeal. On the next two journeys, feet were in turn extricated and held for a moment in the flames. The white mass slithered, like some legless mammal, unwieldily up the steps and vanished inside the houmfor. The second candidate appeared and the operation was repeated. When he was in the temple and lying once more on the floor beside the other candidate, the dancing and the invocations began again. The huddling mambo emptied flasks of oil into the *zins*, and scattered a pool of rum all round the fires which at once burst into a blaze. The houncis, falling to their knees, plunged their hands into the flames. The cauldrons cracked and disintegrated with the heat, the boiling oil was mingled with the rum and a great flame leapt into the air. The remains of the sacrifice were ceremoniously buried and a rhythmic stamping dance took place over the grave.

Soon afterwards the first crisis of possession occurred. Shaking off the usual initial paroxysm, a bulky hounci-canzo rose from the ground in a metamorphosis whose symptoms resembled an amorous delirium. Gabbling and leering, she careered unsteadily round the *tonnelle*, rubbing her loins against every person and object that she encountered, in an erotic simulacrum. Her fellow houncis seized her and began to force her arms into the sleeves of an old morning coat several sizes too small for her. For a Ghédé had been recognized, and these myrmidons of Death all wear the Baron's livery. A hounci-bossale swiftly appeared with a collection of headgear, and, in spite of the Ghédé's shouts and her jerks to free herself, they contrived to hold her while a broken bowler hat was crammed over her ears. A battered trilby was thrust on top of it, and on the very summit of this pagoda, an ancient top-hat. A great pair of black glasses was hastily straddled across her nose, and the moment she was released the Ghédé flew galloping round the *tonnelle* once more, screeching and laughing and firing a child's cap-pistol into the air. The drums thundered, and the drummers roared and snarled over their cylinders like three jaguars. As she cavorted past us, we could see that her eyes were turned back in the revulsion that had become so familiar. Soon another Lwa descended, and by the first light at least half a dozen dancers had fallen and died and risen again, each of them possessed and transformed into members of this ghoulish horde – Baron Cimetièrc, Général Criminel, Capitaine Zombi and the rest, whose rites are celebrated with cracking whips and gunpowder and the wielding of colossal bamboo phalli – until the peristyle seemed to be filled with the top-hats, coat-tails and goggles, the shrieks and the cantrips of a troop of demented and nymphomaniac scarecrows.

GLOSSARY

Baron Samedi: the immensely powerful and magical Lwa of the Dead.

Ghédé: the most benevolent of the Lwas of the Dead, powerful in healing, protector of children, a great jester.

Houmfor: strictly, the inner sanctuary of a site where Voodoo is practised. More generally, it is understood to mean the whole site.

Hounci: accepted devotee at a houmfor. Those not fully initiated are called hounci-bossale, and do the more menial tasks. Those who wish to be fully trained have to undergo the severe canzo initiation – ordeal by fire – becoming hounci-canzos.

Houngan, Mambo: fully initiated voodoo priest and priestess respectively.

Lwa: voodoo deity: that is, the power of a divine archetype, who manifests him or herself in taking possession of a devotee.

Yanvalou: favourite voodoo dance. The name means supplication.

Monastic Life

from *A Time to Keep Silence*

In his introduction to A Time to Keep Silence, *Paddy admits that his main reason for wanting to stay at the Abbey of Saint-Wandrille in Normandy in 1948 was that he needed 'somewhere quiet and cheap to stay while I continued work on a book that I was writing' – that book being* The Traveller's Tree.

The singing of grace continued for several minutes; and, when we sat down, I found myself between two visiting priests, their birettas folded flat beside their plates on the long guest-table in the middle of the refectory, just below the Abbot's dais. Down the walls of this immense hall the tables of the monks were ranged in two unbroken lines, and behind them a row of Romanesque pilasters, with interlocking and engaged Norman arches, formed a shallow arcade. The place had an aura of immense antiquity. Grey stone walls soared to a Gothic timber roof, and, above the Abbot's table, a giant crucifix was suspended. As the monks tucked their napkins into their collars with a simultaneous and uniform gesture, an unearthly voice began to speak in Latin from the shadows overhead and, peering towards it, I caught sight, at the far end of the refectory, of a pillared bay twenty feet up which projected like a martin's nest, accessible only by some hidden stairway. This hanging pulpit framed the head and shoulders of a monk, reading from a desk by the light of a lamp which hollowed a glowing alcove out of the penumbra. Loud-speakers relayed his sing-song voice. Meanwhile, the guest-master and a host of aproned monks waited at the tables, putting tureens of vegetable soup before us and dropping into our plates two boiled eggs, which were followed by a dish of potatoes and lentils, then by an endive salad, and finally by discs of camembert, to be eaten with excellent bread from the Abbey bakery. Every now and then a monk left his place, and knelt for a few minutes before the Abbot's table. At a sign from the Abbot, he would rise, make a deep bow, and with-draw . . . Inspired probably by Victorian oleographs of monastic life,

I had expected a prodigious flow of red wine. The metal jugs on our tables contained, alas, only water.

The recitation had now changed from Latin to French, delivered in the same sepulchral, and, at first, largely unintelligible, monotone. A few proper names emerged – Louis Philippe, Dupanloup, Lacordaire, Guizot, Thiers, Gambetta, Montalembert – it was clear that we were listening to a chapter of French nineteenth-century history. This stilted manner of treating a lay text sounded absurd at first and oddly sanctimonious; its original object, I discovered, had been both to act as a curb on histrionic vanity and to minimize the difficulties of the unlearned reader in the days of St Benedict. Throughout the entire meal no other word was spoken. The tables were cleared, and the monks, their eyes downcast, sat with their hands crossed beneath their scapulars. The Abbot thereupon gave a sharp tap with a little mallet; the reader, abandoning his text, bowed so low over the balustrade that it seemed that he would fall out and then intoned the words *Tu autem Domine miserere nobis*; all rose, and bowing to a rectangular position with their hands crossed on their knees, chanted a long thanksgiving. Straightening, they turned and bowed to the Abbot and, still chanting, moved slowly out of the refectory in double file around two sides of the cloisters, into the church and up the central aisle. Here each pair of monks genuflected, inclined their heads one to another, and made their way to opposite stalls. The chanting continued for about eight minutes, then the entry was gravely reversed. As they reached the cloisters, the files of black figures broke up and dispersed throughout the Abbey.

Back in my cell, I sat down before the new blotter and pens and sheets of clean foolscap. I had asked for quiet and solitude and peace, and here it was; all I had to do now was to write. But an hour passed, and nothing happened. It began to rain over the woods outside, and a mood of depression and of unspeakable loneliness suddenly felled me like a hammer-stroke. On the inner side of my door, the printed 'Rules for the Guests' Wing' contained a mass of cheerless information. The monks' day, I learned, began at 4 a.m., with the offices of Matins and Lauds, followed by periods for private masses and reading and meditation. A guest's day began at 8.15 with the office of Prime and breakfast in silence. At 10 the Conventual High Mass was sandwiched between Tierce and Sext. Luncheon at 1. Nones and Vespers at 5 p.m. Supper at 7.30, then, at 8.30, Compline and to bed in silence at 9. All meals, the rules pointed out, were eaten in silence: one was enjoined to take one's 'recreation' apart, and only to speak to the monks with the Abbot's permission; not to make a noise walking about the Abbey; not to smoke in the cloisters; to talk in a low voice, and rigorously to observe the periods of silence. They struck me as impossibly forbidding. So much silence and sobriety! The place assumed the character of an enormous tomb, a necropolis of which I was the only living inhabitant.

The first bell was already ringing for Vespers, and I went down to the cloisters and watched the monks assemble in silence for their processional entrance. They had put on, over their habits and scapulars, black cowls: flowing gowns with hoods into which those of their ordinary habits fitted, and so voluminous that the wearers appeared to glide rather than walk. Their hands were invisibly joined, like those of mandarins, in the folds of their sleeves, and the stooped faces, deep in the tunnel of their pointed hoods, were almost completely hidden. A wonderful garb for anonymity! They were exact echoes of Mrs Radcliffe's villainous monastics and of the miscreants of Protestant anti-popish literature. Yet they looked not so much sinister as desperately sad. Only in the refectory and the church was I able to see their faces; and, as I sat at Vespers watching them, now cowled, now uncovered, according to the progress of the liturgy, they appeared preternaturally pale, some of them nearly green. The bone structure of their faces lay nearly always close beneath the surface. But, though a deep hollow often accentuated the shadow under the cheekbone, their faces were virtually without a wrinkle, and it was this creaseless haggardness that made their faces so distinct from any others. How different, I thought, from the fierce, whiskered, brigand faces of the Greek monks of Athos or the Meteora, whose eyes smoulder and flash and twinkle under brows that are always tied up in knots of rage or laughter or concentration or suddenly relaxed into bland, Olympian benevolence. The gulf between the cenobites of Rome and those of Byzantium was often in my mind. A cowled figure would flit past in silence, and all at once, with a smile, I would remember Fathers Dionysios and Gabriel, Brothers Theophylaktos,

Christ and Polycarp, my bearded, long-haired, cylinder-hatted war-time hosts and protectors in Crete, pouring out raki, cracking wal-nuts, singing mountain songs, stripping and assembling pistols, cross-questioning me interminably about Churchill, and snoring under olive trees while the sun's beams fell perpendicularly on the Libyan Sea . . . But here, in the Abbey's boreal shadows, there was never a smile or a frown. No seismic shock of hilarity or anger or fear could ever, I felt, have disturbed the tranquil geography of those monastic features. Their eyelids were always downcast; and, if now and then they were raised, no treacherous glint appeared, nothing but a sedulously cultivated calmness, withdrawal and mansuetude and occasionally an expression of remote and burnt-out melancholy. The muted light in the church suspended a filament between us, reproducing the exact atmosphere of an early seventeenth-century Spanish studio in which – tonsured, waxen, austere and exsanguin-ous – were bowed in prayer the models of Zurbarán and El Greco. Not for nothing had these painters followed so closely after St Theresa and St John of the Cross, and so faithfully portrayed the external stigmata of monastic obedience, prayer, meditation, mor-tification and mystical experiment – the traces left by the soul's dark night, by the scaling of heavenly mountains and the exploration of interior mansions. As the monks dispersed after Vespers and, a few hours later, after Compline, I had a sensation of the temperature of life falling to zero, the blood running every second thinner and slower as if the heart might in the end imperceptibly stop beating. These men really lived as if each day were their last, at peace with the world, shriven, fortified by the sacraments, ready at any moment to cease upon the midnight with no pain. Death, when it came, would be the easiest of change-overs. The silence, the appearance, the com-plexion and the gait of ghosts they had already; the final step would be only a matter of detail. 'And then,' I continued to myself, 'when the golden gates swing open with an angelic fanfare, what happens then? Won't these quiet people feel lost among streets paved with beryl and sardonyx and jacinth? After so many years of retirement, they would surely prefer eternal twilight and a cypress or two . . .' The Abbey was now fast asleep but it seemed unnaturally early – about the moment when friends in Paris (whom I suddenly and acutely missed) were still uncertain where to dine. Having finished a flask of Calvados, which I had bought in Rouen, I sat at my desk in a condition of overwhelming gloom and *accidie*. As I looked round the white box of my cell, I suffered what Pascal declared to be the cause of all human evils. [. . .]

My first feelings in the monastery changed: I lost the sensation of circumambient and impending death, of being by mistake locked in a catacomb. I think the alteration must have taken about four days. The mood of dereliction persisted some time, a feeling of loneliness and flatness that always accompanies the transition from urban excess to a life of rustic solitude. Here in the Abbey, in absolutely unfamiliar surroundings, this miserable bridge-passage was immensely widened. One is prone to accept the idea of monastic life as a phenomenon that has always existed, and to dismiss it from the mind without further analysis or comment; only by living for a while in a monastery can one quite grasp its enormous difference from the ordinary life that we lead. The two ways of life do not share a single attribute; and the thoughts, ambitions, sounds, light, time and mood that surround the inhabitants of a cloister are not only unlike anything to which one is accustomed, but in some curious way, seem its exact reverse. The period during which normal standards recede and the strange new world becomes reality is slow, and, at first, acutely painful.

To begin with, I slept badly at night and fell asleep during the day, felt restless alone in my cell and depressed by the lack of alcohol, the disappearance of which had caused a sudden halt in the customary monsoon. The most remarkable preliminary symptoms were the variations of my need of sleep. After initial spells of insomnia, nightmare and falling asleep by day, I found that my capacity for sleep was becoming more and more remarkable: till the hours I spent in or on my bed vastly outnumbered the hours I spent awake; and my sleep was so profound that I might have been under the influence of some hypnotic drug. For two days, meals and the offices in the church – Mass, Vespers and Compline – were almost my only lucid moments. Then began an extraordinary transformation: this extreme lassitude dwindled to nothing; night shrank to five hours of light, dreamless and perfect sleep, followed by awakenings full of energy and limpid freshness. The explanation is simple enough: the desire for talk, movement and nervous expression that I had transported from Paris found, in this silent place, no response or foil, evoked no single echo; after miserably gesticulating for a while in a vacuum, it languished and finally died for lack of any stimulus or nourishment. Then the tremendous accumulation of tiredness, which must be the common property of all our contemporaries, broke loose and swamped everything. No demands, once I had emerged from that flood of sleep, were made upon my nervous energy: there were no automatic drains, such as conversation at meals, small talk, catching trains, or the hundred anxious trivialities that poison everyday life. Even the major causes of guilt and anxiety had slid away into some distant cave and not only failed to emerge in the small hours as tormentors but appeared to have lost their dragonish validity. This new dispensation left nineteen hours a day of absolute and god-like freedom. Work became easier every moment; and, when I was not working, I was either exploring the Abbey and the neighbouring countryside, or reading. The Abbey became the reverse of a tomb – not, indeed, a Thelema or Nepenthe, but a silent university, a country house, a castle hanging in mid-air beyond the reach of ordinary troubles and vexations. A verse from the office of Compline expresses the same thought; and it was no doubt an unconscious memory of it that prompted me to put it down: *Altissimum posuisti refugium tuum . . . non accedet ad te malum et flagellum non appropinquabit tabernaculo tuo.*

Slowly, the monks changed from two-dimensional figures on counter-reformation canvases and became real people, though the guest-master remained almost my only interlocutor. This sympathetic figure, Father Tierce, lived in the guest-house, and was at first my sole link with the monastic life around me. In the rule of St Benedict, the offices of guest-master and cellarer are, after the rank of abbot and prior, those that call for the solidest faith and character, since they bring the holder into daily and hourly contact with the influences and distractions of the outside world. My particular friend was a compendium of charity and unselfishness, whose one study appeared to be the happiness and comfort of his charges; finding places for them during the services, seeing that their cells were comfortable, warning them of mealtimes, and generally steering them through all the reefs and shallows of the monastic routine; beaming through horn-rimmed spectacles, then always bustling away with a swirl of robes on some benevolent errand. It was he who put me in the hands of the librarian, a young and elaborately educated choir-monk who made me free of a vast book-lined labyrinth occupying the whole of a seventeenth-century wing. The library was beautifully kept, and, considering the Abbey's vicissitudes, enormous. Vellum-bound folios and quartos receded in vistas, and thousands of ancient and modern works on theology, canon law, dogma, patrology, patristics, hagiography, mysticism and even magic, and almost as many on secular history, art and travel. Poetry, drama, heraldry, the whole of Greek and Roman literature, a special library on the history and geography of Normandy, an extremely rich and up-to-date reference library, Hebrew, Arabic, Cyriac and Chaldean and hundreds of English books, completed the catalogue. The father librarian gave me a key and his permission to take as many books as I liked to my cell. Like all monastic libraries it possessed a number of volumes that had been placed on the index because they offended against theo-logical orthodoxy; and a number, considered damaging to the peace of monastic life, were locked up in a depository known as the *Enfer*. On various occasions, following up trains of enquiry, I asked for books from both sources, and obtained them without difficulty. Several monks were usually working in the library, reading and writ-ing at the desks, or climbing the ladders in pursuit of recondite knowledge.

As, gradually, I found myself talking to them, I was surprised by the conversation of the monks with whom I came in contact. I found no trace of the Dark Ages here, no hint of necropolitan gloom or bigotry, still less of the ghastly breeziness that is such an embarrass-ing characteristic of many English clerics. There was no doubt of the respect in which they held the cause to which their lives were devoted; but their company was like that of any civilized well-educated Frenchman, with all the balance, erudition and wit that one expected, the only difference being a gentleness, a lack of haste, and a calmness which is common to the whole community. [. . .]

Their values have remained stable while those of the world have passed through kaleidoscopic changes. It is curious to hear, from the outside world in the throes of its yearly metamorphoses, cries of derision levelled at the monastic life. How shallow, whatever views may be held concerning the fundamental truth or fallacy of the Christian religion, are these accusations of hypocrisy, sloth, selfishness and escapism! The life of monks passes in a state of white-hot conviction and striving to which there is never a holiday; and no living man, after all, is in a position to declare their premises true or false. They have foresworn the pleasures and rewards of a world whose values they consider meaningless; and they alone have as a body confronted the terrifying problem of eternity, abandoning everything to help their fellow-men and themselves to meet it.

Worship, then, and prayer are the *raison d'être* of the Benedictine order; and anything else, even their great achievements as scholars and architects and doctors of the church, is subsidiary. They were, however, for centuries the only guardians of literature, the classics, scholarship and the humanities in a world of which the confusion can best be compared to our own atomic era. For a long period, after the great epoch of Benedictine scholarship at Cluny, the Maurist Benedictine Abbey of Saint-Germain-des-Prés was the most important residuary of learning and science in Europe. Only a few ivy-clad ruins remain, just visible between *zazou* suits and existentialist haircuts from the terrace of the Deux Magots. But in scores of abbeys all over Europe, the same liberal traditions survive and prosper. Other by-products of their life were the beautiful buildings in which I was living, and the unparalleled calm that prevailed there. At Saint-Wandrille I was inhabiting at last a tower of solid ivory, and I, not the monks, was the escapist. For my hosts, the Abbey was a springboard into eternity; for me a retiring place to write a book and spring more effectively back into the maelstrom. Strange that the same habitat should prove favourable to ambitions so glaringly opposed.

Serpents of the Abruzzi

The Spectator, 5 June 1953

The Abruzzi is a wild, mountainous region half-way down the leg of Italy, look-
ing over to the Adriatic. Paddy had been on a walking tour of Tuscany and
Umbria with Peter Quennell in the spring of 1953. He continued alone into the
Abruzzi where, at Sulmona, he met an old friend of his called Archie Lyall. The
following day, they proceeded to the village of Cucullo.

Leaving the gentle, Italian primitive landscape of Umbria for the
blank sierras of the Abruzzi was as complete a change as a journey to a different planet. Indeed, these wild grey peaks have an almost
lunar remoteness, and the little village of Cucullo, a grey warren of
houses at the end of a blind alley of the mountains a dozen miles
from Ovid's birthplace at Sulmona, must usually seem a desolate
habitation. The sun beats down from a blazing sky, but in the labyrinthine shadows of the lanes there is a chill bite in the air from the
towering snows of the Gran Sasso.

But once a year, in the first week of May, the mountain silence is
broken, and the village population, normally only a few hundred
souls – shepherds and small cultivators to a man – swells to thousands. Pilgrims, last month, swarmed from all the neighbouring
villages, and, as this is one of the few parts of Italy where regional
costumes survive, the streets were a kaleidoscope of different
colours and fashions. A bearded shepherd, playing an ear-splitting
pibroch on a bagpipe made of a patched inner tube, wore raw-hide
moccasins and his legs were cross-gartered like a Saxon thane's with
thick leather thongs.

The religious occasion was the pretext for a rustic fair. The market
was full of trussed poultry and squealing pigs. Pedlars carried trays
of rosaries, medals, little tin motor-cars, celluloid thumbs-ups and
dried acorn-cups. There were 'lucky' hunchbacks, crippled beggars,
hucksters with fortune-telling canaries and a wandering hypnotist.
Less usual was the presence, wherever one turned, of live snakes,

slung over brown forearms or twisting like bracelets, lying in loose tangles among the funnel-topped bottles in the wine-shops, or held in clusters of four with their unwinking heads all gathered in the palm between the laden fingers of both hands, their long forked tongues sliding in and out of their jaws. Some were nearly two yards in length, and all of them looked alarmingly dangerous.

Most of the *serpari*, or snake-catchers, are under twenty. For weeks past they had been hunting snakes in the mountains where they abound. Capturing them while they are still dazed with their winter sleep, they disarm the poisonous ones by giving them the hem of a garment to bite, which, when snatched away, breaks off their teeth and drains their poison. Then, stored in jars or sewn into goatskins, they are put by until the great day comes round. There were now several hundred of them in the streets of Cucullo – black, grey, greenish, speckled and striped, all hissing and knotting together and impotently darting and biting with their harmless jaws.

The floor of the baroque, and surprisingly large church was deep in crumbs and bundles and debris. Hundreds of visiting peasants, finding the village overflowing, had slept there all night. Queues waited their turn at the confessional, and, under a pink and blue baldachin, relays of priests administered the sacrament. In the north transept a bell clanked almost unceasingly as peasant after peasant, taking a metal ring between his teeth, tugged at a chain that rang the clapper of a bell that had once belonged to St Dominic, to draw his notice to their petition. On waiting trays the crumpled fifty *lire* mounted up. From behind the altar precious lumps of rubble – from the ruins, it is said, of one of St Dominic's foundations – were carried off to be sprinkled over the fields to ensure a good harvest and rid the fields of rats.

A young priest applied a battered silver reliquary to the arms and shoulders of an interminable procession of kneeling pilgrims, or to the upheld crusts of bread they would later feed to their livestock to ward off rabies. Inside the cylindrical casket swung and rattled a wonder-working tooth of St Dominic; now, after a thousand years, a chipped and discoloured fang. Then the devotees moved on to the effigy of St Dominic himself, a life-size wooden figure in black Benedictine habit with a horseshoe in one hand and in the other a crosier. Embracing him with hungry possessiveness, they rubbed little bundles of coloured wool – sovereign thenceforward, when applied to the spot, against toothache and snakebite and hydrophobia – down the grooves of his habit, or lifted their children into kissing distance of the worn and numinous flanks. Silver ex-votos hung round his neck, and pink ribbons with pinned sheaves of offered banknotes fluttered from his shoulders. St Dominic of Sora, or 'the Abbot' – he has nothing to do with the great founder of the Order of the Preachers – was a Benedictine of Umbrian origin, born in 951. He was by turns eremetical and peripatetic, and his countless miracles during his lifetime, and, the Abruzzesi relate, through the agency of his relic ever since, were nearly all connected with the foiling of bears and wolves, and, especially, snakes.

By the time High Mass began, there was no room to move in the crowded church. Yet a passage was cleared and two young women advanced with large baskets balancing unsupported on their heads, each of them containing great hoop-like loaves; both baskets were draped in pink and white silk and decked with carnations and wild cyclamen. They stood like caryatids on either side of the high altar until, at the end of the service, the image of the saint was hoisted shoulder-high and borne swaying into the sunlight before the church door. There, while the compact multitude clapped and cheered and the bells broke into a jubilant peal, the *serpari* clustered round the lowered float. Snakes began flying over the tonsured head like lassoes. Parish elders arranged them feather-boa-like about his shoulders, twisted them round his crosier and wound them over his arms and through the horseshoe and at random all over his body until the image and its pedestal were a squirming tangle. Many fell off or wriggled free, and one over-active reptile was given a crack over the head. The effigy, like a drowned figurehead from the Sargasso Sea, was raised shoulder high once more. A small pink banner pinned all over with notes, then a large green one, were unwieldily hoisted. Village girls intoned a hymn in Abruzzi dialect in St Dominic's honour; then the clergy, one of them bearing the cylinder with its swinging tooth, formed a procession.

The two girls with their peculiar baskets came next. A brass band struck up the triumphal march from *Aida*, and the saint, twisting and coiling with the activity of the bewildered snakes and bristling with their hissing and tongue-darting heads, rocked insecurely forward across the square. The innumerable peasants, the conjurors and pedlars and quacks, fell in step; the wine-shops emptied; pigs and poultry were abandoned in their pens, and the whole immense concourse, now itself forming a gigantic many-coloured serpent, wound slowly along the rising and falling streets. Every few steps the effigy came to a halt while fallen snakes were replaced or yet more banknotes, which floated down from the upper windows, were pinned on the fluttering ribbons. Boys ran alongside, brandishing tangled armfuls of redundant reptiles and, looking up at the bright midday sky, I saw girls on the rooftops flourishing skeins of the now familiar reptiles in both hands.

At last the saint was back at the church door, and there, like a disentangling of cold macaroni, the de-snaking began. It was as if they had frozen to their perch. When St Dominic was in his chapel at last, a strange haggling and chaffering began over the carcasses of his denizens. For snakes are eagerly sought by pedlars, who display them as a reinforcement to their patter, attract a crowd, and then slily open their suitcases of combs or medals or celluloid toys. There was even an atheist patent-medicine manufacturer all the way from Bologna, who boils them down and turns them into ointment against rheumatism. The back of his little car was soon aswarm.

It is tempting to seek a link between these strange doings and some possible pre-Christian worship of Aesculapius, but there was no Aesculapian temple in the area, it seems, though Apollo and Jupiter were worshipped at Sulmona. It is known, however, that the warlike Marsi from whom these Abruzzesi descend were snake-worshippers and snake-charmers and wizards, and there is no reason why these things should have died out by St Dominic's day. Antiquarians also find certain affinities between the Cucullan customs and the fertility rites of the Agathos Daimon. Be that as it may, the strange cult in honour of St Dominic the Abbot shows no signs of dying out. If anything, it grows more popular and more deeply felt as time goes on.

With every mile of the return journey next day through the twisting Sabine gorges and down into the Campagna with the dome of St

Peter's growing larger on the skyline, the proceedings at Cucullo seemed odder and more remote. It was only when I touched my coat-pocket and felt a responsive uneasy wriggle through the tweed, that it seemed real at all. For, by paying a few hundred *lire*, I had become a snake-owner too. It was a fine grey animal over a yard long with clever little black eyes: very active, letting slip no chance of nipping my hand with its unarmed (I hoped) gums. But, when I reached Rome, and my destination on the Tiber island, it had vanished. It must have slid gently away to freedom in the tram between the city walls and the Piazza di Spagna. Perhaps, after a panic in the tram, it was put out of the way. But perhaps it is still rattling its way unobserved round the Seven Hills; or it may be curled up among the pillars of the Forum, or, best of all, basking sleepily on a warm and grassy ledge of the Colosseum, beyond the reach of all harm.

Paradox in the Himalayas

London Magazine, December 1979–January 1980

This piece was written in memory of Paddy's friend Robin Fedden (1908–77), writer, scholar, mountaineer, aesthete and poet. Although he is not mentioned by name, the journey – which took place in 1976 – was the last of many expeditions of which he was the leader. Malana, autonomous and isolated, is up the Parbati valley north of the town of Kulu. It is situated at 9,000 ft.

It was late October when we struck uphill through the golden, auburn and crimson trees, and the air smelled of incense and decay; all sound but the crackle of pine-cones underfoot and the breaking caskets of fallen chestnuts was muffled under heaped-up leaves which occasional breezes lifted in small eddies and then let fall. Our first night's fires lit up a glade near the end of the forest and by noon next day a wisp of birch ended the trees just short of the Chanderkhani pass. This narrow saddle, 12,000 feet up, bristled with tall and enigmatic blades of rock stuck vertically into the grassy ridge, early hints of the idiosyncrasy that lay ahead. Many snow-peaks familiar from recent climbs had kept pace with us on the skyline, but in changed formations, and Deo Tibba had shifted three-quarters round to display a score of new facets. The far side of the pass was an abyss where two lammergeiers were balanced in the hot stillness and our arrival sent them gliding on lazy wings to the next range. An invisible river whispered below. Somewhere, deep in those buttresses and forests, our destination lay.

In under an hour, each in his private landslide, we scrambled 4,000 breakneck feet down a corrie until the thorn-barriers and boulders of a cavernous goat-fold made us halt for breath. The air was stagnant. Flocks scattered the clefts and a white-bearded, white-clad and barefoot shepherd, starting up in consternation, laid aside his ball of yarn and his distaff and only recovered from the shock over a reluctant cigarette. To mitigate defilement, this was offered not by us but by Wangyal, the chief Sherpa; we thought a Buddhist would be better than a Christian. Even so, the shepherd lodged it carefully at the base of a little finger-joint and then, forming an airtight box like a dry hookah with his clasped hands, he filled the hollow with smoke and drew on it, safe from pollution now, by putting his mouth to his joined thumbs, as though about to imitate an owl hooting. Malana, he told Wangyal, was not far below. While they talked he had kept his troubled glance away from our faces, and now he pointed to our boots and our leather belts and watch-straps with an air of distress. The village is protected by a private but all-powerful god called Jamlu to whom leather is an abomination. If they know nothing else, even strangers in these folds of the Himalayas know this and so did we, but we had been caught unawares. If we took these forbidden things into the village, said the shepherd, only the offer and sacrifice of a goat apiece could wipe out the desecration.

A turn in the track brought us above a scattering of roofs put together with irregular slabs. Above them on our side, rock soared to snow-slashed cordilleras; the other side dropped still deeper into a canyon of forest.

It was forbidden, we knew, to enter Malana without permission, so we cast about and found a convenient knoll. But the power of Jamlu came into play at once. Some wild-looking girls, who were huddling there like little crows, took wing, crying a warning, as they fled, not to settle there: it was sacred to Jamlu. Where could we camp without sacrilege? As our search flagged, three hideous boys began to dog our footsteps, squatting wherever we went in a derisive row – two of them witless from inbreeding, the third a vision of nameless evil – until we were rescued by a compassionate villager. He had a D. H. Lawrence beard and wore a round *pahari* cap and he was called Sangat; a man of fine looks and, as we discovered, great good nature. He led us to a pine-clump, a safely unsanctified one, and our tents were soon pitched, fires lit and chapattis baking on the hot stones. Then he left us to consult with the elders. He was back next morning and seeing that all wristwatches were off and our belts and our boots replaced by rope and gym-shoes, he led us downhill and into the village.

Poplars and cypresses and birch-trees rose haphazard among the tall houses. Built of impacted stone and bonded with massive beams, the lower floors were given over to animals and the murk of byres. Higher up, carved and arcaded balconies ran all round the buildings, and primitive looms were set up there among stored hay and purple heaps of amaranth. Instead of stairs, these upper storeys were reached by felled tree-trunks set at a slant, with the branches lopped off short for rungs, and the dwellers sped up and down them like the bandarlog. Aromatic smoke crept between the roof-slabs to float across the village and hang in a blue veil. The villagers in the lanes and the weavers and the spinners on the galleries looked askance at our entry and stopped dead. The spreading silence was soon complete. Men averted their gaze, children ran off as though ogres were coming down the street and the women at the spring – striking figures in homespun tartan, their thick plaits lengthened with black wool, babies slung on their haunches, distaffs in hand and huge brass water-jars on their heads – stood transfixed, and after a long disbelieving glance, turned away with a rictus of bewilderment and pain. Nearly all the village was out of bounds to us. One or two fellow-villagers joined Sangat, less as an escort than to ward off pollution; and even along permitted ways a flutter of anxious hands herded us innocuously to the middle. Malana is a smelly hamlet. To rough mountain folk after dark, all the world's a jakes and all the men and women, etc.; so in some of the by-ways the roles were reversed and our careful steps needed no prompting.

We were halted and bidden to admire the Treasure House. Elaborate triple bands of moulding surrounded the heavy door and many forest-trophies – slender ibex and the heavy crinkled horns of the great Tibetan sheep, the nyam, the urial and, I think, the markhor – adorned the intricately carved wood. It was the storehouse of Jamlu's boundless wealth.

But the heart of the village was a little piazza, sloping and grassy, and enclosed on three sides by arcaded buildings of sacred aspect. The timber façades were wrought with geometric designs and elaborate friezes of peacocks, lions, elephants and horsemen with guns ran right across them, but no Hindu gods were enshrined there, no marigold petals strewn and no camphor flickered in the shadows. But in the very middle of this little piazza, a slab of boldly cut stone lay half-embedded in the grass. It was the holiest place in Malana, Sangat whispered; in fact, Jamlu himself. Following his precept and example, we placed our offerings before him, then lifted joined hands in puja and lay prone for a minute with our brows in the dust.

A feeling of awe dwelt in these lanes; nothing was wholly secular. The hushed devoutness, the anxiety and the lowered lids sealed us away as effectively as helmets of darkness, so it came as a surprise, after a consultation of the elders, to be waved to seats on a stone ledge in this ceremonial square. Our pious homage to Jamlu had made a good impression, it seemed; and here, bit by bit, linguistic curiosity began to break the ice. Among themselves the Malanis talk a language called Kanishta, and the Sherpas, who spoke Tibetan and the Kulu dialect of Hindi, could make nothing of it and least of all Wangyal, who had also picked up more than a smattering of English from earlier mountaineers; and, somehow, so had our local protector. 'What is "house" in Kanishta?' we asked him. '*Kim!*' Sangat answered. And in Hindi? '*Gher!*' Wangyal said, catching on with a collusive look. And in Tibetan? '*Khumps!*' the Sherpas cried in chorus. Then more Malanis began to gather and chime in, doubtfully at first, then as eagerly as children playing Animal Grab. We would point at something – a foot, a knee, an elbow, a tree, a boy, and '*Guding!*' they boomed back in Kanishta, '*Chig!*' '*Yuska!*' '*Biting!*' and '*Tchokts!*' In a few cases, as one would have expected, there were Tibetan or Hindi loan-words from the two great languages Malana is sandwiched between; but most of them resembled neither. Growing more daring we began to dabble in the abstract. 'God?' – pointing up – '*Jong!*' 'Devil?' '*Bhutan!*' 'good?' '*shovilez!*' 'bad?' '*nork!*' 'Sun?' '*Jhari!*' 'Moon?' '*Josta!*' . . . By now we were among friends.

Unlike the nomad herds, the flocks of Malana winter in the mountains. That evening the approaches were a turmoil of bleating; but they had been folded by sundown and in the silence by the camp-fire we pondered the vocabulary of about two hundred words I had jotted down; and later on, kept awake by an owl with a queer double-noted cry, we pondered still: who were the Malanis? Where do they come from? How do they live? Above all, what about Jamlu?

Very few travellers ever climbed to Malana. It was on the way to nowhere. Steep barriers and a bad reputation fended off all but a few lonely scholars; an Asiatic traveller or two, that is, an observant and literate captain on shikar, a clergyman with a bent for languages and some historically minded ICS officers like G. Mackworth-Young, the first outsider to observe a Jamlu ceremony; and, in recent times, Dervla Murphy has splendidly described its winter aspect in *Tibetan Foothold*. But Dr Colin Rosser, a social anthropologist who has studied the place for two years, must remain the chief authority, and source.

The wild local gods have given rise to much speculation. In some ways Jamlu is suzerain of all the deified spirits of trees, caverns, mountains and springs in the region, and Jamlu himself was once the spirit of a mountain, one of twin peaks, and perhaps the younger brother of Gyephang La in Lahul; more important, it is certain, or nearly so, that he was a god in pre-Aryan times. On his way to Malana for the first time, he and his wife Naroi were carrying a box full to the brim with lesser deities. The wind on the Chanderkhani pass blew off the lid and scattered them over Kulu – eighteen of them or more – dropping them at the very points where their shrine later on sprang up when they had sidled into the Hindu pantheon. The only worship of an anthropomorphic deity in Malana itself is the minor cult of Jamlu's wife, now renamed Ranuka, whose little fane stands on the edge of the village. Perhaps out of pre-Aryan pride, the omnipotent Jamlu has neither temple nor image and he has thriven for millennia on this lack of definition. [. . .]

And what of the Malanis? Are they earlier than the Aryans too? Some scholars say so. After all, it was only a few centuries before the Siege of Troy that the chariots of the city-rending invaders stormed into India. Other scholars, bolder still, think they may be pre-Dravidian as well. For the Dravidians, and perhaps their kindred city-dwellers of the Indus valley, like all the successful assailants of India except the English, may also have come here from the north-west and only a few thousand years before the sub-continent turned into Vishnu-land. The Malanis, then – the cloud of surmise expands here like a mushroom – probably descend from the union of pre-Dravidian aboriginals with newcomers of the Vaisia caste when the Aryans, settled in at last, started wandering up the remote Himalayan valleys. Many sources have been suggested for their peculiar language, which must be one of the smallest in the world. The likeliest is Kinnauri, a dialect still spoken in the wild mountains of the former Bashahr state, which stretched from Rampur on the Upper Sutlej to the borders of Tibet. (As far as I can make out this is also the most probable setting for the Himalayan adventures of Kim and the Lama. What Shamleh middens lay beyond those overlapping skylines and shifting visions of Kedarnath and Badrinath?) The region is seventy miles from Malana, as the crow flies; so, sundered as it is by fierce ranges, ten times further for a man. I can find only two Kanishta vocabularies in the Secretariat Library – could my ad hoc collection be the third? – but a rare missionary's handbook of the dialect of Kinnauri – faded, dog-eared and Victorian – divides the dialect between four Sutlej regions, some of which are incomprehensible to each other though only ten miles apart. It makes no mention of Malana, however. A link there plainly is: both are technically subdivisions of the great Tibeto-Burman family; but they must have been parted for hundreds of years and perhaps for thousands. Apart from those few loan-words, the Sherpas could spot no Tibetan admixture; and it is noticeable that Malani faces – which are surprisingly pale and either very beautiful or masks of hideous degeneracy and squalor – have none of the Mongol traits of the Sherpas, or the few Kinnauris that people have pointed out to me in the Lakka Bazaar a mile or so away. The link would be one of language more than race, perhaps, and a thin link at that.

Paradox reigns. Legend, conjecture and fact have plaited a wreath of deviation about the place; their way of life is all but untouched, they say, and akin to nothing else in the Himalayas. Jamlu owns every square inch of the enormous glen and the villagers are only his tenants: the forests and the pastures, even the narrow descending crescents of ploughland, are all his. (Sangat put the population at 560; Rosser, some years ago, at about 500; and Mackworth-Young, in 1911, at 376.) They belong to the *Kanets*-yeomen caste, except for a little group of *Lohar*-blacksmiths, who are allowed no say in affairs; and the village is divided into an upper and a lower half. Haughtily endogamous, but just aware (too late, perhaps) of the dangers of inbreeding, they only marry in theory from one half of Malana to the other and they hope to dodge the threat of imbecility by occasionally taking brides from villages beyond the Rashol pass, the range the two lammergeiers had been heading for; but they never return this favour. Adultery is looked on with mildness, poverty makes polygamy difficult and I think that the polyandry of Lisbeth's range, once rife in the Himalayas, and perhaps here too, has died out.

But it is in proceedings from day to day that Malana differs most noticeably from everywhere else. A council of eleven rules the village. Eight of these, the temporal members as it were, are elected every few years, leaving a triumvirate of spiritual colleagues who take precedence of them; these are drawn from an unvarying clan and their offices are hereditary and for life. The first triumvir is Jamlu's steward, the second his priest and celebrant, the third his oracle. The function of this seer is abetted by prolonged drumming, and, in cold weather, by flinging off all his clothes, which brings on shuddering fits; crises of possession follow soon, when he whirls his uncut locks about in a frenzy and then breaks into prophecy. Apart from this hierarchic trio and the exclusion of women and the *Lohar* caste, the system is egalitarian in temper, democratic in method, ably administered and scrupulous in accounting, though illiteracy is almost universal. [. . .]

'What are those great spikes for on the dogs' collars?' – 'Bears.' The forest is full of them. We spotted a great black pelt hanging from a balcony stretched to dry on crossed poles and when we looked surprised at the presence of leather, they told us that only cow-hide is taboo. (In spite of their ancient origins, this must be part of a post-Vedic belief.) Leopards and deer live in the woods but the favourite quarry of the Malanis, thanks to the enormous prices paid for their scent-pods, is the little musk-deer of Central Asia. Apart from their flocks they have no horned cattle and no chickens; height forbids the double harvests of the valleys and a late thaw can ruin their grudging crops of buckwheat. The village's isolation when the snow has blocked the Chanderkhani and the Rashol passes is hard to imagine. The invisible canyon becomes their only path to the outer world and to Jari (a long day's march away) where they barter ghee, raw wool, game and honeycombs against maize and salt and metal for the *Lohars* to beat into tools. People in the valleys profess scorn for their backwardness, for their insistence in particular on pay in kind rather than cash, even at a loss. But there is awe beneath these sneers, and dread: the powerful god of the Malanis daunts them; they fear the aloofness of his followers, their solidarity, their contempt for strangers; and hearsay augments the fierceness of their wild and uncanny nature by a reputation for universal madness. Jamlu may be an unpredictable god; quick to chide and slow to bless; one who visits backsliding or neglect with blindness, leprosy, insanity, and sudden death; but he is the symbol and safeguard of independence.

The findings of Young and Dr Rosser confirm everything we learnt from Sangat and his friends. But splits are appearing in the xenophobic shell – lamentably, perhaps, scientifically speaking. A school, though shunned till recently by all but one untouchable, will soon begin to erode their ancient ways; and perhaps their growing lenity to us was ethnologically deplorable. For there were return visits to our clump of pines and the next evening, led there by Sangat, half a dozen musicians, including the three terrible boys, all smiles now, settled cross-legged on the grass. A flute trilled and quavered and a drummer in gold earrings hammered at both ends of a long thin drum while the others sang plaintive songs in the Kulu dialect; there was only one song in Kanishta, which I duly noted down. Later, helped by frequent swigs of rice wine poured out of a big brass pot, they trod out the uncomplex figures of mountain dances; the wine mugs were flourished more often; and steps grew swimmingly imprecise, especially when the dancers, with fluttering and clicking fingers, sank unsteadily to their haunches and rotated. There was a bandying of Kanishta toasts – '*Dhalang!*' they cried, and '*Dhalang!*' we answered; – it was turning into a friendly blind. But when we asked for a closer look at the prettily wrought silver flute, decked like Krishna's with tassels and chains and bells, the flute-player was seized with hesitant perplexity; his father was one of the triumvirs, and the instrument could be a conductor of spiritual pollution; passed from hand to hand, a current of defilement might have shot sizzling along the metal. Then he laid it carefully on the grass for us to pick up and his face cleared.

As the shadow-line stole to the tips of the peaks our twilight goings and comings were imperilled by an odd and awkwardly placed hazard. In the centre of our clearing, treacherously overgrown with bracken, yawned a wide, deep hole: why had it been dug there? Pleased at the question, they explained. The oracular triumvir is buried in it on his appointment, but only for half an hour. They dig him up gasping, whereupon he sets off to climb the 16,000 feet to the crest of Girwha Koti – 'God's House', a local name for Deo Tibba – to bring back sprigs of the *losar* and the *gogal* that grow there. Nobody could explain what these plants were but they shook their heads with misgiving. The summit of Deo Tibba is notorious not only for oreads and fairies; any number of mountain spirits of a more uncertain and perhaps dangerous temper are said to haunt the place.

Our exit lay along the hidden gorge. But, like ornithologists lowered down a cliff after rare specimens and finding themselves on a ledge above a still more frightful chasm, we were loath to descend. We set off at last and so steep was the downhill zigzag that the snows and the semicircle of crests were quickly out of sight. In another moment, escalades of tree-tops rushed uphill to surround us and we were sinking through green glooms where the hardwoods soon began to challenge the vertical reign of the conifers. Creepers looped the boughs and ended in tumbling mops, there was falling water and moss and maidenhair ferns in the clefts and grey, curdled, orange, and sulphur-coloured lichens crusted tall buttresses of stone under their fronded overhangs; springs dripped, and snails' tracks of damp gleamed across sheets of split rock . . .

All the last days the sound of the river had risen in a whisper. It was louder now and willow-trees began to spring up. Bamboos soared and spread in green fireworks among rhododendrons the height and thickness of ancient oaks; their branches were heavy with leaves, ragged with Spanish moss and tufted and festooned with a score of parasites; but all their flowers had vanished with the monsoon. Glimpses of running water began to show; we were nearing the bottom of the abyss; and all at once the ravine filled with noise as the river thundered out of the shadows. It fell from shelf to shelf, rushing through the polished troughs it had scooped in the pale metamorphic rock, separating round boulders, rising in fans of spray and then joining again to rotate in deep, slow pools jammed with bleached driftwood; only to break loose once more. High above, the sunbeams sloping across the gorge were almost out of sight. Dropping downhill with scarcely diminishing thunder, the river coiled towards the Parbati in leagues of waterfalls and jade-green flux.

There was a stir in the woods below. A dozen villagers on their way back from market were climbing up the single track. They were gnome-like Malanis stooping under their cone-shaped wicker *kiltas* with bands across their brows. Tattered and barefoot woodland caryatids, balancing heavy loads on their heads, were stepping sinuously up the slanting grass. They must have left Malana before we had arrived; they were wholly unprepared for the shock. Uncorrupted by the familiarities and the bibulous *tamasha* of the night before, they halted in dismay; our attempts at Kanishta greetings, shouted above the crash of a waterfall, must have made our apparition more sinister still. After a glance of incredulous horror they swerved through the rhododendron boles and sped uphill in silence without a single backward glance and the leaves closed after them.

Greece

Abducting a General

Setting the Scene

The most dramatic exploit of Patrick Leigh Fermor's war came in April 1944, when he led the team that planned and executed the abduction of General Heinrich Kreipe. Because it was the subject of a film, in which the role of Paddy was taken by Dirk Bogarde, the operation is often presented as a sort of wildly daring prank. In fact it was meticulously planned. Professor William Mackenzie, commissioned by the Cabinet to write the history of Special Operations Executive immediately after the war, described the Kreipe operation as 'an admirably executed coup . . . The utmost care was taken to avoid involving the Cretans in reprisals, and these were in this instance successful.'*

The operation had its roots in events that had taken place in Crete in the late summer of 1943, by which time Captain Patrick Leigh Fermor had been living on the island as an SOE agent for over a year. When things were at their lowest in 1942 and 1943, he and his three brother officers, plus their signallers and wireless sets, lived hidden in caves and sheepfolds disguised as shepherds. Like their Cretan comrades, they could expect nothing but torture and death if captured. For the Cretans, it was still worse. If found guilty of harbouring agents or escaped prisoners or wandering soldiers left behind after the evacuation, they faced not only execution, but the annihilation and massacre of whole villages in reprisal.

News of the Italian surrender to the Allies reached Crete on 8 September 1943. General Carta, commander of the 32,000 Italians of the Siena Division who garrisoned the eastern part of the island, strongly resisted the Germans' insistence that they should hand over all their arms and ammunition when they left Crete. In anticipation, Carta's chief of counter-intelligence, Lieutenant Tavana, contacted Paddy (then in charge of the Heraklion region) through the Cretan Resistance two months before the armistice was signed. Paddy arranged for as many weapons as possible to be smuggled into Resistance hands, and laid on a large arms drop in the mountains.

British agents in Crete feared that the collapse of Italy might persuade the Cretans that an Allied invasion was imminent. There was a real danger of local bands seizing the moment to strike the Germans before the time was ripe.

---

* William Mackenzie, *The Secret History of SOE* (St Ermin's Press, 2000), p. 483.

Orders went out immediately commanding the local captains to hold their fire, but Kapetan Manoli Bandouvas would not be stopped. He and his men were well armed, having just received a drop of guns and ammunition from SOE in August. On 11 September, his men attacked and wiped out two small German garrisons, then ambushed and annihilated the punitive detachment sent to restore control. The resulting reprisals, ordered by the recently appointed General Müller, were among the most savage that the Germans had ever unleashed on Crete. Between 15 and 16 September, a force of 2,000 Germans slashed and burnt their way through the Viannos region, destroying seven villages and killing over 500 people. Bandouvas and what remained of his band fled to the south coast.

In this harsh new climate, Müller might well have arrested General Carta for his intransigence on the matter of disarmament. So Paddy and his senior SOE officer, the archaeologist and scholar Tom Dunbabin, arranged for the evacuation of General Carta. The General and a handful of his staff were escorted in secret across the mountains to Tsoutsouru on the south coast, where on 23 September they were picked up by the Royal Navy. Paddy and Manoli Paterakis, one of the great Resistance fighters of Crete, boarded the evacuation boat with the idea of disembarking before she sailed – but rough sea prevented them from returning to shore. So it was that Paddy returned to Egypt with General Carta and with much to think about.

Ever since our flight into the mountains with the general, two interweaving thoughts, prompted by the horrible events in Viannos, had been taking shape: how could we respond to General Müller's onslaught, and avoid bringing down trouble? Were such a thing possible, it would have to be some kind of symbolic gesture involving no bloodshed, not even a plane sabotaged or a petrol dump blown up; something which would hit the enemy hard on a different level, and one which would offer no presentable pretext for reprisals. Our recent flight automatically suggested the enemy general as quarry. Looked at like this, our late adventure suddenly took on the guise of a practice run for a much more serious undertaking: an Anglo-Cretan enterprise with old and seasoned mountain friends, rather than a professional Allied *coup de main* entirely organized from outside; something, in fact, that would reflect the close-knit feeling which had grown up during the last two and a half years. Recent disasters had shown that armed confrontation with no external support was foredoomed. But a small party could be dropped on Mount Dikti as easily as the arms to Bandouvas a month before. And it was obvious – as if we didn't know it already! – that a small party, with the whole mountain world on its side to guide, feed, warn and guard it, could move wherever it liked in that vast labyrinth, and much faster than any road-bound military force. The false scent of the captured general's car abandoned with its conspicuous flag not far from deep water would be followed by our flight from those southern coves . . . the stages of our journey were turning into a series of Red Indian smoke signals.*

In Cairo, the plan to kidnap General Müller was given the go-ahead. Paddy found a second in command, a friend who was a captain in the Coldstream Guards called Billy Moss. These two, with Manoli Paterakis and George Tyrakis, another Cretan friend of Paddy's who had been much involved with resistance work on the island, were to form the nucleus of the team. Others would be recruited when they reached Crete.

Paddy was dropped into Crete on 5 February but bad weather prevented Manoli, George and Billy from reaching the island until 4 April. By this time the notorious General Müller had been replaced by a general fresh from the Russian front: General Heinrich Kreipe.

Cairo authorized the mission to proceed despite this change, and preparations began. Taking advantage of the General's regular habits, the plan was that Paddy and Billy Moss, dressed as two Feldpolizei corporals, would stop his car on its way back from his headquarters to the Villa Ariadne at Knossos, where he lived. The General would be abducted and his car would then be abandoned with a letter saying that the General was safe and would be treated with the respect due to his rank. It also emphasized that the operation had been carried out by British officers, with Greek nationals who were serving soldiers in the Forces of his Hellenic Majesty – not Cretan civilians. The point was to give the Germans no excuse for carrying out reprisals in the area.

Paddy is always at pains to stress that most of those involved in the kidnap of General Kreipe were Cretan. Reconnaissance was done by Miki Akoumianakis, SOE's chief agent in Heraklion, who knew the area around Knossos very well. He

* Patrick Leigh Fermor, Afterword to W. Stanley Moss, *Ill Met by Moonlight* (Folio Society, 2001).

also had a house there, next door to the Villa Ariadne. It was Miki who stole the German uniforms for Billy Moss and Paddy. Elias Athanassakis, a young student, was Akoumianakis's lieutenant. It was his idea that the imminent arrival of the General's car should be signalled by an electric bell. Athanassakis also spent a lot of time studying the General's car, the noise of its engine and the shape of its lights. It was thanks to him that the group found the vineyard of Pavlos Zographistos, which was twenty minutes from 'Point A' where the car was to be intercepted. Pavlos and his sister, Anna, both agreed to help. Antoni Zoidakis, who had been helping SOE in its efforts to shelter Allied stragglers, and Stratis Saviolakis, both had good cover as local gendarmes. The other members of the team were Dimitri ('Mitso') Tzatzas, Nikos Komis, and Antoni Papaleonidas from Asia Minor. In the background, in case of trouble, was a band of partisans led by their kapetan, Athanasios Bourdzalis.

On the night of 26 April, as the General's car swept up the road towards Heraklion, the two German corporals stepped out of the dark. All went according to plan, and having captured the General, the party split into two groups. Accompanied by George Tyrakis, Paddy drove the car to the spot where it was to be found, with its letter. He and Tyrakis then walked south to the village of Anoyeia.

Meanwhile the General, escorted by Billy Moss and Manoli Paterakis, was being guided by Stratis to a cave outside Anoyeia. Here Paddy (known as 'Mihali' to the Cretans) and Tyrakis would join them next day.

from 'Abducting a General', a personal report of the Kreipe Operation written at the request of the Imperial War Museum, 1969

Anoyeia, the largest village in Crete, was too remote and isolated for a permanent garrison. High on the northern slopes of Mount Ida, it is the key foothold for crossing that great mass. Famous for its independent spirit, its idiosyncrasy of dress and accent, it had always been a great hideout of ours. The year before, Mike Stockbridge and I had baptized the daughter of brave local Kapetan, Stephanoyanni Dramountanes, and thus became his god-brothers. He had been killed – shot down while trying to make a break for it, by jumping over a wall with his hands tied – after the German encirclement of the village. But I knew we could find all the backing we needed from his relations and followers, and from his successor in command, Kapetan Mihali Xylouris. We, George Tyrakis and I, climbed uphill all night to Anoyeia, and when we reached those windy and dawn-lit cobbles, I was still wearing German uniform. For the first time I realized how an isolated German soldier in a Cretan village was treated. Cloaked shepherds, in answer to greeting, gazed past us in silence; then stood and watched us out of sight. An old crone spat on the ground. The white-whiskered and bristling elders with jutting beards shorn under the chin were all seated outside the coffee shop; baggy trousered, high-booted, turbaned men leaning on their gnarled sticks. (I knew all of them.) They stopped talking for a moment, then loudly resumed, pointedly shifting their stools to offer their backs or their elbows in postures of studied hostility. Doors and windows slammed along the lane. In a moment we could hear women's voices wailing into the hills: 'The black cattle have strayed into the wheat!' and 'Our in-laws have come!', island-wide warnings of enemy arrival.

We were glad to plunge into a side-alley and the friendly shelter of Father Skoulas's house. (We had sent him to the Middle East for SOE and parachute training; when he got back he was known as 'the flying priest'.) His wife, retreating down the corridor in alarm, refused to recognize me; it is amazing what a strange uniform and the removal of a moustache (or of the beards that we all grew at one time or another) would do. 'It's me, Pappadia, Mihali!' – 'What Mihali? I don't know any Mihali!' Deadlock. Alerted by a neighbour, the priest arrived, and at last, amid amazement and laughter, all was well.* The village were told we were harmless scroungers; later, that we had left. The give-away garments were peeled off. Raki and mezze appeared under the great arch of the house and, sitting on the cross-beam of her loom plucking a chicken in a cloud of feathers, the priestess was all smiles and teasing now. Nobody had heard of the capture yet . . .

Thank heavens for Stratis's police uniform. He soon appeared. The ascent had been laborious – the General's leg had received a bad

---

* Years later, the son of Father Skoulas told me that what convinced his mother that the young German soldier in front of her was indeed Mihali was the gap between his front teeth.

bang during the struggle at the car – but safe. They were now sheltering in a gulley a mile or two away. A basket of food and drink was stealthily despatched, and I was to join them after dark with a guide and a mule for the General.

In the late afternoon the noise of an aircraft flying low over the roofs brought us all to our feet. Running up the ladder to the flat roof, we saw a single-winged Feiseler-Storck reconnaissance plane circling above, moulting a steady snowfall of leaflets. It wheeled round several times, whirring its way up and down the foothills, vanished westwards still trailing its white cloud; then turned back towards Heraklion. Several leaflets had landed on the roof.

'To all Cretans,' the text went in smudged type still damp from the press,

Last night the German General Kreipe was abducted by bandits. He is now being concealed in the Cretan mountains and his whereabouts cannot be unknown to the inhabitants. If the General is not returned within three days, all rebel villages in the Heraklion district will be razed to the ground and the severest reprisals exacted on the civilian population.

The room was convulsed by incredulity, then excitement and finally by triumphant hilarity. We could hear running feet in the streets, and shouts and laughter.

'Just think, we've stolen their *General*!' – 'The horn-wearers won't dare look us in the eyes!' – 'The horn-wearers came here looking for wool, and we'll send them away shorn!'

How had it happened? Where? Who had done it? The priest, who was in the know, and god-brother George, winked at us and Stratis and I lowered our eyes innocently. I told them it was the work of an Anglo-Cretan commando; mostly Cretan; 'And you'll see! Three days will pass and there won't be any villages burnt or even shooting!' (I hoped this was true. I seemed to be the only one in the room disturbed by the German threat and I prayed that urgency would lend wings to the messengers' heels and scatter our counter-leaflets and the BBC news of the General's departure from the island. Had the Germans found the car yet, with my letter pinned on the upholstery?

Had they followed our paperchase of clues down to the submarine beach?)

'Eh!' one old man said, 'They'll burn down all the houses one day. And what then? My house was burnt down four times by the Turks; let the Germans burn it down for the fifth time! And they killed scores of my family, scores of them, my child. Yet here I am! We're at war, and war has all these things. *You can't have a wedding feast without meat.* Fill up the glasses, Pappadia.'

An hour after sunset our two parties had rejoined, and we were winding up a steep and scarcely discernible goat path. On a mule in our midst, muffled against the cold in Stratis's green gendarme's greatcoat with Manoli by his side, rode the General: or rather, Theophilos: the words 'Kreipe' or 'Strategos' had been forbidden even as far back as Kastamonitza. Billy told me they had had a German alarm during the day and had moved their hideout. Perhaps the alarm had been raised by the distant glimpse, from above Anoyeia, of me in German uniform, and George openly armed and in battledress, but not too obvious with his black beret stuffed into his pocket. The General, they all said, had been reasonable and cooperative; his most immediate worry – which he repeated to me during our first rest for a smoke among the rocks – was the loss of his Knight's Cross of the Iron Cross, a decoration worn around the neck. I said it had probably come off in the struggle; perhaps it had been found during the cleanup in which case I would see that it was returned, and he thanked me. A propos of the leaflets, which I translated, he said: 'Well, you surely didn't expect my colleague Bräuer to remain inactive when he learnt of – my rape (*mein Raub*)?' – 'No, General, but the Germans won't catch us' (I prudently touched a handy ilex trunk here). 'The Cretans are all on our side, you know.' 'Yes, I see they are. And, of course, you've always got me.' 'Yes, General, we've always got you.' At another of these halts he said, after a sigh and almost to himself, '*Post coitum triste.*' Astonished at this comment, I told him that only a few minutes before, and far out of earshot, Billy and I had decided that the same phrase exactly suited the mood of deflation that had followed the capture. 'It's all right for you, Major,' the General said, 'military glory, I suppose. But my whole career has come to bits. (*Meine ganze Karriere ist kaputt gegangen*.) The war is over for me, as you said. And to think that my promotion from *Generalmajor* to *Generalleutnant* has just come through!' His heavy face – he had a jutting chin, straight hair cropped at the sides but long enough to fall over his brow, and clear blue eyes – looked morose and sad. 'I wish I'd never come to this accursed island.' He laughed mirthlessly. 'It was supposed to be a nice change after the Russian front . . .' Here, we both laughed. It was all rather extraordinary. Unfortunately for the journey ahead, he was wearing the same light field grey as we were, and the loose ski trousers of mountain troops. Thank heavens he had thick mountain boots. There were many ribbons over the left breast, the Wehrmacht eagle over the right, the Iron Cross First Class – won at the battle of Verdun, low on the left breast, but no small emblem of the Crimea on his left arm like the rest of the Bremen-Sebastopol division he had commanded until a few hours before. The red tabs and the gold oak-leaves blazed with newness. No eye-glass, no *mensur* scars. He was the thirteenth son of a Lutheran pastor in Hanover and had been brought up in the Classics (*'die humanitäten'*). For '*zwei*' he always said '*zwo*', which must be a Hanoverian foible. He was a professional soldier to the backbone and must have had, in surroundings where there was more scope, a solid and commanding presence.

In the small hours we climbed off the track and curled up on the bracken floor of an old shepherd's hut; the fire in the middle lit up a conical stone igloo, cobwebbed and sooty, and lined with tiers of cheeses like minor millstones and dripping bags of whey. The others had had some sleep, but George and I hadn't slept since Skalani. We rose again in the dark and continued our journey. As dawn broke, we were hailed from an overhanging ledge by one of Mihali Xylouris's lookouts, sitting with a gun across his knees. In a moment he was bounding down the hill; he threw his gun aside with a yell and flung his arms round me, Billy, Manoli and George, only stopping just in time at the astounded General. It was Kosta Kephaloyannis, one of my honorary god-brothers. He was about nineteen, lithe and wild-looking, with bronze complexion, huge green eyes and flashing teeth like a young panther. Other lookouts had joined us from their spurs and soon we were in Xilouris's cave, surrounded by welcoming guerrillas. Mihali, with his clear eyes, snowy hair and moustache and white goats-hair cape, was one of the best and most reliable leaders in Crete. There were formal introductions, and the cat, as far as the General's whereabouts and the identity of his captors went, was out of the bag.

There, too, were a cheerful trio of English colleagues. John Houseman, a young subaltern in the Bays, John Lewis, heavily booted and bearded, and, miraculously, Tom Dunbabin's wireless operator and his set. He had been informed, via Cairo, of our messages to Sandy, and Tom had sent his wireless station on to Mount Ida to help us. Our communications problem was solved. I joyfully wrote out a signal, breaking the news, urging BBC and RAF action and asking for a boat in any cove the Navy found convenient south of Mount Ida, but preferably at Sachtouria. Fortunately a timely schedule to Cairo was just coming up; we could wait there, arrange things at our ease, cross Ida, slip down to the sea, and then away to Egypt. With any luck, the BBC would have convinced the enemy that we'd left and reduce their opposition to a token show of force or even none at all.

It was a day of meetings. Our binoculars spotted three figures coming from the east: the two Anthonys (Zoidakis and Papaleonidas) and Gregori Khanarakis, but no driver. I was filled with misgiving. We all – the reconstituted abduction party, that is – went aside among the boulders. 'It was no good, *Kyrie Mihali*,' Antoni Zoidakis explained, handing me a German paybook and some faded family snaps. He was very upset. Hans, the driver, had been half stunned, poor devil. He could only walk at the rate of a tortoise. They'd almost carried him across the plain to the eastern foothills; then, during the afternoon, the hunt was up: motorized infantry had de-trucked in all the villages round the eastern flanks of the mountains and begun to advance up the hillside in open order. If they left the driver behind for the Germans to overtake, the whole plan, and the fiction of non-local participation, was exploded; the entire region would be laid waste with flame and massacre; if they stayed with him, they themselves would have been captured. There was only one thing for it; the enemy were too close to risk a gun's report; how then? Antoni leant forwards urgently, put one hand on the branching ivory hilt of his silver-scabbarded dagger and, with the side of his other hand, made a violent slash through the air. 'By surprise. In one second.' 'He didn't know a thing,' said one of the others. There was a deep crevasse handy and lots of stones; he would never be found. 'It was a pity. He seemed quite a nice chap, even though he was a German.'*

The turn things had taken was deeply upsetting. I had planned that there should be no bloodshed on the operation, and that the driver, Corporal Frunze, would leave with the rest of the party. It was shattering news; the silence of malefactors hung over us, broken at last by Manoli Paterakis. 'Don't fret about it! We did our best. Just remember what those horn-wearers have done to Crete, Greece, Europe, England!' Predictably, he repeated the grim Cretan proverb about the wedding feast (quoted above). We all stood up. I told them they'd acted in the only possible way and so it seemed.

After an hour trying to get the message to Cairo, the operator discovered that some vital part of the set had broken down; a part, moreover, that was unreplaceable in Crete. It was a lack only to be remedied by sea, like our own problem, or by parachute. Both these, of course, could only be arranged by wireless contact. The prospect was dark.

Our first runner to Tom arrived back with the news that nobody in the south knew exactly where he was. He'd sent us his wireless, then gone to ground with a bad attack of malaria. There were two other stations in the province of Retimno, far away in the north-west; but as there had been a lot of moving about, Tom was our only link with them. Anyway in the present commotion, they would almost certainly be shifting too. The messenger also brought news of troop movements at Timbaki, Melabes, Spyli and Armenioi; columns of dust were heading towards Mount Ida from the heavily garrisoned Bad Lands of the Messara; observation planes were scattering over the southern foothills. A runner from Anoyeia brought reports of identical enemy doings in the north: lorried infantry unloading in all the foothills as far west as the great monastery of Arkadi (a notorious haunt of all of our friends until it was blown), where the German

---

* A different, and perhaps more exact account of the driver's end may be found in Antony Beevor, *Crete: The Battle and the Resistance* (John Murray, 1991), p. 306 which I strongly recommend. There were a number of details about the operation that I only learnt later on. For all the rest, the reader is referred to Billy Moss's *Ill Met by Moonlight*.

troops had bombarded the pro-abbot Dionysios and his monks with the same question that they were asking everywhere: *Where is General Kreipe?* But so far, and most untrue to form, there had been little violence, few arrests, no shooting. There was a glimmer of hope, attributed to the letter I had left for the German authorities stating that this British Commando was guided by Greek regular soldiers serving in the Middle East.

Otherwise, the scene was beginning to cloud. Mihali Xylouris and god-brother George picked out an escort for the next stage of our journey; our god-brother would accompany us. 'Whatever happens,' Mihali said, 'we'll block the way for the Germans. We know all the passes. We can blow them to bits; and if they get on your tracks, we'll shoot into the gristle' – i.e. to kill. I begged him not to fire a single shot, just to keep cover, watch where the enemy was and let us know if they got anywhere near. (The Germans nearly always stuck to the main paths; when they wandered away from them, they usually got lost; all guides commandeered locally would lead them to the foot of unscaleable cliffs and over landslides and up and down steep torrent beds of shank-smashing boulders.) Everything ahead was a looming wilderness of peaks and canyons, and in the rougher bits it would be impossible for a large party to keep formation, or even contact, except at a slow crawl which could be heard and seen for miles. The whole massif was riddled with clefts and grottoes to hide in. We must all vanish into thin air and let the enemy draw a total blank.

For the General, breaking bread with Kapetan Mihali and his men and us must have seemed very odd: the many signs of the cross before falling to and then the glasses clashed together with the usual resistance toasts. 'Victory!', 'Freedom!', 'Blessed Virgin stand close to us!', 'May she scour the rust from our guns!', and 'May we die without shame!' Mihali and his band were scrupulously polite; but they found it hard to wrench their glance from our strange prize.

Two days later, through lack of covering, Billy, the General and I ended up, not for the last time, all three sleeping under the same blanket, with Manoli and George on either side, nursing their Marlin guns and taking it in turns to sleep.

We woke up among the rocks, just as a brilliant dawn was breaking over the crest of Mount Ida which we had been struggling across for two days. We were all three lying smoking in silence, when the General, half to himself, slowly said:

> 'Vides ut alta stet nive candidum
> Soracte . . .'

I was in luck. It is the opening line of one of the few odes of Horace I know by heart (*Ad Thaliarchum*, I.ix). I went on reciting where he had broken off:

> '. . . Nec iam sustineant onus
> Silvae laborantes, geluque
> Flumina constiterint acuto'

and so on, through the remaining five stanzas to the end.

The General's blue eyes swivelled away from the mountain-top to mine – and when I'd finished, after a long silence, he said: 'Ach so, Herr Major!' It was very strange. 'Ja, Herr General.' As though, for a long moment, the war had ceased to exist. We had both drunk at the same fountains long before; and things were different between us for the rest of our time together.

The Island of *Leventeiá*

from *Roumeli*

The part that Paddy and his colleagues played in the Cretan resistance, and the way that the Cretans protected and sheltered them while putting themselves at terrible risk, made an unbreakable bond, one strengthened by mutual empathy, complicity and companionship. In this passage from Roumeli, *Paddy describes the island, and its indomitable inhabitants.*

Crete gave my retrogressive hankerings their final twist. In spite of the insular pride of the inhabitants, their aloofness from the mainland and the idiosyncrasy of their dialect and their customs, this island is an epitome of Greece. Greek virtues and vices, under sharper mountains and a hotter sun, reach exasperation point. It is, in the unpejorative sense with which I have been trying to rehabilitate the word, the most Romaic region of all; the last region the Turks relinquished. In another sense it is the least; Crete fell to the Turks two centuries later than the rest of the Byzantine Empire. This reprieve was the last half of four hundred years of restless subjection to Venice. In 1669, after a long siege, Candia fell to the Turks, and for two hundred and forty-six years Crete was the worst governed province of the Ottoman Empire and the one where the conquering race was thickest on the ground. It was the fault of the Great Powers, not Crete, that her liberation was so long delayed. Revolts against the Venetians had been leavened by interregna of literary and artistic activity. But her history under the Turks was a sequence of insurrections, massacres, raids, pursuits and wars almost without a break. Enosis with Greece was only achieved in 1915.

Like certain ranges of Epirus and the Mani, the Cretan mountains were never entirely subdued. The struggle could only have been carried on in a land of wild mountains by people of exceptional vitality and determination. There is hardly a village where the old men are unable to recall at least one rebellion and remember with advantages the deeds they did. (Until a few years ago, an old woman in the nome of Retimno still survived from the siege of the Abbey of Arkadi. Having turned it into a fortress and refuge against the besieging Turks, the abbot, when supplies at last ran short, touched off the powder magazine and sent himself and his fellow-defenders sky high. One tiny swaddled girl, blown a couple of furlongs, landed in a thicket and lived . . .) The memory of these times was still fresh in 1941, when the island was invaded by the German parachutists. Following the instinct of centuries, the old men and boys and women (for the retreat had marooned nearly everyone of military age on the mainland) leapt to arms and fell on the invaders alongside their allies. Instead of three years of docile subjection these acts ushered in bitter resistance.

The grandeurs and miseries of the occupation are well known. But that is not, here, the point. It is this. When a scattered handful of Englishmen, of whom I was one, found themselves involved in these doings, the ranges strung between Ida and the White Mountains were our refuge; the people we lived among were mountaineers, shepherds and villagers living high above the plains and the cities in circumstances which exactly tallied with the life and the background of the Klephts in revolt at any time during the past few hundred years. Modern life had only found the most hazardous foothold; many of the blemishes of lawless mountain life ran riot. There were leaders of guerrilla bands who were paragons of courage and unselfishness; a few, equally brave, were as ruthless and ambitious as Tamburlaine. The habit of centuries, as we have seen, impelled resistance to the occupation at all costs. It had also bequeathed lawless customs which now wreaked havoc among the Cretans themselves. They are virtually weaned on powder and shot; every shepherd goes armed, and a worship of guns and great skill in handling them dominate the highlands. The rustling of flocks, though it is on the wane, still goes on. Marriages sometimes begin by the armed abduction of the bride by her suitor and his friends, and blood feuds, initiated, perhaps, by one of these two causes or by an insult, by rage or an exchange of shots, can decimate opposing families over a space of decades and seal up neighbouring villages in hostile deadlock. Harsh and terrible deeds are done in the name of family honour. The wildness of the country puts these things beyond the reach of the law and fills the mountains, even in peacetime, with a scattered population of outlaws; in war, when all shadow of authority except the hostile and impotent writ of the enemy was swept aside, lawless ways doubly prospered. In spite of the occupation, in which these mountaineers were so resolute and determined, private vengeance (especially in Sphakia and Selino) laid many villagers low.

All this is confined to a few regions and it is on the wane. Obviously, it is the duty of the state to stamp out these fierce customs. Yet I can never hear or read of a Cretan mountaineer being hunted down and brought to book for participating in one of these mountain feuds without a feeling of compunction: the juxtaposition of modern law and those eagle-haunted wildernesses seems somehow as incongruous as the idea of Orestes bundled into a Black Maria. For many of these tragedies are, by age-old standards, innocent; they are prompted by feelings of duty and conducted with honour. There was much to deplore; much more, however, to admire; in particular their courage and the compassion that prompted them to shelter, clothe and feed the straggling army of their marooned allies. For this hundreds of Cretans were killed in reprisal massacres, and scores of villages were burnt to ashes; and, when their protégés were safely spirited away to Africa, their ardour was poured into resistance, and, most mercifully for us, into backing up the handful of foreign emissaries who had been dropped into their midst to help carry on the secret war. It was no mean thing for these solitary allies in their midst to feel that they had the support of a dozen mountain-ranges and of several hundred villages; indeed, if need be – and there was need, now and then – of the whole island.

But, apart from these general qualities, so propitious to the struggle which was afoot, it was the detail and the structure of their life – in which we aspired, in speech and manner, to drown ourselves – which invited fascination and respect.

Little in these crags and ravines had changed for centuries. One felt that each village must have existed since Minoan times. There was little there but a church filled with flaking Byzantine frescoes and a slanting maze of stepped and cobbled lanes; but there were subtle differences in the weave and the pattern of blankets and knapsacks and the way that men tied their fringed headkerchiefs, and in the cut of their hooded capes, and in some of them, a distinguishing accent, a variant of the Cretan dialect, and even of physical appearance. However often these villages had been sacked and burned they were always built again and according to an unbreakable formula. I remember sitting on the flat roof of a friend's house in Anoyeia, on the slopes of Mount Ida, and, as I gazed at the moonlit jigsaw of roofs and houses all round, calling to mind Aristotle's ideal for the capitals of the Greek states: cities small enough to hear the voice of one herald.

We seldom stayed in villages; not through fear of treachery, but lest innocent garrulity should endanger them. The houses contained little: a semicircular arch across the living-room, a smoke-blackened hearth, a low ledge of divan round the walls spread with coloured blankets, a loom, a wooden table and stools, the icons and their lamp and a pitcher with thorn twigs in the mouth against flying insects. Onions, garlic and tomatoes hung from the cobwebbed beams; faded pictures of Venizelos looked down from the walls and enlarged sepia photographs of turbaned grandsires armed to the teeth. Hens, pecking their way indoors, were always being shooed out, and swallows dived to and from their nest in the rafters with a swish; when we were there, rifles leaned in the corner and lay across the tables; some were adorned with silver plaques and cartridge-belts heavy with flashing clips festooned them. The thick embrasures of the windows and the doors framed downhill cascades of olives and a canyon twisting between dovetailing scarps; often these vistas ended in a triangle of the Aegean or the Libyan Sea; they were nearly always commanded by the upheaval of Ida or the White Mountains. Sometimes, with sentries posted, after a banquet with the Olympianly bearded priest, the mayor and the village elders, we would stay the night. At these meals, the women, coiffed and clad in black – saviours of numberless British, New Zealand and Australians – served and stood near with arms akimbo; they joined in the conversation spiritedly but, in this masculine and patriarchal society, seldom sat with us. In villages like this I was treated for small maladies now and then – for rheumatism, due to constant sleeping out in wet clothes – and for persistent headaches. The universal remedy of cupping was followed, in every case, by darker therapies administered by clever old women: many candlelit signs of the cross were performed over the afflicted part; incantations accompanied them, and oil dropped slowly into a glass of water in ritual quantities. Once a beautiful young witch knotted a pinch of salt in one corner of my turban and murmured spells for half an hour. Impossible to discover the words: '*mystiká prágmata! Kalá prágmata! Vaskaníes!*' was the only answer, through lips across which forefingers were conspiratorially laid; words followed by peals of laughter from the women and the girls who gather at such times: 'Secret things! Good things! Charms . . .!' They worked at once.

But the high mountains, for nearly three years, were our real home. It was there, at the end of hours climbing and higher than the dizziest village, that devotion to the Greek mountains and their population took root. We lived in goat-folds and abandoned conical cheese-makers' huts and above all, in the myriad caverns that mercifully riddle the island's stiff spine. Some were too shallow to keep out the snow, others could house a Cyclops and all his flocks. Here, at ibex- and eagle-height, we settled with our small retinues. Enemy searches kept us on the move and it was in a hundred of these eyries that we got to know an older Crete and an older Greece than anyone dreams of in the plains. Under the dripping firelit stalactites we sprawled and sat cross-legged, our eyes red with smoke, on the branches that padded the cave's floor and spooned our suppers out of a communal tin plate: beans, lentils, cooked snails and herbs, accompanied by that twice-baked herdsman's bread that must be soaked in water or goats' milk before it is eaten. Toasting goats' cheese sizzled on the points of long daggers and oil dewed our whiskers.* These sessions were often cheered by flasks of raki, occasionally distilled from mulberries, sent from the guardian village below. On lucky nights, calabashes of powerful amber-coloured wine loosened all our tongues. Over the shoulders of each figure was slung a bristly white cloak stiff as bark, with the sleeves hanging loose like penguins' wings; the hoods raised against the wind gave the

---

* Before beginning, all signed themselves with the cross, their thumb and two first fingers conjoined to honour the Trinity, the cross-bar going from right shoulder to left in the Orthodox way; and, at the meal's end, before storing away any fragments of bread left over, they would kiss them in memory of the Mystic Feast.

bearded and moustachioed faces a look of Cistercians turned bandit. Someone would be smashing shells with his pistol-butt and offering peeled walnuts in a horny palm; another sliced tobacco on the stock of a rifle: for hours we forgot the war with talk and singing and stories; laughter echoed along minotaurish warrens.

Few of the old men could write or read, those in middle age found reading hard and writing a grind; the young were defter penmen, but, owing to their short time at school and the disorder of the war, they were not advanced in the craft, apart from an occasional student on the run from the underground in one of the towns. A by-product of this scholastic void was a universal gift for lively and original talk; the flow and style of their discourse were unhindered by the self-consciousness which hobbles and hamstrings the rest of us. They had astonishing memories. These often reached back to their great-grandfathers' day, and, by hearsay, far beyond. In an island of long lives, this made all the past seem recent: compelling proof of the continuity of history. It reduced the war to just another struggle, the worst and the most recent of many, with which we were perfectly able to deal, and, though the Germans had overrun Greece and driven the British back to El Alamein, win. 'Never fear, my child,' some greybeard would say, prophetically prodding the smoke with a forefinger like a fossil, 'with Christ and the Virgin's help, we'll eat them.' All agreed, and the conversation wandered to the First World War and Asia Minor and arguments about the respective merits of Lloyd George and Clemenceau, to Bismarck and the assassination of Abraham Lincoln, or the governments, constitutions and electoral systems of different countries. Then the level of this far-ranging chat, much of it far beyond the scope of their literate equivalents in England, might suddenly be reduced by another old man, simpler than his fellows, asking, and evoking general derision and amusement by his question, whether the English were Christians or, like the Moslems, polygamous . . . Intelligence, humour, curiosity, the rapid assimilation of ideas and their quick deployment, an incomparable narrative knack, arguments resolved by a sudden twist, the inability to leave facts and ideas undeveloped – they are objects to play with like nuggets – all these graces flowered in this stony terrain. The Cretan dialect, with its ancient survivals and turns of phrase and a

vocabulary that changed from valley to valley and an accent unpol-
luted by the metropolis, was an unstaunchable fountain of delight
and fascination.

Their clothes, however ragged and patched, were emblematic of
the dash and spirit they prize so highly: black boots to the knee,
baggy, pleated, dark-blue trousers – breeches among the young* –
wasp-waisted at the middle by a twisted mulberry silk sash eight feet
long in which was often stuck a long dagger with a branching ivory
hilt and an embossed silver sheath; above this came a black shirt and
sometimes a blue waistcoat as tight as a bullfighter's, stiff with
embroidered whorls. A black silk turban with a heavy fringe was
twisted at a rakish tilt round every brow. Bandoliers and a slung gun
came next – fittings which often accompanied the frocks of abbots,
monks and priests – and over them, in winter, the white hooded cape.
A curly handled stick, never a crook as on the mainland, with as many
wriggles along its shaft as could be found, finishes everything off. All,
however tattered and frayed by mountain life, is taut and streamlined,
a garb in which, as I well know, it is impossible not to swagger. This
bravura was accentuated among the old men by the odd archaic cut
of their beards; shorn under the jaw-line, they jutted from their chins
like the beards of ancient warriors on vases. This look was under-
scored by their deceptively frowning eyebrows and the high hawklike
bridges of their noses. The ferocity of those swooping brows was
contradicted by the eyes beneath. These are seldom wary and
reserved, as they are in the Mani: alert, confident, wide, humorous
and unguarded, they blaze like lamps.† Everything about these men
spells alacrity and vigour. They are lean, sweated to the bone, strong
and resilient; the old are as hard as the limestone that surrounds
them, the young as fast across the mountains as Hurons, as untamed
as ibexes. Nowhere in Greece is the quality of *leventeiá* so clearly

---

* Cretans of the towns and the lowlands who had abandoned this mode were referred
to, with some scorn but more pity, as *makrypantalonádes*: 'longtrousermen'.

† The island was captured from the Byzantines by the Saracens of Spain in the eighth
century, and turned into a nest of corsairs. Rather more than a century later they were driven
into the sea; the island was seized for Byzantium again by Nicephorus Phocas and seven
half-legendary princes. Here and there, especially in the south, one can detect a line of nose,
a curl of brow, that may ultimately spring from this piratical sojourn.

manifest. This attribute embraces a range of characteristics: youth, health, nerve, high spirits, humour, quickness of mind and action, skill with weapons, the knack of pleasing girls, love for singing and drinking, generosity, capacity to improvise *mantinades* – those intricate rhyming couplets sung with a sting in the second line – and 'flying like a bird' in the quick and violent dances. *Leventeiá* often includes virtuosity on the *lyra*: it is universal zest for life, the love of living dangerously and a readiness for anything.

Rather unexpectedly, this supercharge of energy and extroversion is shot with a most delicately poised sensitiveness, sometimes by a touchiness, where a mishap or a slight, even an imaginary one, can turn the world black and drive its victim into melancholy and languor, almost to pining away. It is the task of friends to diagnose the anguish and exorcize it; not always an easy task. This lurking demon, resembling the *tribulatio et angustia* of the Psalms, the Greeks call *stenochoria*. But the problem acts both ways: should distress assault one, they recognize its symptoms with an almost feminine intuitiveness and try, with tact and solicitude, to resolve it; and even if they are mistaken about the cause, this kindness may allay the effect. Their need and their talent for friendship is the obverse of implacable hatred for enemies.

Stenochoria finds them helpless; but, with the major calamities that shower down upon them, they are better fitted to deal; ancestral reactions come to the rescue. The loss of a kinsman in a mountain affray or a reprisal holocaust would unloose grief and rage which, ungovernable at first, the longing for vengeance would channel and the anodynes of fatalism slowly allay. The Cretans see life in tragic and heroic terms. This being so, it is fortunate that their feeling of comedy is also pronounced. They are preternaturally quick at locating the ludicrous aspects of things; they seize the point and throw it back in a different shape. (The gift for laughter in Greece becomes still more remarkable when we think of her neighbours. Turkey, the Slav states, Albania and Southern Italy weave a dark garland of literalness and scarce jokes . . .) This blessing lightened many of our troubles. It gave a marvellous zest to those long troglodytic sessions which, especially in winter, often kept us pent.

These were the times when one heard how to foretell the future by dreams and by gazing at the markings on the scraped shoulder blades of sheep and learnt about the superstitions and beliefs which still survive there; about gorgons and nereids and vampires; of the 'light-shadowed ones', who can see more than ordinary mortals; of how an ancestor of the Manouras family fought with a dragon outside his village, and how, at each anniversary of the Battle of Frangokástello, phantom hosts of Greeks and Turks – 'the people of the dew' – complete with guns and cannon and banners, are seen to fight the battle all over again. The hours were often whiled away with singing *mantinades*. Some of us even learnt to improvise them ourselves, which was considered a feat for strangers, and hailed with applause. There were many songs. But *ta rizitika*, 'the foothill ones', were far beyond our scope, so intricate are they, so unseizable in key and rhythm and changes of tempo. One called *Chelidonáki mou gorgó*, 'my swift little swallow', especially sticks in my memory . . . The *lyra* often accompanied these songs; it is a three-stringed instrument* a foot-and-a-half long, propped upright on the musician's knee and played with a bow. Beautifully hollowed and carved out of walnut, this smooth and polished instrument is light as a feather and capable of a great range of moods. Exciting and violin-like, the melodic line swoops, soars, twirls, laments and exults with a manic-depressive fluidity. It was good luck to have a *lyra*-player in one's party, not only for the sake of the music; the players are great fun, as a rule, fast runners, and crack shots; nonpareils of *leventeiá*, in fact.

* Identical with the rebeck which angels play in *trecento* paintings and on the capitals in cloisters.

Trade Secrets of the Kravarites

from *Roumeli*

The Kravara is a wild region of western Greece, whose inhabitants had been famous for living exclusively by mendicity. They were quack doctors, relic-pedlars, beggars and pickpockets – in fact every means of parting the unwary from their money had been raised, by the Kravarites, to a fine art. Paddy longed to find out whether these stories were based on fact, though he feared that raising the subject at all might cause indignation among the modern-day Kravarites. To his surprise, they were willing and eager to talk about the skills of their ancestors.

'Uncle Elias is the man,' they told me in the lamp-lit tavern. 'He'll tell you all about the old Kravarites in the epoch' – this vague term, '*stin ipochí*', always refers to an indeterminate yore, a vague period of old days long sped. 'He's ninety.'

His long, clean-shaven face was a network of wrinkles but his dark eyes darted eagerly. When he took off his cloth cap of mock-leopard's skin – headgear which has long enjoyed an intermittent proletarian vogue in Greece – a snowy shock fell thick and straight over his corrugated brow. A handsome, humorous and slightly actor-ish mobility stamped his features. He looked much younger than ninety and I said so. The compliment called two new fans of wrinkles into play and his smile revealed long palisades of teeth from which not one was missing.

'Those teeth are all his own, too,' the hunchback said.

'The teeth are all right,' Uncle Elias observed, flashing them once more, 'but they're out of work.'

Everyone laughed. He came from a different village and the locals treated him with a mixture of affectionate teasing and respect. Laying his thick stick across the lamp-lit table he slowly crushed tobacco leaves in the palm of his hand and stuffed them into a home-made pipe. 'Contraband from Agrinion,' someone murmured. 'Don't tell the *patellos* [the Kravara code word for policeman] . . .'

As we talked, he fished a little bar of steel out of his pocket and then, holding it between finger and thumb with a disc of dried fungus held tight against it, he struck it repeatedly with a chip of flint. A faint whiff as of singeing cloth told us that the sparks had ignited it. Blowing until the glow had spread, he laid the smouldering fungus on his pipe-bowl and puffed until a cloud of illegal and aromatic smoke embowered him.

'*Barba Elia*,' someone said, pointing to his disintegrating footgear, 'you ought to get a new pair of boots. Those have seen their day.' 'Don't you worry about them,' Uncle Elias answered from his cloud. 'They are laughing.' It is true that the gaps between the uppers and the soles curled in the semblance of dark smiles.

The old days in the Kravara . . . The utterances of this fluent old man revived them with great vividness. A mass of circumstantial detail suggested that he had played a considerable part in those ancient doings; but it was never explicit. I expected in vain that his narrative would slip at some point from *oratio obliqua* to *oratio recta*; the collusion of his glance, however, was something more than a hint.

The first impediment a young beggar had to discard, Uncle Elias instructed us, was an attribute called the *tseberi*, or the *tsipa*, of shame. The *tseberi* is the headkerchief that village women wear and the symbol of their modesty; the *tsipa* is a thin layer or membrane, and in some regions a foreskin; its loss was a kind of psychological circumcision. Those handicapped by the stigma of its presence, which was detectable to initiates at once by the expression on their foreheads, could never come to much; they must be armed by a brazen front that no insult could shake. Old Kravarites dismissed their daughters' suitors with the words: 'Go away, boy! You've still got your *tsipa tis dropis*. Get rid of that shame-brow and then we'll see.' The emblem of success was the heavy staff, or *matsoúka*, which accompanied each new journey. An array of these, hanging on the wall, proved the owner a man of substance. They were polished with handling and scarred by the fangs of a hundred dogs; these gnashing and hysterical foes invested the approach to a village with the hazards of an invasion. The trophies accumulated like quarterings of nobility and dynastic alliances were contracted between the children of households boasting an equal display. These sticks, it was said, were sometimes hollowed for the concealment of the gold coins: the weight of small change was intolerable until it was converted. British sovereigns were highly treasured. Normally the gold coins were dispersed and sewn about the owner's rags. The *tagari*, a roomy woven bag, slung on a cord, was essential. This they filled with *paximadia*, bread twice-baked and hard as a stone, once the diet of the hermits of the Thebaid and now the sustenance of shepherds. Accoutred with staves and sacks and this almost unfissile food, they set out; usually alone, occasionally in couples. Sometimes their professional devices were a handicap. Uncle Elias cited a duumvirate in which one member pretended to be one-legged and the other one-armed: but the one-legged partner could eat at twice the speed of his mate, so they split up. 'Dumbness', too, had drawbacks: 'mute' beggars had been bitten to the bone by dogs rather than give themselves away . . . Did they always manage to keep up their disguises? Not always. Uncle Elias told us of a champion beggar, a tall and burly man, who had perfected the knack of extreme malformation: his legs and arms became a tangle, his head lolled, his eyes rolled and his tongue hung out: 'like this!' With these words, Uncle Elias shifted on his chair, and with a click, as it were, became a scarecrow. His face switched to a burlesque mask of tragedy; a maimed arm shot out, a suppliant litany streamed from his lips: 'Kind people, spare a mouthful of bread or a copper for a fellow-Christian who has lost the use of his limbs from birth and has eaten neither crust nor crumb for a week. God and Christ and the All-Holy-One and all the Saints and prophets and martyrs shower their blessings on you!' The metamorphosis, total and astonishing, had taken place in a flash. Just as suddenly, he relaxed into his normal self. 'He used to almost overdo it,' he said with an engaging laugh. 'But he made plenty of money. A very bright fellow.'

'Well,' he went on, 'one day he arrived in a Bulgarian village inhabited by Pomaks, terrible men. But instead of alms, he got sneers, insults, shoves, pinches, kicks. He stood it as long as he could, but his blood was beginning to boil, and suddenly——' Here the old narrator uncoiled from his chair, jumped to his feet and soared above the lamp-lit circle. Under those hoary brows his eyes fired glances like harpoons from face to face. '. . . suddenly he straightened up and set about them!' Uncle Elias' clenched fists mowed through the air in a whirlwind of scything sweeps and jabs and upper cuts. '*Dang! Ding! Boom! Bim! Bam!* Down they went like the dead! *Pam! Poom!* There must have been ten of the horn-wearers flat on the ground! And the others! You should have seen their faces! Their eyes were starting out of their sockets as though the Devil had sprung from Hell! They took to their heels; the village square was empty.' He sat down again grinning. What happened to the beggar? 'Why,' he said, mopping his brow from the exertion, 'he ran for it too, far, far, far away over the hills! When they came round he was kilometres off! *Paraxena pragmata!* Strange doings!'

The Last Emperor of Byzantium

from *Mani*

Castles in the air do not require very rigid foundations; their enchantment lies in the fact that they are built on almost nothing. In the early 1950s when Paddy was exploring the Mani, he met a fisherman from the village of Kardamyli whose family name suggested that he might be descended from the last Byzantine dynasty, the Palaeologi – which was enough to fuel the following magnificent day-dream.

I woke up thinking of the Mourtzini and the Palaeologi. It occurred to me, drinking mountain-tea in the street, that I had clean forgotten to ask when the Mourtzinos family had died out. 'But it hasn't,' Mr Phaliréas said. 'Stratis, the last of them, lives just down the road.'

Evstratios Mourtzinos was sitting in his doorway weaving, out of split cane and string, a huge globular fish-trap more complex than any compass design or abstract composition of geometrical wire. The reel of twine revolved on the floor, the thread unwinding between his big toe and its neighbour as the airy sphere turned and shifted in his skilful brown fingers with a dazzling interplay of symmetrical parabolas. The sunlight streamed through the rust-coloured loops and canopies of drying nets. A tang of salt, tar, seaweed and warm cork hung in the air. Cut reeds were stacked in sheaves, two canaries sang in a cage in the rafters, our host's wife was slicing onions into a copper saucepan. Mourtzinos shrugged his shoulders with a smile at my rather absurd questions and his shy and lean face, which brine and the sun's glare had cured to a deep russet, wore an expression of dubious amusement. 'That's what they say,' he said, 'but we don't know anything about it. They are just old stories . . .' He poured out hospitable glasses of ouzo, and the conversation switched to the difficulties of finding a market for fish: there was so much competition. There is a special delight in this early-morning drinking in Greece.

Old stories, indeed. But supposing every link were verified, each

shaky detail proved? Supposing this modest and distinguished looking fisherman were really heir of the Palaeologi, descendant of
Constantine XI and of Michael VIII the Liberator, successor to
Alexis Comnene and Basil the Bulgar-Slayer and Leo the Isaurian
and Justinian and Theodosius and St Constantine the Great? And,
for that matter, to Diocletian and Heliogabalus and Marcus Aurelius,
to the Antonines, the Flavians, the Claudians and the Julians, all the
way back to the Throne of Augustus Caesar on the Palatine, where
Romulus had laid the earliest foundations of Rome? ... The generous strength of a second glass of ouzo accelerated these cogitations.
It was just the face for a constitutional monarch, if only Byzantium
were free. For the sheer luxury of credulity I lulled all scepticism to
sleep and, parallel to an unexacting discourse of currents and baits
and shoals, a kind of fairy-tale began assembling in my mind: 'Once
upon a time, in a far-away land, a poor fisherman and his wife lived
by the sea-shore ... One day a stranger from the city of Byzantium
knocked on the door and begged for alms. The old couple laid meat
and drink before him ...' Here the mood and period painlessly
changed into a hypothetic future and the stranger had a queer story
to tell: the process of Westernization in Turkey, the study of
European letters, of the classics and the humanities had borne such
fruit that the Turks, in token of friendship and historical appropri-
ateness, had decided to give the Byzantine Empire back to the
Greeks and withdraw to the Central Asian steppes beyond the Volga
from which they originally came, in order to plant their newly-won
civilization in the Mongol wilderness ... The Greeks were streaming
back into Constantinople and Asia Minor. Immense flotillas were
dropping anchor off Smyrna and Adana and Halicarnassus and
Alexandretta. The seaboard villages were coming back to life; joyful
concourses of Greeks were streaming into Adrianople, Rhodosto,
Broussa, Nicaea, Caesaraea, Iconium, Antioch and Trebizond. The
sound of rejoicing rang through eastern Thrace and banners with the
Cross and the double-headed eagle and the Four Betas back-to-back
were fluttering over Cappadocia and Karamania and Pontus and
Bithynia and Paphlagonia and the Taurus mountains ... But in the
City itself, the throne of the Emperors was vacant ...

Stratis, our host, had put the fish-trap on the ground to pour out

a third round of ouzo. Mrs Mourtzinos chopped up an octopus tentacle and arranged the cross-sections on a plate. Stratis, to illustrate
his tale, was measuring off a distance by placing his right hand in the
crook of his left elbow, 'a grey mullet that long,' he was saying,
'weighing five okas if it weighed a dram . . .'

Then, in the rebuilt palace of Blachernae, the search for the heir
had begun. What a crackling of parchment and chrysobuls, what
clashing of seals and unfolding of scrolls! What furious wagging of
beards and flourishes of scholarly forefingers! The Cantacuzeni,
though the most authenticated of the claimants, were turned down;
they were descendants only from the last emperor but four . . .
Dozens of doubtful Palaeologi were sent packing . . . the
Stephanopoli de Comnene of Corsica, the Melissino-Comnenes of
Athens were regretfully declined. Tactful letters had to be written to
the Argyropoli; a polite firmness was needed, too, with the Courtney
family of Powderham Castle in Devonshire, kinsmen of Pierre de
Courtenai, who, in 1218, was Frankish Emperor of Constantinople;
and a Lascaris maniac from Saragossa was constantly hanging about
the gates . . . Envoys returned empty-handed from Barbados and the
London docks . . . Some Russian families allied to Ivan the Terrible
and the Palaeologue Princess Anastasia Tzarogorodskaia had to be
considered . . . Then all at once a new casket of documents came to
light and a foreign emissary was despatched hot-foot to the
Peloponnese; over the Taygetus to the forgotten hamlet of
Kardamyli . . . By now all doubt had vanished. The Emperor
Eustratius leant forward to refill the glasses with ouzo for the fifth
time. The Basilissa shooed away a speckled hen which had wandered
indoors after crumbs. On a sunny doorstep, stroking a marmalade
cat, sat the small Diadoch and Despot of Mistra.

Our host heaved a sigh . . . 'The trouble with dyes made from pine-
cones,' he went on – 'the ordinary brown kind – is that the fish can
see the nets a mile off. They swim away! But you have to use them or
the twine rots in a week. Now, the new *white* dyes in Europe would
solve all that! But you would hunt in vain for them in the ships' chan-
dlers of Kalamata and Gytheion . . .'

The recognition over, the rest seemed like a dream. The removal
of the threadbare garments, the donning of the cloth-of-gold

dalmatics, the diamond-studded girdles, the purple cloaks. All three were shod with purple buskins embroidered with bicephalous eagles, and when the sword and the sceptre had been proffered and the glittering diadem with its hanging pearls, the little party descended to a waiting ship. The fifth ouzo carried us, in a ruffle of white foam, across the Aegean archipelago and at every island a score of vessels joined the convoy. By the time we entered the Hellespont, it stretched from Troy to Sestos and Abydos . . . on we went, past the islands of the shining Propontis until, like a magical city hanging in mid-air, Constantinople appeared beyond our bows, its towers and bastions glittering, its countless domes and cupolas bubbling among pinnacles and dark sheaves of cypresses, all of them climbing to the single great dome topped with the flashing cross that Constantine had seen in a vision on the Milvian bridge. There, by the Golden Gate, in the heart of a mighty concourse, waited the lords of Byzantium: the lesser Caesars and Despots and Sebastocrators, the Grand Logothete in his globular headgear, the Counts of the Palace, the Sword Bearer, the Chartophylax, the Great Duke, the thalassocrats and polemarchs, the Strateges of the Cretan archers, of the hoplites and the peltasts and the cataphracts; the Silentiaries, the Count of the Excubitors, the governors of the Asian Themes, the Clissourarchs, the Grand Eunuch, and (for by now all Byzantine history had melted into a single anachronistic maelstrom) the Prefects of Sicily and Nubia and Ethiopia and Egypt and Armenia, the Exarchs of Ravenna and Carthage, the Nomarch of Tarentum, the Catapan of Bari, the Abbot of Studium. As a reward for bringing good tidings, I had by this time assumed the Captaincy of the Varangian Guard; and there they were, beyond the galleons and the quinqueremes, in coruscating ranks of winged helmets, clashing their battle-axes in homage; you could tell they were Anglo-Saxons by their long thick plaits and their flaxen whiskers . . . Bells clanged. Semantra hammered and cannon thundered as the Emperor stepped ashore; then, with a sudden reek of naphtha, Greek fire roared saluting in a hundred blood-red parabolas from the warships' brazen beaks. As he passed through the Golden Gate a continual paean of cheering rose from the hordes which darkened the battlement of the Theodosian Walls. Every window and roof-top was a-bristle with citizens and as the great company processed along the purple-carpeted street from the Arcadian to the Amastrian Square, I saw that all the minarets had vanished ... We crossed the Philadelphia and passed under the Statue of the Winds. Now, instead of the minarets, statuary crowded the skyline. A population of ivory and marble gleamed overhead and, among the fluttering of a thousand silken banners, above the awnings and the crossed festoons of olive-leaves and bay, the sky was bright with silver and gold and garlanded chryselephantine ... Each carpeted step seemed to carry us into a denser rose-coloured rain of petals softly falling.

The heat had become stifling. In the packed square of Constantine, a Serbian furrier fell from a roof-top and broke his neck; an astrologer from Ctesiphon, a Spanish coppersmith and a moneylender from the Persian Gulf were trampled to death; a Bactrian lancer fainted, and, as we proceeded round the Triple Delphic Serpent of the Hippodrome, the voices of the Blues and the Greens, for once in concord, lifted a long howl of applause. The Imperial horses neighed in their stables, the hunting cheetahs strained yelping at their silver chains. Mechanical gold lions roared in the throne room, gold birds on the jewelled branches of artificial trees set up a tinkling and a twitter. The general hysteria penetrated the public jail: in dark cells, monophysites and bogomils and iconoclasts rattled their fetters across the dungeon bars. High in the glare on his Corinthian capital, a capering stylite, immobile for three decades, hammered his calabash with a wooden spoon ...

Mrs Mourtzinos spooned a couple of onions and potatoes out of the pot, laid them before us and sprinkled them with a pinch of rock salt. 'When we were a couple of hours off Cerigo,' Stratis observed, splashing out the ouzo, 'the wind grew stronger – a real *meltemi* – a roaring *boucadoura*! – so we hauled the sails down, and made everything fast ...'

There, before the great bronze doors of St Sophia, gigantic in his pontificalia, stood Athenagoras the Oecumenical Patriarch, whom I had seen a few months before in the Phanar; surrounded now with all the Patriarchs and Archbishops of the East, the Holy Synod and all the pomp of Orthodoxy in brocade vestments of scarlet and purple and gold and lilac and sea blue and emerald green: a forest of gold pastoral staves topped with their twin coiling serpents, a hundred yard-long beards cascading beneath a hundred onion-mitres crusted with gems; and, as in the old Greek song about the City's fall, the great fane rang with sixty clanging bells and four hundred gongs, with a priest for every bell and a deacon for every priest. The procession advanced, and the coruscating penumbra, the flickering jungle of hanging lamps and the bright groves and the undergrowth of candles swallowed them. Marble and porphyry and lapis lazuli soared on all sides, a myriad glimmering haloes indicated the entire mosaic hagiography of the Orient and, high above, suspended as though on a chain from heaven and ribbed to its summit like the concavity of an immense celestial umbrella, floated the golden dome. Through the prostrate swarm of his subjects and the fog of incense the imperial theocrat advanced to the iconostasis. The great basilica rang with the anthem of the Cherubim and as the Emperor stood on the right of the Katholikon and the Patriarch on the left, a voice as though from an archangel's mouth sounded from the dome, followed by the fanfare of scores of long shafted trumpets, while across Byzantium the heralds proclaimed the Emperor Eustratius, Servant of God, King of Kings, Most August Caesar and Basileus and Autocrator of Constantinople and New Rome. The whole City was shaken by an unending, ear-splitting roar. Entwined in whorls of incense, the pillars turned in their sockets, and tears of felicity ran down the mosaic Virgin's and the cold ikons' cheeks . . .

Leaning forward urgently, Stratis crossed himself. '*Holy Virgin and all the Saints!*' he said. 'I was never in a worse situation! It was pitch dark and pouring with rain, the mast and the rudder were broken, the bung was lost, and the waves were the size of a house. There I was, on all fours in the bilge water, baling for life, in the Straits between the Elaphonisi and Cape Malea! . . .'

. . . the whole of Constantinople seemed to be rising on a dazzling golden cloud and the central dome began to revolve as the redoubled clamour of the Byzantines hoisted it aloft. Loud with bells and gongs, with cannon flashing from the walls and a cloud-borne fleet firing long crimson radii of Greek fire, the entire visionary city, turning in faster and faster spirals, sailed to a blinding and unconjecturable zenith . . . The rain had turned to hail, the wind had risen to a scream; the boat had broken and sunk and, through the ink-black storm, Stratis was swimming for life towards the thunderous rocks of Laconia . . .

. . . The bottle was empty . . .

The schoolmaster's shadow darkened the doorway. 'You'd better hurry,' he said, 'the caique for Areopolis is just leaving.' We all rose to our feet, upsetting, in our farewells, a basket of freshly cut bait and a couple of tridents which fell to the floor with a clatter. We stepped out into the sobering glare of noon.

Supper in the Sky

from *Mani*

The towers of the Mani were built in the seventeenth and eighteenth centuries, when the Maniots were rich from piracy. The taller the tower, the more fire-power and damage its owners could inflict on rival clans or vendetta-embroiled neigh-bours. The Maniots were fierce, proud, and bloodthirsty: when a woman gave birth to a son, the family rejoiced that another 'gun' had been born. By the middle of the twentieth century, however, the Maniots were living more peaceful lives. The inhabitant of this tower was a farmer, whose daughter Vasilio had met Paddy and Joan on the road and invited them to stay.

Many things in Greece have remained unchanged since the time of the *Odyssey* and perhaps the most striking of these is the hospitality shown to strangers; the more remote and mountainous the region, the less this has altered. Arrival at a village or farmstead is much the same as that of Telemachus at the palaces of Nestor at Pylos and of Menelaus at Sparta – so near, as the crow flies, to Vatheia – or of Odysseus himself, led by the king's daughter to the hall of Alcinöus. No better description exists of a stranger's sojourn at a Greek herdsman's fold than that of Odysseus when he stepped disguised into the hut of the swineherd Eumaeus in Ithaca. There is still the same unquestioning acceptance, the attention to the stranger's needs before even finding out his name: the daughter of the house pouring water over his hands and offering him a clean towel, the table laid first and then brought in, the solicitous plying of wine and food, the exchange of identities and autobiographies; the spreading of bedclothes in the best part of the house – the coolest or warmest according to the season – the entreaties to stay as long as the stranger wishes, and, finally, at his departure, the bestowal of gifts, even if these are only a pocketful of walnuts or apples, a carnation or a bunch of basil; and the care with which he is directed on his way, accompanied some distance, and wished godspeed.

In the *Odyssey*, the newcomer often strikes a banquet in progress, and very often a stranger in Greece today will find himself led to an honourable place at a long table of villagers celebrating a wedding, a baptism, a betrothal or a name-day and his plate and glass are filled and refilled as though by magic. Often, by a little chapel (dedicated to the prophet Elijah, the Assumption or the Transfiguration on a mountain top, or, outside some built-up cave, to a *Chryssospiliotissa* – a Virgin of the Golden Grotto – or St Anthony of the Desert), he will find the rocks and the grass starred with recumbent pilgrims honouring a pious anniversary with singing and dancing, their baskets open and napkins of food spread out under the branches, the wine flowing freely from gourds and demijohns; and here, as at the village festivals, the traveller is grasped by horny hands, a place is made smooth for him on the cut brushwood, a glass put between his fingers and a slice of roast lamb offered on a fork or a broad leaf. This general hospitality on feast days is less remarkable than the individual care of strangers at all seasons. It is the dislocation of an entire household at a moment's notice that arouses astonishment. All is performed with simplicity and lack of fuss and prompted by a kindness so unfeigned that it invests the most ramshackle hut with magnificence and style.

Tonight, however, there was a change in the accustomed Homeric ritual. After drinking *ouzo* in the walled yard at the tower's foot, Vasilio's father said, 'It's a hot night. Let's eat in the cool.' He took a lantern and led the way into the tower. We followed him up the steep ladders through storey after storey until, breathless with climbing, we were on a flat roof about eight yards square surrounded by a low parapet. Chairs appeared from below and Vasilio took a coil of rope and paid it into the night; hauling it up the sixty-foot drop after an exchange of shouts, with a round tin table tied to the end. She took out and spread a clean white tablecloth and put the lantern in the centre, installing a circle of gold in the moonlight. Our faces, which were soon gathered round a roast lamb which I hoped we had not met before, were lit up by an irrelevant glow of gold which changed to the moonlit pallor of silver while jaw-bones and eye sockets were stressed with shadow if anyone leaned out of the lantern's range. The rope, to the end of which a huge basket had now been tied, was lowered into the dark again and again for more wine and food.

The night was still. As our tower-top was the highest in Vatheia, the others were invisible and we might have been dining in mid-air on a magic carpet floating across dim folds in the mountains. Standing up, the other tower tops came into sight, all of them empty and clear under the enormous moon. Not a light showed, and the only sounds were the shrill drilling note of two crickets, a nightingale and a faint chorus of frogs, hinting of water somewhere in the dry sierra. I tried to imagine how this little group, dining formally round a solitary golden star of lamplight on this little hovering quadrilateral, would look to a passing bird. I asked our host if they often had meals up here: 'Only when we feel like it,' he answered.

He had been talking of the winter, and the familiar theme of the Mani wind. 'It makes a noise that could deafen you, when the tramontana blows through these towers,' he said; and all at once, in the silence and the hot moonlight, I had a vision of that lamentable blast screaming past the shutters, of maelstroms of hail and snow coiling through those perpendiculars. 'And when there's a thunderstorm, you think the world has come to an end with all the noise and the lightning! That's when the young think of marrying, to have company in bed to keep them warm . . .'

The table was cleared and lowered swinging into the gulf and blankets and pillows, glasses and pitchers of drinking water laid out for the guests. 'I'll put this on the trap door,' he said, picking up an iron cannon ball from the parapet and cupping it in his palm like an orb, 'in case the wind should blow up and slam it shut. It's all they are good for now.'

We sauntered to the end of the village before going to bed. Beyond the cactuses a few miles to the south, a long row of twinkling lights, sailing westward under an upright pale pillar of smoke, suddenly slid out of the lee of Cape Matapan. It must have been an enormous liner lit up for a gala night. Could we hear the sound of music? One could almost imagine it. '*Megálo*,' said our host, 'Big'; truthfully enough. It disappeared behind the leaf of a prickly pear and emerged a minute later. I wondered where it was coming from. Beirut? Alexandria? Bombay? Colombo? Hong Kong? I thought of the passengers in tropical mess-jackets and low dresses and comic paper hats, the brandy revolving in balloon glasses, cigar smoke

ascending, shipboard romances ripening, cliques cohering and splin-
tering, plans forming and couples pairing off for the sights of Naples
and trips to Vesuvius; of the gallant ship's doctor, of the life and soul
of the party, of the ship's bore and the ship's vamp. Perhaps they
were wearing false noses fitted with burlesque moustaches and large
cardboard spectacles? To what tunes were they dancing, and were
streamers being thrown? I remembered once, sailing past the southern Peloponnese and Calabria, leaning across the bulwarks as many
of the passengers must have been leaning at that moment and wondering what happened in those wild and secret looking mountains to
the north. 'Look,' perhaps they were saying, 'there's a light up there!
How lonely it must be . . .'

The lights grew smaller as the liner followed the same path as
many a Phoenician galley and many a quinquereme; heading northward in the invisible groove of Harald Hardraada's ships, sailing
shield-hung and dragon-prowed from the Byzantine splendour of
Mickelgard for grey northern fjords at the world's furthest edge. At
last it shrank to a faint glow and was swallowed up by an immense
obliterating cactus.

There was much, it occurred to me next day, to be said for tower-
dwelling, especially in summer. Eating and sleeping on the roof while
the lanes below hoard the stagnant air, one catches every passing
shred of wind. One sleeps in the sky surrounded by stars and with
the moon almost within arm's reach. Dawn breaks early, and, by chasing the sleeper down the ladder out of the sunlight, solves the daily
martyrdom of getting up; and the Bastille-thick walls cool the rooms
with a freshness that grows with each descending storey as the layers
of ceiling accumulate overhead: six gradations of temperature from
the crucifying blaze of the roof to the arctic chill of the excavated
cellar. And towers ensure the rare and inestimable boon, that non-
existent commodity of Greek village life, privacy. The turmoil of
domestic life, insulated by the absorbent vacua of the intervening
chambers, swirls and bubbles fifty feet below. Who is going to climb
all those belfry ladders? (Alas, no physical barrier can daunt the thirst
for company; but for the moment all was quiet.) There was another
negative benefit of the Mani, and one which it had taken some time

to appreciate: not since Areopolis had there been a single wireless set; nothing but that delightful horned gramophone in Yeroliména. [. . .] In the heart of the country, the silence of the most desolate places is suddenly rent by the blood-curdling howl of a rogue wireless set . . . But, like religion, it has been late in reaching the Mani, and among the towers a blessed silence prevails. The only sound at the moment, as I sat over my long neglected diary among piles of sacks, was Vasilio half singing and half humming to herself in the room below.

She had demanded, the night before, all the washing which had accumulated since Sparta, and I had seen her foreshortened torso thumping and rinsing before daybreak in a stone trough in the yard and later spreading the laundry to dry on boulders and cactus branches. Now with this soft singing the delicious childhood smell of ironing floated up through the trap door. A floor further down her mother was weaving at her great loom which sent forth a muted and regular click-clack of treadles.

Beyond the bars of my window the towers descended, their walls blazoned with diagonals of light and shade; and, through a wide gap, castellated villages were poised above the sea on coils of terraces. Through another gap our host's second daughter, wide hatted and perched on the back of a wooden sledge and grasping three reins, was sliding round and round a threshing floor behind a horse, a mule and a cow – the first cow I had seen in the Mani – all of them linked in a triple yoke. On a bank above this busy stone disc, the rest of the family were flinging wooden shovelfuls of wheat in the air for the grain to fall on outstretched coloured blankets while the husks drifted away. Others shook large sieves. The sun which climbed behind them outlined this group with a rim of gold and each time a winnower sent up his great fan, for long seconds the floating chaff embowered him in a golden mist.

The sun poured into this stone casket through deep embrasures. Dust gyrated along the shafts of sunlight like plankton under a microscope, and the room was full of the aroma of decay. There was a rusty double-barrelled gun in the corner, a couple of dog-eared Orthodox missals on the shelf, and, pinned to the wall above the table, a faded oleograph of King Constantine and Queen Sophia, with King George and the Queen Mother, Olga Feodorovna, smiling with time-dimmed benevolence through wreaths of laurel. Another picture showed King Constantine's entry into reconquered Salonika at the end of the first Balkan war. On a poster, Petro Mavromichalis, the ex-war minister, between a pin-up girl cut out from the cover of *Romantzo* and a 1926 calendar for the Be Smart Tailors of Madison Avenue, flashed good-will from his paper monocle. Across this, in a hand unaccustomed to Latin script, *Long live Uncle Truman* was painstakingly inscribed. I felt like staying there for ever.

Delphinia

from *Mani*

The Aphrodite, *from Cythera, was a well-trimmed caique which took Paddy and Joan up the eastern coast of the Mani, from Kypriano to Kotronas. They shared the space on board with several passengers and their livestock, which included chickens, pigs, a flock of goats, and a female donkey with her foal. They had not been long at sea before the dolphins appeared.*

Soon the delighted cry of *'Delphinia!'* went up: a school of dolphins was gambolling half a mile further out to sea. They seemed to have spotted us at the same moment, for in a second half a dozen were tearing their way towards us, all surfacing in the same parabola and plunging together as though they were in some invisible harness. Soon they were careering alongside and round the bows and under the bowsprit, glittering mussel-blue on top, fading at the sides throught gun-metal dune-like markings to pure white, streamlined and gleaming from their elegant beaks to the clean-cut flukes of their tails. They were beautiful abstractions of speed, energy, power and ecstasy leaping out of the water and plunging and spiralling and vanishing like swift shadows, each soon to materialize again and sail into the air in another great loop so fast that they seemed to draw the sea after them and shake it off in mid-air, to plunge forward again tearing two great frothing bow-waves with their beaks; diving down again, falling behind and criss-crossing under the keel and deviating and returning. Sometimes they flung themselves out of the sea with the insane abandon, in reverse, of a suicide from a skyscraper; up, up, until they hung poised in mid-air shaking in a muscular convulsion from beak to tail as though resolved to abandon their element for ever. But gravity, as though hauling on an oblique fishing-line, dragged them forward and down again into their rifled and bubbling green tunnels. The headlong speed through the water filled the air with a noise of rending and searing. Each leap into the air called forth a chorus of gasps, each plunge a sigh.

These creatures bring a blessing with them. No day in which they have played a part is like other days. I first saw them at dusk, many years ago, on the way to Mount Athos. A whole troop appeared alongside the steamer, racing her and keeping us company for three-quarters of an hour. Slowly it grew darker and as night fell the phosphorescent water turned them into fishes of pale fire. White-hot flames whirled from them. When they leapt from the water they shook off a million fiery diamonds, and when they plunged, it was a fall of comets spinning down fathom after fathom – league upon league of dark sky, it seemed – in whirling incandescent vortices, always to rise again; till at last, streaming down all together as though the heavens were falling and each trailing a ribbon of blazing and feathery wake they became a far-away constellation on the sea's floor. They suddenly turned and vanished, dying away along the abyss like ghosts. Again, four years ago, when I was sailing in a yacht with six friends through the Outer Cyclades in the late afternoon of a long and dreamlike day, there was another visitation. The music from the deck floated over the water and the first champagne cork had fired its sighting-shot over the side. The steep flank of Sikinos, tinkling with goat bells and a-flutter with birds, rose up to starboard, and, close to port, the sheer cliffs of nereid-haunted Pholegandros. Islands enclosed the still sea like a lake at the end of the world. A few bars of unlikely midsummer cloud lay across the west. All at once the sun's rim appeared blood-red under the lowest bar, hemming the clouds with gold wire and sending a Japanese flag of widening sunbeams alternating with expanding spokes of deeper sky into the air for miles and spreading rose petals and sulphur green across this silk lake. Then, some distance off, a dolphin sailed into the air, summoned from the depths, perhaps, by the strains of *Water Music*, then another and yet another, until a small company were flying and diving and chasing each other and hovering in mid-air in static semicircles, gambolling and curvetting and almost playing leapfrog, trying to stand on tip-toe, pirouetting and jumping over the sinking sun. All we could hear was an occasional splash, and so smooth was the water that one could see spreading rings when they swooped below the surface. The sea became a meadow and these antics like the last game of children on a lawn before going to bed. Leaning spellbound over the bulwarks and in the rigging we watched them in silence. All at once, on a sudden decision, they vanished; just as they vanish from the side of the *Aphrodite* in this chapter, off the stern and shadowless rocks of the Mani.

'*Kala einai ta delphinia*,' the captain said when they had gone. 'Dolphins are good.'

Sash Windows Opening on the Foam

Architectural Digest, November 1986

In March 1964, Paddy and Joan finally signed the contract for the land on which they were to build their house. Their property consisted of a rocky promontory surrounded by olive groves, looking out towards an island in the bay of Messenia. For a while they lived in tents on the site, pacing it out, arguing over enfilades and proportions as the house rose up around them.

'Where a man's Eleventh Edition of the *Encyclopaedia Britannica* is, there shall his heart be also'; and, of course, Lemprière, Fowler, Brewer, Liddell and Scott, Dr Smith, Harrap and Larousse and a battery of atlases, bibles, concordances, Loeb classics, Pléiade editions, Oxford Companions and Cambridge histories; anthologies and books on painting, sculpture, architecture, birds, beasts, fishes trees and stars; for if one is settling in the wilds, a dozen reference shelves is the minimum; and they must be near the dinner table where arguments spring up which have to be settled then or never. This being so, two roles for the chief room in a still unbuilt house were clear from the start.

Twenty-two years ago, when we were the only strangers in the Mani, it was possible to build a house for very little. But it was a challenge. Our headland jutted between a bay and a small cove and there was nothing on it but olive terraces, thistles, asphodels and an occasional tortoise and here we pitched our tents exactly where the chief room was to be. There was rock for building everywhere; friendly and excellent workmen; the occasional visits of an architect friend from Athens helped us with stresses and strains and we found Niku Kolokatrones, a brilliant master-mason, in the mountain village above, and prudently became relatives by standing god-parents to his small son. Ideas abounded, but it was while it was actually taking shape that we decided how the house should be. In the end, all our mugging up and our drawings and pacings and fiery arguments brought – or so it seemed to us – splendid results.

In two years the house was standing, and because of the rough-hewn, fast-weathering limestone – all prised out of the Taygetus range in whose foothills we live – it looked like a monastery which had been crumbling there for centuries. A wing shot out over the drop of the terraces, outside staircases went up, and the whole thing was roofed over with faded tiles that we picked up for almost nothing, like carrion crows, after the earthquakes in the central Peloponnese.

You enter from the east along the gallery through the leaves of a heavy beech door. This is framed in a massive bolection of russet stone that we rashly designed without books: the moulding is a foot wide and the torus rises seven inches from the scotia. (There was no road, and except for heavy items, every stick came by mule; but the six-foot lintel of this doorway took twelve men and a ladder and we were sweating and tottering under it when an artless goatherd under the olives asked where we were taking it. 'To the sea,' our god-brother said between his teeth, 'to chuck it in, just in case it floats.') When it was up, we were awed by the mad splendour; it went to our heads and set the pace for all the rest. The long wall opposite was pierced by a French window with a heavy stone beam for a lintel, and above this we put an old marble slab from Paros, perforated by an oval holding a star.

The room's large fireplace soars tapering to a wide wooden cornice, and the cornice surrounds a wooden ceiling. Both of these are only pine, but twenty years have given them a patina like cypress-wood or cedar. Thirty slim beams divide the ceiling up into an infinity of squares which recede in vistas and, by a stroke of luck, these and the shape of the room are as acoustically right for music as the inside of a violin. The floor is paved with unpolished rectangles of grey-green stone quarried from Mount Pelion and, in the middle, a large intricate star of purple stone bordered with white pulls the whole thing together.

A divan runs all round the north end of the room. Like the long sofa by the fire, it is covered in white linen woven in Arachova. Widened still more by a ledge along the back, this looks very handsome but it makes the shelves there harder to reach, and the ledges get cluttered with papers, dictionaries, shears and secateurs and books get lost there for weeks. The bookcases with no divan in front rise nine feet from the floor and we have discovered a brilliant way of reaching the upper shelves without steps: an elephant-pole of brass-bound teak made by the Hong Kong Chinese to help minor rajahs to climb into their howdahs: it splits down the middle and half the pole drops away parallel with a heartening bang like grounded arms; the rungs, slotted and hinged in hidden grooves, fall horizontal and up one goes.

But at the south-facing end, everything changes. A central opening runs across three-quarters of it and the coffered soffit, the same height as the other lintels, is supported at both ends by a disengaged hexagonal pillar. You go through, and down a step, into something which, throughout the Levant, is called a *hayáti*. This winter chamber lighted by scores of panes can become a cavern of shade in summer, and perfect for an afternoon snooze, by drawing curtains of mattress-ticking, with the stripes running horizontal. In winter, rugs cover the wooden floor of this miniature Hardwick (but secret plans are afoot for a Cosmati floor with roundels of porphyry and serpentine edged with bands of black-and-white zig-zag looped together in interlocking figures of eight; perhaps next year). The flagstones of the big room are covered in winter too; near the fire, by *flokkáti* rugs of shaggy goats' hair from Epirus; and kilims from Konia, Smyrna and Ak-Shehir, with light-hearted flower and geometric patterns of blue, green, white, ochre and orange, strew the rest of the room and make it rather like an emir's tent.

Writing-tables to the left of the French window and behind the sofa, and occasional things here and there like faded William Morris armchairs, strike an English note. The fireplace wall to the east has been left free for pictures: two large Japanese seventeenth-century paintings of young goshawks jessed in blue and crimson; Jamaica foliage by Lucian Freud; some Craxton goats; a semi-geometric roofscape and a design of plants by Nico Ghika; three small Edward Lear Cretan scenes; and a Robin Ironside of a recumbent statue waking up in a museum. A Javanese bust of Shiva Mahadeva and odd fragments of sculpture are scattered about the divan ledge, and, on a slab, two marble legs stand there beside a marble tree-stump which the vanished god or shepherd must have leant on; they were dug up near Palestrina at the same time as the headless Cybele in a niche in the gallery.

A visiting friend unsettlingly hinted that a Victorian mahogany dining-table was not up to the rest; so, years later, we ruinously exorcized this complex with an inlaid marble table made by Dame Freya Stark's *marmorista* in Venice. Based on a *tondo* in the chancel of S. Anastasio in Mantua, white flames of Udine stone radiate from the centre of a design of subtle grey carsico and *rosso di Verona*. When it arrived, lugging the triple plinth of Istrian stone down from the road and then trundling the heavy circular top through the trees was as bad as the earlier struggles with the lintel. But the friend was right. Here it is, beautiful and immovable for ever, and when set about with glasses and candles, it turns the humblest meal – even oil and lentils – into a feast. The east door, then, looks out on a row of arches; the north windows, on to a green thought in a green shade – cypresses and olive trees, that is, and clipped rosemary hedges; and to the south, charmed magic sash-windows opening on the foam of, first, descending tree-tops, and then the sea. But the axis of the room – and thus of the whole house – is planned so the west windows, winter and summer, catch the sunset till the last gasp.

The terrace outside is a continuation of the room: you go down two semicircular steps from the French window to an expanse of terracotta tiles (successfully fired in a local kiln after many attempts), about half the width (paced out last year) of the Place Fürstemberg. The olives here are girded by stone seats and surrounded by rings of pebble-mosaic – garlands, waves, wreaths and cables – and, beyond a low fountain with Seljuk affinities, the terrace ends in a sort of exedra-like outdoor *hayáti* near the cliff's edge: you go down two more steps to a geometric pebble-pattern rectangle with a big stone table for dinner in summer – once a marble balcony and bought for a fiver from a housebreaker in Tripoli. There are solemn clumps of cypresses on either side of this, and looking from the drawing-room, one's eye shoots on between them, over the cove, past a theatrically placed island and a sequence of dragon-capes and then across the Messenian Gulf to where the mountains of the Morea rumble away to the north.

The room and its offshoots sound grander than they are; but from the stern Mitford test – 'All nice rooms are a bit shabby' – the place comes out with flying colours; time, wear, and four-footed fellow inmates – born downholsterers and interior desecrators – have put the place out of all danger. Luckily, decent proportions (worked out in our tents from Vitruvius and Palladio) and rough building materials, have the knack of swallowing up disorder and incongruity. Occasionally a far-wandering hen that would be hopelessly out of place in a smarter room, stalks jerkily indoors, peers round, stalks out again and everything seems normal. Last month a white goat entered from the terrace, followed by six more in single file; they trooped across the floor looking as much at home as Jamshyd's lions and lizards, then out into the gallery, down twenty steps and into the landscape again without the goats or the house seeming in any way out of countenance.

But the great advantage of a long room is that different things can go on without impinging: reading, music, letter-writing, talk by the fire, eyelids closing in the *hayáti*, 'a wildcat snooze': or chess at one end of the room and friends' children on the floor with tiddlywinks at the other. Every seventh of November, which is the Feast of SS. Michael and Gabriel – and also my name-day (*Mihali*, in Greek) – the room fills a special role. The Archangels have a minute chapel three groves away and after the yearly Mass, a swarm of friends from the village, sometimes fifty or sixty, led by the bearded vicar, come in for a long chat and drinks and *mézé*. Thanks to the divans – suddenly packed with venerable figures in black coifs – the room can hold them all without too much of a squash and in spite of the immobility of the table, there is space in the middle for dancing; and when, later on, the complicated steps of the *syrtos* and the *kalamantiano*, accompanied by clapping and singing, begin to weave their nimble circles round the central star, the room seems to have come into its own at last.

People

The Polymath

from *A Time of Gifts*

The Polymath was one of those scholars whose knowledge was such that he could talk about history in the broadest possible sweeps, and in the minutest detail. His meeting with Paddy, beside the Austrian Danube early in 1934, was fortuitous. Paddy was full of questions and the Polymath must have enjoyed teaching such an enthusiastic student.

After supper and filling in my diary in the front room of the inn in Persenbeug – I think I must have been staying there on the charitable-burgomaster principle – I started to sketch the innkeeper's daughter Maria while she busied herself over a basket of darning. I was talking to her about my visit to St Florian: either it had been the wrong time for sightseers or a day when the Abbey was officially shut. The janitor was adamant. I told him it was my only chance – I had come all the way across Europe to see the Abbey; and at last, when I must have sounded on the brink of tears, he had begun to melt. He had handed me over to the friendly Canon in the end, who showed me all. Maria laughed. So did a man at the next table who lowered the *Neue Freie Presse*, and looked over his spectacles. He was a tall and scholarly-looking figure with a long amusing face and large blue eyes. He was dressed in leather breeches and a loden-jacket, and a big dark dog with Breughel tendencies called Dick lay quietly beside his chair. 'You did the right thing,' he said. 'In Germany you would only have got in by shouting.' Maria and two watermen, the only other people in the Gastzimmer, laughed and agreed. [. . .]

[In my new acquaintance] I had chanced on a gold mine. 'Enquire Within About Everything': flora, fauna, history, literature, music, archaeology – he was a richer source than any castle library. His English, mastered from governesses with his brothers, was wide in range, flawless in its idiom and polished by many sojourns in England. He was full of stories about the inhabitants of Danubian castles, of which he was one, as I had more or less gathered from the others' style in addressing him: his lair was a battered Schloss near Eferding, and it was the empty heronry I had noticed there which had first excited him when he was a boy about the fauna of the river. He had a delightful Bohemian, scholar-gipsy touch.

He was on his way back from an antiquarian visit to Ybbs, the little town immediately across the river. His goal there had been the carved tomb of Hans, Knight of Ybbs: 'A figure', he said, 'of knock-out elegance!' He showed me a snapshot the parish priest had given him. (It was so striking that I crossed the river to see it next day. The Knight, standing in high relief in a rectangle which is deeply incised with gothic lettering, was carved in 1358. Falling in battle in the same decade as Crécy and Poitiers, he was an exact contemporary of du Guesclin and the Black Prince: at the very pinnacle, that is, of the age of chivalry. [. . .]

At the mention of the Ritter von Ybbs, I asked him the exact meaning of *von*. He explained how a 'Ritter von' and an 'Edler von' – Knight, or Nobleman, 'of' somewhere – were originally feudal landowners holding a fief, and usually an eponymous one, in knight's fee. Later it simply became the lowest rank in the scale of titles. Its fiendish aura in England, due to the military bent of Prussian junkers, is absent in Austria where a milder, squire-ish feeling hovers about the prefix. This was the cue for an excursus on central European aristocracy, conducted with great brio and the detachment of a zoologist. I had got the hang of it on broad lines; but what about those figures who had intrigued me in Germany: landgraves, margraves, wildgraves and Rhinegraves? Who was the Margravine of Bayreuth and Anspach? The answers led him to a lightning disquisition on the Holy Roman Empire and how the tremendous title had pervaded and haunted Europe from Charlemagne to the Napoleonic Wars. The roles of the Electors – the princes and prelates who chose the Emperors until the Crown became an unofficial Habsburg heirloom, when they ratified it still – were at last made clear. Between his election and accession, I learnt, a prospective Emperor was styled King of the Romans. 'Why!' he said, 'there was an English one, King John's son, Richard of Cornwall! And his sister Isabella married the Emperor Frederick II, the *stupor mundi*! But Richard never succeeded, poor fellow – as you know' – a tacit, all-purpose nod seemed the best response here – 'he died of grief when his son Henry of Almain was murdered by Guy de Montfort at Viterbo in revenge for his father's barbarous death at the battle of Evesham. Dante writes about it . . .' By this time I had stopped being surprised at anything. He explained the mediatization of lesser sovereign states when the Empire was dissolved; and from here, at a dizzy pace, he branched into the history of the Teutonic Knights, the Polish szlachta and their elective kings, the Moldowallachian hospodars and the great boyars of Rumania. He paid brief tribute to the prolific loins of Rurik and the princely progeny they scattered across the Russias, and the Grand Princes of Kiev and Novgorod, the Khans of Krim Tartary and the Kagans of the Mongol Hordes. If nothing had interrupted, we would have reached the Great Wall of China and flown across the sea to the Samurai world.* But something recalled us nearer home: to the ancient, almost Brahminic Austrian rules of eligibility and the stifling Spanish ceremony of the Court which had survived from the times of Charles V. He was critical of the failures of the nobility at crucial moments, but he was attached to it nevertheless. The proliferation of central European titles came under mild fire. 'It's much better in England, where all but one reverts to Mister in the end. Look at me and my brothers! All handle and no jug.' Would he have liked titles to be done away with? 'No, no!' he said, rather contradictorily. 'They should be preserved at all costs – the world is getting quite dull enough. And they are not *really* multiplying – history and ecology are against them. Think of the Oryx! Think of the Auckland Island Merganser! The Great Auk! The Dodo!' His face was divided by a grin: 'You ought to see some of my aunts and uncles.' But a moment later his brow was clouded by concern. 'Everything is going to vanish! They talk of building power-dams across the Danube and I tremble whenever I think of it! They'll make the wildest river in Europe as tame as a municipal waterworks. All those fish from the East – they would never come back! Never, never, never!' He looked so depressed that I changed the subject by asking him about the

---

* I loved all this. I was soon suspiciously expert in all the relevant sociohistorical lore, to which others might give a grosser name. But I would have been genuinely taken aback if anyone had taxed me with snobbery.

Germanic tribes that had once lived here – the Marcomanni and the Quadi – I couldn't get their odd names out of my head. 'What?' He cheered up at once. Those long-haired Wotan-worshippers, who peered for centuries between the tree-boles, while the legionaries drilled and formed tortoise on the other bank? His eyes kindled, and I drank in more about the Völkerwanderungen in a quarter of an hour than I could have gleaned in a week with the most massive historical atlases. [. . .]

I mentioned earlier that we – or rather, the polymath – had talked about the Marcomanni and the Quadi, who had lived north of the river hereabouts. The habitat of the Marcomanni lay a little further west; the Quadi dwelt exactly where we were sitting. 'Yes,' he had said, 'things were more or less static for a while . . .' He illustrated this with a pencil-stub on the back of the *Neue Freie Presse*. A long sweep represented the Danube; a row of buns indicated the races that had settled along the banks; then he filled in the outlines of eastern Europe. '. . . and suddenly, at last,' he said, 'something happens!' An enormous arrow entered the picture on the right, and bore down on the riverside buns. 'The Huns arrive! Everything starts changing place at full speed!' His pencil leaped feverishly into action. The buns put forth their own arrows of migration and began coiling sinuously about the paper till Mitteleuropa and the Balkans were alive with demons' tails. 'Chaos! The Visigoths take shelter south of the lower Danube, and defeat the Emperor Valens at Adrianople, *here!*', he twisted the lead on the paper – 'in 476. Then – in only a couple of decades' – a great loop of pencil swept round the tip of the Adriatic and descended a swiftly outlined Italy '– we get Alaric! Rome is captured! The Empire splits in two –' the pace of his delivery reminded me of a sports commentator '– and the West totters on for half a century or so. But the Visigoths are heading westwards', an arrow curved to the left and looped into France, which rapidly took shape, followed by the Iberian peninsula. 'Go West, young Goth!' he murmured as his pencil threw off Visigothic kingdoms across France and Spain at a dizzy speed. 'There we are!' he said; then, as an afterthought, he absentmindedly pencilled in an oval across northern Portugal and Galicia, and I asked him what it was. 'The Suevi, same as the Swabians, more or less: part of the whole movement. But *now*,' he went on, '*here go the Vandals!*' A few vague lines from what looked like Slovakia and Hungary joined together and then swept west in a broad bar that mounted the Danube and advanced into Germany. 'Over the Rhine in 406: then clean across Gaul –' here the speed of his pencil tore a ragged furrow across the paper '– through the Pyrenees three years later – here they come! – then down into Andalucia – hence the name – and *hop!* –' the pencil skipped the imaginary straits of Gibraltar and began rippling castwards again '– along the north African coast to' – he improvised the coast as he went, then stopped with a large black blob – '*Carthage!* And all in thirty-three years from start to finish!' His pencil was busy again, so I asked him the meaning of all the dotted lines he had started sending out from Carthage into the Mediterranean. 'Those are Genseric's fleets, making a nuisance of themselves. Here he goes, sacking Rome in 455! There was lots of sea activity just about then.' Swooping to the top of the sheet, he drew a coast, a river's mouth and a peninsula: 'That's the Elbe, there's Jutland.' Then, right away in the left hand corner, an acute angle appeared, and above it, a curve like an ample rump; Kent and East Anglia, I was told. In a moment, from the Elbe's mouth, showers of dots were curving down on them. '– and there go your ancestors, the first Angles and Saxons, pouring into Britain only a couple of years before Genseric sacked Rome.' Close to the Saxon shore, he inserted two tadpole figures among the invading dots: what were they? 'Hengist and Horsa,' he said, and refilled the glasses.

This was the way to be taught history! It was just about now that a second bottle of Langenlois appeared. His survey had only taken about five minutes; but we had left the Marcomanni and the Quadi far behind . . . The polymath laughed. 'I forgot about them in the excitement! There's no problem about the Marcomanni,' he said. 'They crossed the river and became the Bayuvars – and the Bayuvars are the Bavarians – I've got a Markoman grandmother. But the Quadi! There are plenty of mentions of them in Roman history. Then, all of a sudden – none! They vanished just about the time of the Vandals' drive westward . . .' They probably went along with them too, he explained, as part of the slipstream . . . 'A whole nation shimmering upstream like elvers – not that there are any eels in the

Danube,' he interrupted himself parenthetically, on a different note. 'Not native ones, unfortunately: only visitors – suddenly, the forests are empty. But, as nature hates a vacuum, not for long. A new swarm takes their place. Enter the Rugii, all the way from southern Sweden!' There was no room on the *Neue Freie Presse*, so he shifted a glass and drew the tip of Scandinavia on the scrubbed table top. 'This is the Baltic Sea, and here they come.' A diagram like the descent of a jellyfish illustrated their itinerary. 'By the middle of the fifth century they were settled all along the left bank of the Middle Danube – if "settled" is the word – they were all such fidgets.' I'd never heard of the Rugii. 'But I expect you've heard of Odoaker? He was a Rugian.' The name, pronounced in the German way, did suggest something. There were hints of historical twilight in the syllables, something momentous and gloomy . . . but what? Inklings began to flicker.

Hence my ascent to this ruin. For it was Odoacer, the first barbarian king after the eclipse of the last Roman Emperor. ('Romulus Augustulus!' the polymath had said. 'What a name! Poor chap, he was very good-looking, it seems, and only sixteen.')

Behind the little town of Aggsbach Markt on the other bank, the woods which had once teemed with Rugians rippled away in a fleece of tree-tops. Odoacer came from a point on the north bank only ten miles downstream. He dressed in skins, but he may have been a chieftain's, even a king's son. He enlisted as a legionary, and by the age of forty-two he was at the head of the winning immigrant clique in control of the Empire's ruins, and finally King. After the preceding imperial phantoms, his fourteen years' reign seemed – humiliatingly to the Romans – an improvement. It was not a sudden night at all, but an afterglow, rather, of a faintly lighter hue and lit with glimmers of good government and even of justice. When Theodoric replaced him (by slicing him in half with his broadsword from the collarbone to the loins at a banquet in Ravenna) it was still not absolutely the end of Roman civilization. Not quite; for the great Ostrogoth was the patron of Cassiodorus and of Boëthius, 'the last of the Romans whom Cato or Tully could have acknowledged for their countryman'. But he slew them both and then died of remorse; and the Dark Ages had come, with nothing but candles and plainsong left to lighten the shadows. 'Back to the start,' as the polymath had put it, 'and lose ten centuries.'

Konrad

from *A Time of Gifts*

Paddy spent the night after his nineteenth birthday, 12 February 1934, in a Salvation Army hostel on the outskirts of Vienna. He was broke, and was hoping that his monthly allowance of £4 would be waiting at the British Consulate. It wasn't; but his new friend Konrad hit upon an excellent solution to the problem.

An arresting figure in blue-striped pyjamas was sitting up reading in the next bed when I awoke. The fleeting look of Don Quixote in his profile would have been pronounced if his whiskers had been springier but they drooped instead of jutting. His face was narrow-boned and his silky, pale brown hair was in premature retreat from his brow and thin on top. His light blue eyes were of an almost calf-like gentleness. Between the benign curve of his moustache and a well-shaped but receding chin the lower lip drooped a little, revealing two large front teeth, and his head, poised on a long neck with a prominent Adam's apple, was attached to a tall and gangling frame. No appearance could have tallied more closely with foreign caricatures of a certain kind of Englishman; but instead of the classical half-witted complacency – *Un Anglais à Mabille* – a mild, rather distinguished benevolence stamped my neighbour. When he saw that I was awake, he said, in English, 'I hope your slumbers were peaceful and mated with quiet dreams?' The accent, though unmistakably foreign, was good, but the turn of phrase puzzling. No trace of facetiousness marred an expression of sincere and gentle concern.

His name was Konrad, and he was the son of a pastor in the Frisian Islands. I hadn't read *The Riddle of the Sands* and I wasn't sure of their whereabouts but I soon learnt that they follow the coasts of Holland and Germany and Denmark in a long-drawn-out archipelago from the Zuider Zee to the Heligoland Bight where they turn north and die away off the Jutish coast. Tapered by tides and winds, interspersed with reefs, always crumbling and changing shape, littered with wrecks, surrounded by submerged villages, clouded with birds, and heavily invaded, some of them, by summer bathers, the islands scarcely rise above sea-level. Konrad belonged to the German central stretch. He had learnt English at school and had continued his studies, during his spare time from a multiplicity of jobs, almost exclusively by reading Shakespeare and this sometimes gave his utterances an incongruous and even archaic turn. I can't remember what mishaps had brought him, in his late thirties, into such low water and he didn't dwell on them. He was not a dynamic personality. The quiet good humour, the poise and the mild but unmistakable dignity of bearing that glowed from him, were strikingly at odds with the feckless morning hubbub of the enormous room. Holding up a disintegrating volume, he told me he was rereading *Titus Andronicus*. [. . .]

We shared some of his bread and cheese at one of the scrubbed tables down the middle of the room and, as we ate, I learnt that his feelings for the English language – and for England in general – sprang from a theory about his native archipelago. Before they were driven to the islands, the Frisians had been a powerful and important mainland race and it seems that they and their language were more akin to the ultimate English than any of the other Germanic tribes that invaded Britain. He was convinced that Hengist and Horsa were Frisians. (Where was the polymath? As Konrad spoke, I began to see the two invaders in a new light: instead of meaty, freckled and tow-haired giants barging their berserker way into Kent, I now saw two balding, slightly equine and Konrad-like figures wading ashore with diffident coughs.) He cited a further proof of the closeness of the two nations: a couple of centuries after Hengist, when the ship-wrecked St Wilfred of York began to preach to the still heathen Frisians, no interpreter was needed. It was the same when St Willibrod arrived from Northumbria. I asked him to say something in the Frisian dialect. I couldn't understand his answer, but the short words and flat vowels sounded just as English must to someone who doesn't know the language.

I drew him as he talked, and it came out well – one couldn't go wrong! He gazed at the result with thoughtful approval and offered to guide me to the British Consulate, where I hoped salvation lay. We left our effects, as he called them, in the office. 'We must beware,' he said.

'Among good and luckless men there is no lack of base ones, foot-pads and knaves who never shrink from purloining. Some love to filch.' Tall and bony in a long, threadbare overcoat and a rather wide-brimmed trilby, he looked serious and imposing, though something in his bearing and in his wide, soft gaze lent a touch of absurdity. His stylish and well-brushed hat was on the point of disintegration. With unexpected worldliness, he showed me the maker's name inside: 'Habig,' he said. 'He is the most renowned of the hatters of Vienna.'

The surroundings were even more depressing by daylight. The Hostel lay in the Kolonitzgasse in the Third District between the loading bays of the Customs House and the grimy arches of a via-duct and an overhead railway track, silent now like the whole derelict quarter. Rubbish seemed to cover everything. Our track took us over the Radetzky Bridge and beside the Danube Canal through a dismal scene of sad buildings and dirty snow under a cloudy sky. We turned up the Rotenturmstrasse and, as we made our way into the Inner City, things began to change. We passed St Stephen's Cathedral and its single gothic spire. The barriers and the road-blocks of the day before were still there, but passage was free and for the moment no gunfire sounded in the distance. The city seemed to have returned to normal. Palaces began to assemble, fountains rose, and monuments with fantastical elaboration. We crossed the Graben to the Am Hof-Platz: passing a tall pillar with a statue of the Virgin, we headed for a street the other side, where a flagpole and a tin oval with the lion and the unicorn indicated the British Consulate. The clerk inside looked in all the pigeon-holes for a registered letter. There was nothing.

If Vienna had looked grim and overcast before, it was doubly so as I joined Konrad below in the Wallnerstrasse. A few drops of sleety drizzle were falling. 'Be not downcast, my dear young,' Konrad said, when he saw me. 'We must take counsel.' We walked down the Kohlmarkt. At the other end a great archway opened into the court-yard of the Hofburg and zinc-green domes assembled over rows of windows. We turned left into the Michaelerkirche. It was dark inside and after the classical surroundings, unexpectedly gothic and empty except for a beadle who was lighting candles for an impending Mass. We settled in a pew, and after perfunctory prayers for the beadle's benefit, Konrad said: 'Hark, Michael! All is not lost. I have been ripening a plan. Have you your sketch-block by you?' I tapped the pocket of my greatcoat, and he unfolded his plan, which was that I should sketch professionally from house to house. I was appalled, firstly from timidity, secondly out of very well-founded modesty. I protested that my drawing of him had been a lucky exception. Usually they were very amateurish; putting his suggestion into practice would almost be taking money under false pretences. Konrad quickly overrode these objections. Think of wandering artists at fairs! Where was my spirit of enterprise? His siege was mild but firm.

I gave in and soon I began to feel rather excited. Before we left, I thought of lighting a candle to bring us luck, but we hadn't a single coin between us. We headed for the Mariahilf Quarter. Falling into step, he said: 'We will commence with the small buggers' – to my surprise, for his usual discourse was rather prim. I asked him: what small buggers? He stopped dead, and a blush began to spread until it had entirely mantled his long face. 'Oh! dear young!' he cried. 'I am sorry! Ich meinte, wir würden mit *Kleinbürgern* anfangen – with little burghers! The rich and the noble here,' he waved his hand round the old city, 'have always lackeys, many and proud, and sometimes they are not deigning to vouchsafe.' As we walked, he rehearsed me in what to say. He thought I should ask for five *schillinge* a picture. I said it was too much: I would ask for two: a bit more than an English shilling, in fact. Why didn't he keep me company for the first few times? 'Ah, dear young!' he said, 'I am of ripe years already! I would be always frightening them! You, so tender, will melt hearts.' He told me that Viennese front doors were pierced by peepholes at eye level, through which the inhabitants always surveyed prospective visitors before they unlatched. 'Never cast your eye on it,' he advised me: 'Ring, then gaze upward at the Everlasting with innocence and soul.' He took my walking stick, and advised me to carry my coat folded over my arm and to hold my sketching book and pencil in the other hand. My outfit looked a little odd, but it was still clean and tidy: boots, puttees, cord breeches, leather jerkin and a grey shirt and a pale blue hand-woven and rather artistic tie. I combed my hair in a shop window, and the closer we got to our field of action, the more I felt we must have resembled Fagin and the Artful Dodger. We shook hands earnestly in the hall of an old-fashioned block of flats and I mounted and rang the first bell on the mezzanine floor.

The little brass peep-hole gleamed cyclopically. I pretended not to notice that an eye had replaced the lid on the other side but bent my gaze on vacancy; and when the door opened and a little maid asked me what I wanted, I spoke up on cue: 'Darf ich mit der Gnä' Frau sprechen, bitte?' ('Please may I speak to the gracious lady?') She left me in the open doorway, and I waited, eagerly poised for my next utterance, which was to be: 'Guten Tag, Gnä' Frau! Ich bin ein englischer Student, der zu Fuss nach Konstantinopel wandert, und ich möchte so gern eine Skizze von Ihnen machen!'* But it remained unuttered, for the maid's embassy to the drawing-room, almost before she could have opened her mouth, produced results that neither Konrad nor I could have foreseen. A man's shrill voice cried: 'Ach nein! Es ist nicht mehr zu leiden!' 'It's not to be borne! I must make an end!'; and, hot-foot on these words, a small bald figure in a red flannel dressing-gown came hurtling down the passage with the speed of a cannon ball. His head was averted and his eyes were tight shut as though to exclude some loathed vision and his palms were repellingly spread at the ends of his arms. 'Aber nein, Helmut!' he cried. 'Nein, nein, nein! Not again, Helmut! Weg! Weg! Weg! Weg! Away, away, away!' His hands by now were against my chest and thrusting. He carried me before him like snow before a snowplough and the two of us, one advancing and one retreating, flowed out through the door and across the landing in a confused and stumbling progress. Meanwhile the little maid was squeaking 'Herr Direktor! It's *not* Herr Helmut!' Suddenly he stopped; and his reopened eyes sprang from their sockets. 'My dear young man!' he cried aghast. 'A thousand times, my apologies! I thought you were my brother-in-law! Come in! Come in!' Then he shouted to the room we had left, 'Anna! It's not Helmut!' and a woman in a dressing-gown was soon at hand and anxiously seconding her husband's apologies. 'My dear sir!' he continued, 'please come in!' I was whirled into the drawing-room. 'Gretl! Bring a glass of wine and a slice of cake! There! Sit down! A cigar?' I found myself in an

---

* 'Good morning, Madam! I am an English student walking to Constantinople on foot, and I would so much like to do a sketch of you.'

armchair, facing the man and his wife, who were beaming at me. His rosy face was adorned with one of those waxed and curled moustaches that are kept in position overnight by a gauze bandage. His eyes sparkled and his fingers drummed arpeggios in double time on his knees as he talked. His wife murmured something and he said: 'Oh yes! Who are you?' I slipped into my second phase ('Student', 'Constantinople', 'sketch', etc.). He listened intently and I had barely finished before he shot into his bedroom. He emerged two minutes later in a stand-up collar, a speckled bow tie and a velvet jacket trimmed with braid. His moustache had a fresh twist to it and two carefully trained strands of hair were arranged across his scalp with great skill. Sitting on the edge of his chair, he folded his hands palm to palm on his joined knees with a challenging jut to his elbows, and, gazing nobly into the middle distance with one toe tapping at high speed, froze into a bust. I got to work, and his wife poured out another glass of wine. The sketch didn't seem very good to me, but when it was finished, my sitter was delighted. He sprang to his feet and flew buoyantly about the room with the sketch at arm's length, the forefinger and thumb of the other hand joined in connoisseurship. 'Ein chef d'oeuvre!' he said – 'Ein wirkliches Meisterstück!' They declared themselves astonished at the low fee demanded. I graciously accepted a handful of cigars as well, and did a sketch of his wife. He persisted, as she sat, in using the bun on the crown of her head as a pivot for swivelling her face to more telling angles; and when this was finished they led me across the landing to do a sketch of a retired lady singer who in her turn passed me on to the wife of a music publisher. I was launched! When I found Konrad again, he was patiently mooning about the pavement. I approached him as though I had just slain the Jabberwock, and was suitably acclaimed. In a few minutes, we were in a snug Gastzimmer, toying with Krenwurst, ordering delicious Jungfernbraten and geröstete potatoes and wine. Thanks to Trudi, Major Brock and, that morning, Konrad and my recent sitter, body and soul had been kept firmly together; but it was the first actual meal since dinner at the castle two days earlier. It seemed a long time ago. For Konrad, I think, it was the first real spread for much longer. A little flustered at first, he professed to deplore all this extravagance. My attitude, from a phrase in *The Winter's*

Tale which we had been looking at earlier, was "'Tis fairy gold, boy, and 'twill prove so'; and, as we clinked glasses, my elation affected him. 'You see, dear young, how boldness is always prospering?' After this feast, I went back to work, leaving Konrad in a café reading *Venus and Adonis*.

The Postmaster's Widow

from *A Time of Gifts*

In Mitter Arnsdorf I stayed under the friendly roof of Frau Oberpostkommandeurs-Witwe Hübner – the widow, that is, of Chief-Postmaster Hübner – and sat talking late.

She was between sixty and seventy, rather plump and jolly, with a high-buttoned collar and grey hair arranged like a cottage loaf. The photograph of her husband showed an upright figure in a many-buttoned uniform, sword, shako, pince-nez and whiskers that were twisted into two martial rings. She was glad of someone to talk to, she told me. Usually her only companion in the evenings was her parrot Toni, a beautiful and accomplished macaw that whistled and answered questions pertly in Viennese dialect, and sang fragments of popular songs in a quavering and beery voice. He could even manage the first two lines of *Prinz Eugen, der edle Ritter*, in celebration of Marlborough's ally, the conqueror of Belgrade.

But his mistress was a born monologuist. Ensconced in mahogany and plush, I learnt all about her parents, her marriage and her husband, who had been, she said, a thorough gentleman and always beautifully turned out – 'ein Herr durch und durch! Und immer tip-top angezogen'. One son had been killed on the Galician Front, one was a postmaster in Klagenfurt, another, the giver of the parrot, was settled in Brazil, one daughter had married a civil engineer in Vienna, and another – here she heaved a sigh – was married to a Czech who was very high up in a carpet-manufacturing firm in Brno – 'but a very decent kind of man', she hastened to add: 'sehr aständig'. I soon knew all about their children, and their illnesses and bereavements and joys. This staunchless monologue treated of everyday, even humdrum matters but the resilience and the style of the telling saved it from any trace of dullness. It needed neither prompting nor response, nothing beyond an occasional nod, a few deprecating clicks of the tongue, or an assenting smile. Once, when she asked rhetorically, and with extended hands: 'So what was I to do?', I tried to answer, a little confusedly, as I had lost the thread. But my words were drowned in swelling tones: 'There was only one thing to do! I gave that umbrella away next morning to the first stranger I could find! I couldn't keep it in the house, not after what happened. And it would have been a pity to burn it . . .' Arguments were confronted and demolished, condemnations and warnings uttered with the lifting of an admonitory forefinger. Comic and absurd experiences, as she recalled them, seemed to take possession of her: at first, with the unsuccessful stifling of a giggle, then leaning back with laughter until finally she rocked forward with her hands raised and then slapped on her knees in the throes of total hilarity while her tears flowed freely. She would pull herself together, dabbing at her cheeks and straightening her dress and her hair with deprecating self-reproof. A few minutes later, tragedy began to build up; there would be a catch in her voice: '. . . and next morning all seven goslings were dead, laid out in a row. All seven! They were the only things that poor old man still cared about!' She choked back sobs at the memory until sniffs and renewed dabs with her handkerchief and the self-administered consolations of philosophy came to the rescue and launched her on a fresh sequence. At the first of these climaxes the parrot interrupted a pregnant pause with a series of quacks and clicks and the start of a comic song. She got up, saying crossly, 'Schweig, du blöder Trottel!',* threw a green cloth over the cage and silenced the bird; then picked up the thread in her former sad key. But in five minutes the parrot began to mutter 'Der arme Toni!' – (Poor Toni) – and, relenting, she would unveil him again. It happened several times. Her soliloquy flowed on as voluminously as the Danube under her window, and the most remarkable aspect of it was the speaker's complete and almost hypnotic control of her listener. Following her raptly, I found myself, with complete sincerity, merrily laughing, then puckering my brows in commiseration, and a few minutes later, melting in sympathetic sorrow, and never quite sure why. I was putty in her hands.

Sleep was creeping on. Gradually Frau Hübner's face, the parrot's cage, the lamp, the stuffed furniture and the thousand buttons on the upholstery began to lose their outlines and merge. The rise and fall

---

* 'Shut up, you silly fool!'

of her rhetoric and Toni's heckling would be blotted out for seconds, or even minutes. At last she saw I was nodding, and broke off with a repentant cry of self-accusation. I was sorry, as I could have gone on listening for ever.

Lady Wentworth and Byron's Slippers

from *Roumeli*

Judith Blunt-Lytton, Baroness Wentworth (1879–1957), was Byron's great-granddaughter, and the owner of a great hoard of Byroniana. Her descent from the poet was through his daughter Ada, who married the 1st Earl of Lovelace; and their daughter Lady Anne King married Wilfrid Scawen Blunt. Judith was their only child, who grew into a very remarkable woman: a world-champion tennis player, horse-breeder, and author of several books about horses.

Antony Holland was a great favourite of Lady Wentworth; she seemed really pleased that we had come to see her. Her talk ranged with dark humour over life in the desert and the breaking and training of Arab horses; famous figures long dead were stood up and bowled over like ninepins. Answering a question about a tremendous Edwardian statesman and grandee, she said, 'Oh, charmin', charmin', but such a milksop . . .' She liked the idea of her great-grandfather: 'But Lady Byron had rotten bad luck with him,' she said. 'You just read my uncle Lovelace's book about it!' The row might have taken place only a few years ago. Afterwards we hunted through a huge, disused and heavily cumbered room for a full-face portrait of Byron as a young man, but we could not find it. 'It's all a bit topsy-turvy,' she murmured, hopping nimbly over corded trunks and japanned tin cases. I saw, with excitement, that these were labelled on the side, in chalk or in white paint, 'Ld Byron's letters' and 'Ly Byron's letters'. 'Yes, they're all in there,' Lady Wentworth said sombrely, 'and it's the best place for them.' We looked at a case with Byron's Greek-Albanian velvet jacket with its gold lace and hanging sleeves. There were his velvet-scabbarded scimitar and his heavily embroidered velvet greaves – the same accoutrements, I think, that he wears in the famous Phillips portrait. We explored the amassed relics for an hour. Struck by a sudden idea, she led us to her study. It was crammed with portraits, miniatures, framed eighteenth-century silhouettes; books, keepsakes and trophies were gathered in a jungle: rummaging in her desk, she turned over a chaos of farm accounts, horse-breeding literature, lawyers' letters, a battered missal, seedsmen's catalogues, a rosary, farriers' bills and circulars for cattle cake, until at last she found what she was after.

They were some letters, dated a few years back, from an Australian sergeant in Missolonghi. The Greek he was billeted on, he wrote, owned a pair of shoes belonging to Lord Byron; he said the owner would like to return them to one of Byron's descendants. 'But, of course, knowin' no Greek, I couldn't do anythin' about it,' Lady Wentworth said. 'I'd like to have them, if they were really my great-grandfather's.' She turned the letter over. 'He must be a nice kind of a chap, to take all that trouble. I hope I wrote to thank him . . .' So she lent me the sergeant's letters and I promised to write to the owner of the shoes. She also gave me a copy of Lord Lovelace's *Astarte* and a sheaf of her own poems, printed, I think, in Horsham. They were violent, very colloquial rhyming diatribes against the Germans, written during the war after a stray bomb had destroyed the royal tennis court. (Crabbet was on the direct Luftwaffe route to London.) Her polemic gifts had at last discovered a universal rather than a private target. 'You're smilin',' she said. 'They're no great shakes, I fear. It doesn't always run in families . . .' There was a pause. Then Lady Wentworth said: 'You're not in a hurry, are you? Let's have a hundred up.'

She led us along a passage and up three steps into the dim and glaucous vista of a billiard room. A log fire was blazing; brandy and whisky and soda water flashed their welcome. Lady Wentworth gazed out at the dark afternoon. Through the lashing rain we contemplated the sodden park, the weeping trees and a sudden cavalcade of Arab ponies. 'What a shockin' afternoon,' she said. 'Let's draw the curtains.' We sent the tall curtains clashing along their rods and blotted out the diluvial scene and the daylight and switched on the shaded prism of lamps above the enormous table. She slipped off her many rings and lay them by the grog tray in a twinkling heap; then, after interlocking and flexing her fingers for a few moments like a concert pianist, she chose a cue, sighing 'spot or plain?'

We played in rapt silence. A feeling of timeless and remote seclusion hung all about us, a half-delightful, half-mournful spell which the house and our companion conspired to cast. She had taken on both of us and it was soon clear she was a brilliant player: our turns were spaced out between longer and longer breaks. All was quiet, except for the occasional squeak of French chalk, the fall of a log, a splutter of raindrops down the chimney, the occasional hiss of the siphon. Sudden gusts made the trunks of the huge trees creak ominously outside. 'I shouldn't be surprised if it doesn't fetch one of them down,' Lady Wentworth said, pausing before a difficult shot. 'It's been a rotten winter.' She played the shot facing away from the table and behind her back, which she arched as pliantly as a girl's. The balls sped unerringly to their destination and the soft clicks and the thuds on the cushion were followed by two plops. 'Put red back, would you, Antony?' She crossed to the other side on silent plim-soled feet . . . The huge scores mounted up in game after lost game. The whole world seemed reduced to this shadowy room with its glowing green quadrilateral; the slow eddies of our cigar smoke under the lamps and the flickering firelight and the trundling balls. The light caught a brooch here and a locket there as our hostess moved mercilessly to and fro at her effortless, demolishing task. Tea, brought in by a housekeeper and two Irishwomen (identical twins, quite plainly), was no interruption. Lady Wentworth lifted a silver lid. 'Oh, good,' she murmured sadly. 'Muffins.' We ate them cue in hand, and the massacre went on. She looked disappointed when, night having long ago invisibly fallen, the time came to go. Why didn't we stay and take pot luck . . . ? Her slim silhouette and the anachronistic headdress were dark in the doorway and she still held a cue in her hand as she waved us goodbye. We drove away through stormy folds of woodland. The 1950s waited outside the park gates. Meanwhile, shadowy cohorts from Arabia shifted about among the soaking timber. The whites of a score of eyes flashed hysterically or gazed for a moment in the headlamps. Then with a wheel and a flounder they vanished into the dark like rainy ghosts.

The looming prospect of Missolonghi, as we mooned about Astakos and brooded on our wrongs, had brought all this rushing back.

I had written to the owner from England and he had sent a friendly answer. Indeed, he said, he longed to send the shoes of the illustrious Lord Byron to his descendant, but he was anxious lest the precious relics should go astray in the post; better wait till some reliable emissary could be found. Since then all had been silence. Well, I had thought in Astakos, I'll be able to clear everything up in a day or two, when the boat comes. I'll simply ask the way to the house of Kyrios —

That was the trouble! Mr Who? I had forgotten the name. It shouldn't be hard to find in a little town like Missolonghi. But, to leave nothing to chance, I went to the post office and sent a telegram to Lady Wentworth.

Her answer was waiting in the Missolonghi *poste restante*; *Sorry very provoking*, it read, *correspondence mislaid good luck Wentworth*. I asked the man behind the counter if he knew anything about a fellow-citizen who owned a pair of Lord Byron's shoes. No, he had never heard of them, nor had his colleagues, not even the postmaster himself. They and the other people in the post office were full of concern. The words '*Tà papóutsia toù Lórdou Vyrónou*' began to hum through the building. 'Ask at the town hall. They've got some Byron things there. The mayor might know . . .' The mayor, a distinguished, spectacled figure, knew nothing either. We contented ourselves by peering at the sparse Byron relics in the glass cases. There was a cross-section of the last surviving branch of the elm tree under which the poet had reclined at Harrow; an envelope, addressed in the familiar writing, sere with age, to 'the Honble Mrs Leigh, Six Mile Bottom, Newmarket'; a letter beginning, 'My dearest Caroline'; the document declaring Byron an honorary citizen of the town; a picture of his daughter, Augusta Ada, as a girl; Solomos's commemorative hymn and the broadsheets announcing his death; an aquatint of Newstead Abbey and another of 'the Shade of Byron contemplating the ruins of Missolonghi'. A third print, published in 1827, depicted Archbishop Germanos, who had raised the standard of revolt at Kalavryta. The beard and the canonicals vaguely approximated to the attributes of an Orthodox prelate; but the background was a soaring Beckfordian complex of lancets, triforia, clerestories and crocketed finials: a telling proof of how dimly western Europe apprehended what Greece, during the eclipse of Ottoman power, was like.

But no trace of the shoes.

We drew blank everywhere; with the clergy, the police, the various banks. There was scarcely a bar in which we did not order a swig as a prelude to enquiry. In desperation, we even accosted likely strangers in the street.

Maddened by frustration, at a restaurant table near a statue of President Tricoupis under a clump of palm trees, we scarcely touched our luncheon octopus, swallowing glass after glass of cold Fix beer to replace the salt cataract which the heat summoned from every pore. We fretted through fitful siestas and surged into the streets long before the town had woken up, and soon found ourselves at the *Kypos tôn Eroôn*. I had begun to wonder whether the conversations at Crabbet and the exchange of letters had all been hallucinations.

This Garden of Heroes is a stirring place. There, among the drooping and dusty trees of midsummer, stood the marble busts and the monuments of the heroes of Missolonghi. It is a mark of the importance of Lord Byron in Greek eyes that his statue, the only full-length figure there, has been accorded the central position in this Valhalla. Dotted about, too, are monuments to the other philhellenes who fought or died for the liberation of Greece: the numerous Germans, the French, the Americans, the English, and, symbolized by a huge granite totem surrounded by boulders, the Swedes; on every side, mingling with these guest-warriors, are the great Greek paladins of the Siege.

We were sitting rather dejectedly on the low wall outside, and meditating on how to resume our quest, when a flutter of coloured flounces and a plaintive murmur heralded the onslaught of a gypsy woman. But we were in no mood for fortune-telling, and when, driven away at last by the persistence of her litany, which alms had failed to stem, we rose wearily to return to the town, she gazed balefully in our faces and said she saw unhappiness and failure written there. Further dejected by these tidings, we returned to our quarters.

But she was wrong. A nice-looking young woman was waiting for us. Her face brightened as we appeared: were we looking for Lord

Byron's shoes? She had heard we had been asking about them. They belonged to her uncle: she told us his name; I recognized it in a flash as that of my correspondent. Could we call at his house in an hour's time?

Can a duck swim?

We climbed the stairs to the guest room of a substantial house built of yellow stone not far from the site of the house where Byron died. The shutters were still closed against the afternoon heat. Solid Victorian furniture fitted with antimacassars materialized in the shadows round the welcoming figure of our host. He was a large and robust man, between sixty and seventy, with jutting black eyebrows and a tufted crop of grey hair and the simple and friendly manner of an old sea captain, which indeed he was. His niece was there with an artillery subaltern, her fiancé. The punctilio of their dress put our tired travelling outfits to shame. The niece busied herself with the ceremonial of a visit, administering spoonfuls of cherry jam, then a glass of water, a thimbleful of coffee and a scruple of *mastika*. Less forgetful than me, our host had politely greeted me by name at once and fished out my letters; he also placed on the table, among other treasures, a neatly stitched canvas parcel about a foot long, from which we couldn't take our eyes; in laborious indelible-ink lettering of someone unused to Latin characters were traced the words: *The Baroness Wentworth, Crabbet Park, Three Bridges, Sussex . . .*

I congratulated him on ferreting out Byron's descendant and asked, rather tentatively, how Byron's shoes had come his way. Had he inherited them?

'No,' he said. 'Though my grandparents, who were both Missolonghiots, must have seen Lord Byron often. Why, my grandpa was forty-two at the time of the siege, and my granny was thirty. He was born in 1784 and he died at the age of a hundred and four, when I was three years old! A hundred and four! He had pre-war bones! *Propolémika kókkala!* Not like our thin modern ones . . . I can't remember him, of course, I'm only seventy-eight, but they all said he was a fine old man. He and my granny took part in the great exodus, fighting their way through the besieging Turks, and God be praised,' he paused to cross himself, 'they got away safely. This is his yataghan.'

He handed me the curving weapon with its bossed silver sheath and branching bone hilt, I drew it and ran my finger along the notched blade, and wondered whether the edge was dented as he hacked his way out on that terrible day. 'There are his barkers' – we toyed with a heavy brace of pistols, almost straight ones encrusted with filigree, the butts ending in pearshaped knobs of Yanina silverwork – 'and this is his *balaska*, the metal pouch they kept their bullets in, and here's his powder flask. And this is his pen-case and its little inkwell; the lid clicks open – all silver! – though he wasn't much of a scribe. But everybody wore them, even the ones without any letters at all, stuck into their belts,' he said with a smile, making a jutting gesture towards his middle, 'for the dash of it, *dia leventeiá*. The more they had in their belts, the better. Well, my absolved* grandparents got away all right, and came back after the battle of Navarino, when the storm had blown over, and went into shipping. In a small way, at first; then he built more and more caiques, carrying cargoes and trading up and down the Gulf and in the Ionian Islands to start with, and especially to Zante – our town has always had a strong link with that place – and then into the Aegean, and, finally, all over the archipelago and the Mediterranean. They were good times. My father carried on and so did I. You see this house? It was built in my father's day, and every block of it, *every block of it*, was brought in our own bottoms from – guess where? From Savona in Italy, near Genoa! Every block of it.' He tapped the wall behind his chair with a bent knuckle. 'There! As sound and as solid as when it was built!'

As he spoke we tried to keep our eyes from staring too pointedly at the canvas parcel. It grew darker; his daughter opened the shutters. The grape-green evening light flowed in through the mosquito wire. 'Things have changed now,' he went on. 'We're not what we used to be, though we've still got a roof over our head. But those were the days. They had everything! They could tie up their dogs with strings of sausages.'

He fell silent as though all had been said. The inrush of evening light revealed that his right eyelid had suffered some mishap on the

---

* This word – *synchoriménos* – together with *makarítes*, blessed, is a slightly more pious way of saying 'the late'.

high seas which gave the illusion of a wink. After a long silence, I ran a forefinger absent-mindedly along the top of the canvas parcel.

'Ah, yes,' our host said with a sigh. 'Lord Byron's shoes . . . This is how they came my way. When *O Výron* was in Missolonghi, he used to go duck-shooting in the lagoon in a *monóxylo* – one of those dug-out canoes they still use – belonging to a young boatman called Yanni Kazis. Kazis had three daughters. Two of them married and left our town and the third went away to Jerusalem,' he pointed out of the window, 'and became a nun in an Orthodox convent. Many years later she came back. She was a frail old woman, all skin and bones, in a nun's habit. Her family had been scattered to the winds and she had nowhere to go, so I gave the poor old woman a room in my house. That was in 1920 – or was it 1921? Anyway, she lived with us for the last few years of her life. Just before she died she gave me this box' – he pulled a battered casket from under the table – 'and in it were these papers and books, and the shoes of the Lordos. Also an icon of St Spiridion, which I hung up in the Cathedral.' The yellowed and flyblown papers turned out to be the black-edged broadsheets published by the Provisional Government of Western Greece and signed by Mavrocordato, announcing Lord Byron's death and decreeing a salute of thirty-seven cannon – a salvo for each year of the poet's life – and three days of deep mourning, in spite of the impending Easter celebration. The books were a dog-eared Orthodox missal and two devotional works, all deep in mould.

'The shoes,' he continued, 'were given to her father by Lord Byron. Byron used to wear them about the house, when her father had rowed him back from the lagoon. Kazis never wore them, but kept them as sacred relics and when he died, he gave them to his daughter; and when *she* had no more days left, she gave them to me as a thanks-offering for her bed and board. We buried her, and here they are. She was a good old woman and may the ground rest light on her.'

He seemed rather loath to undo the neat parcel, but at last snipped through the stitches in the canvas with the tip of his grandfather's yataghan and began to unwrap the tissue paper. We all craned forward.

Perhaps with Byron's Greek costume at Crabbet in mind, I had been expecting a pair of *tsarouchia*, those heavy Greek mountain footwear, beaked and clouted, sometimes with velvet tufts across the toe, that are the traditional accompaniment of the *fustanella*. But when the innermost cocoon of tissue paper had been shed, the two faded things that my host gently deposited in my hands were light, slender, faded slippers, with their morocco leather soles and the uppers embroidered with a delicate criss-cross of yellow silk and their toes turning up at the tip in the Eastern mode. They suggested Morocco or Algiers and a carpeted and latticed penumbra, rather than the rocky Aetolian foothills; or, even more, slippers in the oriental taste that a regency dandy might have bought in the Burlington Arcade or at some fashionable shoemakers' or haberdashers' in the galleries of Genoa or Venice . . . The two flimsy trophies passed in silence from hand to hand. Something about them carried instant conviction. When we turned them upside down and examined the thin soles this conviction deepened: the worn parts of the soles were different on each. Those of the left were normal; the right showed a different imprint, particularly in the instep. We pointed this out to their owner, but, as he had never heard that there was anything out of the ordinary about Byron's feet, it evoked no more than polite interest. For us, perhaps because we were so near the scene of the harrowing last moments of the poet's life, perhaps because of our frustrating search and the sudden simplicity of its solution, these humble relics were poignant and moving to an extreme degree. It was as though that strange young man, as Hobhouse called him, had limped into the twilit room . . .

The lamps were turned on, and when we had photographed and measured and sketched them, our host wrapped them up once more with a look of slight embarrassment. At last he confessed that, now that it had come to the point, he could not bear to let them leave the family: his niece was about to be married – 'She's taking this young *pallikari* here,' he said, waving the shoes in the direction of the sub-altern, 'and I want to make them part of her dowry. They could hand them on to their descendants, and they to theirs, and so on for ever . . .' He felt guilty about changing his mind. We assured him no one would dream of blaming him, least of all Byron's great-grand-daughter. She would wish the young couple luck and prosperity and a dozen offspring, as we did. His embarrassment vanished in a moment. We drank a final glass of *mastíka*, standing up, to toast the coming marriage. Then after a last look at the slippers and vicelike valedictory handshakes, we left our host still holding the slippers in his hand and wishing us godspeed. The town was wide-awake with evening doings and we felt as elated as though we were taking those elusive trophies with us.

Auberon Herbert

from *Auberon Herbert: A Composite Portrait*, ed. John Jolliffe
(Compton Russell, 1976)

Auberon Herbert (1922–74) always felt a particular loyalty to the Poles, who had accepted him as a private in the 14th Jazlowiecki Lancers in 1942 after the British, Free French and Dutch armed forces had all turned him down. After the war, he did all he could for the dispossessed Poles in England, and also championed the cause of the Ukraine and Belorussia. A devout Catholic and gifted linguist, he spent his time between his wide acres at Pixton Park, Dulverton, and his house in Portofino.

It was twelve o'clock on a dirty and rainy morning towards the end of the war, but inside the old Wilton's just off St James's Square everything was lamplit and snug. The only other customer was a spectacular young Polish officer who was ordering a double vodka at the bar in such way that I had to cast a second glance at the white eagles on the collar, the coloured flashes and the blue and white decorations and medal ribbons.

'. . . put in the tomato juice next,' he was saying, 'and a lot of Worcester sauce, then a squeeze of lemon and, finally, plenty of pepper and salt.'

'You want a Bloody Mary,' the barman said.

'No. That's precisely what I don't want.' The Captain in the Carpathian Lancers spoke with a convinced but unruffled affability. 'The odious roadhouse jauntiness of that name turns a magnificent drink into wormwood and simultaneously traduces the memory of a noble and deeply wronged Queen.'

At this moment a Polish private came discreetly through the curtained doorway out of the rain. Spotting his officer, he approached, saluted, murmured something in Polish and then handed over a number of banknotes which the Captain thrust into a side pocket in an untidy ball with one hand, while he smote his brow with the back of the other and reinforced the gesture with a cry of *Mój Boze!* and a stream of Polish self-reproach.

'He's my soldier-servant,' he explained when the soldier had gone. 'Such a dear, good, intelligent man! I had forgotten all my cash on my dressing-table at the Cavendish and it was brilliant of him to find me. May I please offer you a drink?'

He went on to explain, I think, that the name of the mixture was less an impious misnomer than a failure to pronounce the Slav syllables of a drink called a Vladimir; but I'm not sure; for, as our parallel plates of oysters, escorted by numberless glasses of Chablis, were demolished and replaced and then replaced again, we were soon so deep in the etymology and syntax of half a dozen languages that both the topics and their sequence, even at the time, were hard to keep disentangled. I think he was home on leave from a Polish brigade in the Low Countries, for he was talking about the subjunctive in Dutch and citing useful examples, and this led the way to analogous foibles in the dialects of the Wends, the Sorbs and the Kashubes; and thence to the range of variations that separates the Goidelic from the Brythonic branches of the Celtic tongues. He was tall and thin, and preternaturally pale, and his large green eyes and a cleft jutting chin gave him the good looks of a Bulwer-Lytton or a Disraeli hero. The urgent volubility of his discourse, swelling to vehemence or sinking to confidential apostrophe and adorned with a dazzling escort of similes and tropes, was beautifully under control. It was impossible not to be charmed and amused and a little bewildered. Who *could* he be? As he enlarged with a puckered brow on the plight of the Mirdites of northern Albania, I kept wondering. The problems of the Tosks south of the Skumbi river were causing him deep concern, also the future of the Chams, the Liaps and the Ghegs, and the movement of political notions among the Kossovars of the old Sanjak of Novipazar and along the banks of the Black Drin. His periods often ended in a wide, sinuous and tightly clenched smile that was half-saturnine and half-comic. He had a habit of holding his cigarette between forefinger and thumb and flourishing it like a piece of chalk to underline the stages of his discourse; it looked as though he might put the wrong end to his lips but it always righted itself just in time. Wilton's had filled up and emptied again while we were talking. 'The whole trouble with the *Bosnian* Moslems,' he was saying, when suddenly a fiercer gust of rain slashed across the window-panes and a clap of thunder drowned the end of his sentence.

'Shocking weather,' the barman said.

'It is indeed,' my neighbour agreed. 'I'm afraid there's nothing for it but some more Stilton and another glass of port. I'm so delighted to meet someone who appreciates the importance of midday stoking-up in foul weather.'

I can't remember whether it was then or later on that he explained the colours under which he was sailing, 'I tried the Irish Guards,' he said, sadly, 'but they wouldn't take me, because of health. But the Poles did, bless them. And here I am.'

This was not his only reason for loving the Poles. Shocked at their fate at the beginning of the war, when he was seventeen, and doubly outraged after the Yalta conference, he took their cause to heart as though it were his personal duty to right it. In a post-war world which had become the abomination of desolation for the Poles, this Quixotic and lasting passion, manifesting itself in a wide range of kind acts and moral and material help and backing and solicitude, spread feelings of friendship, warmth and concern exactly when they were needed. There was something very noble about this. Auberon's devotion to the cause of Poland, and his later championship, as the years passed, of other victims of Eastern oppression, sprang from several sources. He felt a kind of collective guilt on behalf of the West: we had failed to see justice done; and deep feelings of Christian charity and of chivalry impelled him to help wherever he thought help was needed. Finally, he followed the promptings of a heart of gold. In spite of predictable bias and fruity diatribes against his natural foes, he couldn't bear anyone to be unhappy. There were times both in London and in the country when he seemed swamped under pensioners and protégés: but his good deeds, hidden in a thick smokescreen of humour and deprecation, were always carried out with self-effacing tact. Alongside these, there was, I think, another impulse still: the half-unconscious survival of an atavistic and unhesitating family tendency to attempt, when public justice failed, to take whole nations under their wing. This intuitive, unprovincial and uninsular sympathy with injustice in remote places was a kind of Neville-Chamberlainism in reverse: the farther off a country, and the less that was known about it, the more urgent the need and the darker the wrongs crying out for redress.

It was not in Auberon's nature to do things by halves. On a quite different level, uncircumspect recklessness surrounded him with adventures and scrapes and odd events. He hated going to bed. Sharing this noctambulist bent, I found myself, as time passed, sitting up late with him among many changes of scenery: in many pubs and clubs, and, when they closed, in splendid or shady night-haunts; in cafés in Paris and Rome and Portofino; in his own house in Neville Terrace – looked after by Karol, the resourceful soldier of Wilton's, and his wife – and at Pixton; and finally, in the Mani, where these notes are written. Our meetings were invariably protracted, always stimulating, often full of surprises. I remember him sitting, very late one night, on the end of my bed and analysing point by point the merits and the mistakes of the Council of Ferrara–Florence. Sleep must have supervened for a moment, or even for longer, for my next vision reveals the posture unchanged except that one of his arms was wound about his neck in such a way that a cigarette was setting fire to the back of his dressing-gown collar and a thin column of smoke was ascending. Outside the dawn was beginning to break, and his discourse had shifted to the early colonization of Brazil.

Auberon's zest for hunting had none of the grim monomania of a congenital Nimrod. It was love for the country round Pixton – those tall hangers and deep valleys, the rock-strewn brooks that suddenly open in the wild sweeps of Exmoor – that hoisted him into the saddle; this, and the enjoyment of the oddity and variety of the companions that the chase scattered all round him over the map. He would fix up a visiting friend with a horse borrowed from a kind sister or niece living nearby, but his own mounts were becoming steadily more of a problem. The vicissitudes of life were rearranging the contours of the slender Uhlan of Wilton's into a still long-legged but sometimes pear-shaped equestrian of a kind that Leech would have loved to depict, and on misty mornings a vast, un-spectacled, utterly benevolent Scamperdale beamed across the tree-tops of Somerset from the back of some almost Trojan steed. He had a gift for naming horses. His last one was called Four Poster. (Auberon always had a look of belonging to a more ancient and rarer species than his neighbours and the gradual change of outline accentuated this: it could make him appear, coming down club steps at the top of

St James's Street, as unexpected as some obsolete creature of the deeps or the forests, an archaeopteryx perhaps, alighting from a glade in the Miocene Age, mopping a pearled brow with a spotted bandanna and radiant with the news that the Slovenes had lost the aorist even earlier than he had thought.) How charming these sojourns at Pixton were! Countless miles across wild and various country and tired hacks homeward long after dark were followed by happy fireside evenings under a lamplit Montagna; one of them, marked by his mother Mary Herbert reading Browning aloud to us in her beautiful voice, survives with a particular lustre.

Visually, Auberon's aesthetic sense was not highly developed, but he wrote with feeling and verve and great skill and he should have written a great deal more. Dispersal and restlessness were his enemies here. His ear for the run of a sentence was faultless, a part of his astonishing gift for languages; and I shall always remember a brilliant disquisition – in the small hours in Normandy, fittingly enough – on the double English language heirloom and the importance of keeping a proper balance between words of Anglo-Saxon and Latin root; how a Latin preponderance endangered one's themes and sent them ballooning away in abstract drifts of Ciceronian rotundities that could only be rescued by tethering them to the ground and reality with short Anglo-Saxon pegs. He had an equal fondness for classical and for liturgical Latin: it was a sensibility on which vernacular innovations were bound to jar and the recoil led him far afield – all the way, eventually, to the Old Slavonic liturgy, hallowed by thirteen centuries of use in Eastern Europe, of SS Cyril and Methodius. It was an ingenious solution, triumphantly characteristic of Auberon's unusual turn of mind. Those hoary Slavonic sounds consoled him for the Latin cadences he had revered and lost; they effaced the memory of their contemned replacements; they were an added bond with the Ukrainians and Ruthenians whose causes he had made his own; above all – and this was crucial for someone with Auberon's overmastering sense of loyalty – his new fellow-worshippers had for three centuries been in union with the Holy See: a fact which left the allegiance of a lifetime intact. (Perhaps the ancient Mozarabic rite of Visigothic Spain – which, after weathering the centuries of Moorish suzerainty, is celebrated daily in one of the side-chapels of Toledo

Cathedral, and always in Latin – might have suited him. Liturgical rock-pools antedating the Tridentine Mass by seven centuries, only half a dozen Mozarabic parishes survive, all of them in Castile. The scarcity and the abstruseness would have been more of a lure than a deterrent.)

All the auspices conspired to make our last encounter a memorable one. Taking wing for this headland on a sudden impulse he arrived at the very moment when a beautiful yacht – a rare apparition in this wilderness – came ruffling into the small bay. She was the *Dirk Hatterick*, belonging to Aymer Maxwell, who in a minute hailed half a dozen of us on board. Then, turning her about, he pointed her bowsprit south. We glided through the brilliant spring morning, past the succeeding promontories and the deep ravines and the towers that clustered in sheaves along the inland sierras; under the gull-haunted, perpendicular walls of Cape Grosso; past the legendary cave leading to Hades, until we had left Cape Matapan far astern. Gazing northward from the open sea, we could descry, faintly looming, the three great peninsulas of the Peloponnese. On the way back, we dropped anchor and swam to the shore on which the ruined palace of Petrobey Mavromichalis was reflected at the end of its long, still gulf. It was an apposite halt. Auberon's great-grandfather was one of the few early travellers to venture into the Mani when it was still a fastness of the vendetta and piracy and revolt. He had been the guest of Petrobey here: of the last of the irredentist Beys of the Mani, that is, and one of the great leaders in the Greek War of Independence. Though geography had given me the linguistic advantage for once – not that Auberon was by any means tongue-tied in Greek – he had somehow stolen a march by proxy. During the last century and a half his far-wandering family had spread a wide net over the Balkans and the Levant. One had explored the vampire-haunted canyons of the Morea and the strongholds of the Jebel Druse; another was captured and cut down by bandits on the Boeotian shore; another had met his death by the freshly opened tomb of Tutankhamen. Yet another – indeed, Auberon's father – had toiled across waterless Arabian wastes and ridden through the passes of the Anatolian hinterland and been acclaimed at last as a saviour in a hundred Albanian glens. (The name of Aubrey Herbert emerges again and again, in many remote and widely separated regions of the Near and Middle East, and always with wonder. 'Antres vast and deserts idle' – these were his haunts. How far they seem from the streams and hills of the West Country.)

As we skimmed homewards, flying corks saluted the sunset off our port bow and at lighting-up time we climbed up the cliff and feasted by candlelight among the cypresses there. Auberon had to leave at dawn. When everyone else had stolen off to bed, we sat up, sending our voices across the all but inaudible water as we spanned the remainder of the night with talk and laughter – not for the first time, but alas, for the last – until the constellations became less distinct and a giveaway pallor began to spread beyond the ridge of the Taygetus.

Roger Hinks

from A Portrait Memoir in *The Gymnasium of the Mind: The Journals of Roger Hinks, 1933–1963*, ed. John Goldsmith (Michael Russell, 1984)

Kenneth Clark described Roger Hinks (1903–63) as 'one of the most learned and perceptive art historians of his generation'. Appointed Assistant Keeper in the Department of Greek and Roman Antiquities in the British Museum, he was forced to resign in 1940 following the uproar over the cleaning of the Elgin Marbles. After the war Hinks joined the British Council, and was Representative in Rome, The Hague and Athens.

There are older and closer friends who perhaps should be writing instead of me, but few can have liked him more, and at least our first meeting was a respectably long time ago. It happened on the evening of 12 August 1934, when I was trudging across Europe at the age of nineteen. Stained with travel, I had ordered a drink in the Boulevard Tzar Ozvoboditel in Sofia. There was only one other foreigner in the Café Bulgaria, who turned out to be Professor Whittemore, the famous Bostonian authority on Byzantium. We automatically plunged into talk and were soon joined by two of his friends, Steven Runciman and Roger Hinks: it was an international congress of Byzantine experts and art historians which had gathered these scholars under Mount Vitosha. They were impeccable in Panama hats and suits of cream-coloured Athenian raw silk and their bi-coloured shoes were beautifully blancoed and polished. Both were in their early thirties and they belonged much more to the deck of an Edith Wharton yacht or to the cypress-alley of a palazzo in Henry James than to this hot little Balkan capital. We met several times; their conversation was dazzlingly erudite and comic; then the end of the conference scattered them again. 'I'm off to stay in a Tuscan villa with one of those delightful Italian gardens,' I remember Roger Hinks saying. 'You know, solid mud all winter and in the summer nothing but dust.'

Later, in London or Rome or Paris, I came across Roger several times in rooms full of people, by chance and for moments only, but always with pleasure; and each time I was puzzled by a fugitive resemblance to someone; but whom? The touch of episcopal aplomb, the gravity, when he was seated, of a monumental bust; the full, pale cheek, the exorbitant eye that could change so quickly from diffident aloofness to kindness and amusement . . . ? He was too well-covered to be in any sense good looking but there was about him something infinitely civilized and urbane. Years passed before I hit on the identity of his alter ego, and I found it at last in an engraved frontispiece by Sir Joshua Reynolds in the 1809 edition of the *Decline and Fall of the Roman Empire*. He was Gibbon! Later on I sought corroboration and found it in a picture by Henry Walton in the National Portrait Gallery. Roger had the underside of his chin under much more stringent control than the famous historian, but, once again, he struck me as the spitting image. This revelation happened in the fifties during his tour of duty in Athens as Representative of the British Council, when we finally got to know each other well and became firm friends. We often met later on but most of this memoir belongs to that Athenian interlude.

Roger had a pronounced foible about capital cities. He complained bitterly about each one that he happened to be living in: everything was wrong – the food, the drink, the language, the architecture, the inhabitants, the weather – and he cast his mind back unceasingly to his last habitat, however uncongenial it had seemed at the time, and sighed as though he had been expelled from Paradise. Amsterdam, Stockholm, Rome, Paris – they all went through the same perverse sequence of indignity and rehabilitation and Athens conformed to this process through damaging and, of course, unfair comparison to the Rome he had just left. But this time his feelings went deeper, indeed they never quite emerged again. The architectural disparity meant much to someone with his ruthless optical awareness; but there were other reasons for his disfavour. The charm of Athens was just beginning to succumb to the indiscriminate concrete and the thickening skies which a decade or two later were to steep the city in real ugliness. Worse still, his time there coincided with the acutest period of the Cyprus trouble. These years of intemperate feeling on both sides inflicted great distress on Greeks who were attached to England and perhaps even more on their English equivalents, of which I was one: more so, because they felt that the policy of their country was at fault. A newcomer to all this, Roger was comparatively uninvolved, but he was in an official position and the isolation imposed by strong feelings nearly brought his work at the Council to a standstill. Many passages in the diaries reveal his thoughts about mass opinion, propaganda and organized outcry: they are akin to Dr Johnson's dictum about patriots; and all these things – unjustly, I think, but understandably – deeply coloured his attitude to this unhappy time. Exasperation was his prevailing mood, coupled with pitying resignation.

We were living in the painter Niko Ghika's house on Hydra and the amazing surroundings had prompted me to write a long article on the influence on a painter of his native landscape, the Greek in this case, comparing its spare and bony nobility with the facile and accessible softness of Italy. Roger devoted several diary pages to it and, predictably and rather convincingly, took the opposite view. He put it much more succinctly on a postcard:

> Excellent, your piece: it brought out all the amaurotic, blue-sclerotic, cleido-cranial, dysostotic, epidermolytic, filthy, grimy, haemato-chromatic, ichthyotic, jaundiced, ketonuric, Laurence-Moon-Niemann-Oguchi-Pelizaeus-Merzbacher-syndromic, radio-isotopic, schizophrenic, telangiecstatic, ugly, vicious, web-toed, xerodermic, yawy and zymotic quality of the Greek landscape to a T. But give me the men of Vernon and Les Andelys every time.* Et in Arcadia Ego . . . R.

He raised the writing of postcards – with his perfect spacing, lack of erasure, studied prose and sometimes verse – to a minor art and many of those that have survived strike a note of homesickness and exile from western Europe. My own postcard of George Sand's house, posted to him from Bourges, brought the answer:

* I think he mentions the two Norman towns because Vernon had come into the landscape article apropos of nearby Giverny, where Monet's *Nymphéas* was painted; and Les Andelys is Poussin's birthplace.

How nice to think of you at Nohant: did the ghost of Madame
d'Agoult pacing up and down in the garden while Franz played the
Erlkönig Fantasia haunt you? Oh, how *commosso* I should have been
. . . Our favourite *claveciniste* is now Padre Narciso Casanova. R.

Whatever the depth of his prejudices, which he sometimes exag-
gerated in order to tease or to stoke up an argument, they were always
entertainingly conveyed. He thought – or pretended to think – that
everyone, especially 'Philhellenes', and even, retrospectively, his old
friend Robert Byron, made too much of a fuss about the different
schools of Greek ikon-painting. (Secretly, they interested him very
much.) He arrived for luncheon one day with a smile of triumph: 'I'm
off to Italy to look at some proper *painting* for a change! And by painting,' he said, fixing me accusingly, 'I *don't* mean the daubed planks that
masquerade under the name in *this* part of the world. Nobody here
has ever had an inkling of the meanings of *chiaroscuro* or *morbidezza*.'
This at once gave rise to a song, to the tune of *Giovinezza*, beginning
'Morbidezza morbidezza! Chiaroscuro, che bellezza!' Nancy Mitford,
who was there, joined in joyfully and many verses were improvised.
He loved this sort of thing; he was as good at being teased himself as
he was at teasing. There was a mild hint of the latter – on the principle that all Grecophils are supposed to be Turcophobes – when he
wrote: 'I am thinking of going to Ankara for the Orthodox Easter to
escape all the crackers and candlegrease, and I am practising my
domes and minarets in my sketch-book.'

Questioning accepted notions is one of the characteristics of his
writing; its conversational equivalent, the pinpointing of clichés, was
salutary but quelling. I once described someone as bright as a button
and he dampingly observed that some buttons were bright, others
not. He often gave his contradictory bent free play, and once, when
the conversation had wandered to Lapland and from there to reindeer, I remarked on the thick moss that seemed to grow on their
antlers.

'No,' Roger said. 'They *graze* on moss. Sphagnum moss, I believe.'
'I'm talking about the moss their antlers are covered with.'
He shook his head with a smile.
'But Roger, you can see it quite clearly in photographs.'

'Reindeer are very nervous animals,' he said. 'When they see some-one pointing a camera, they start fidgeting.' He shook his own head quickly from side to side. 'So the antlers always come out blurred on the snaps.'

'Have you ever been to Lapland, Roger?'

'No.'

In spite of a certain austere touch, he loved pleasure. The diaries talk with some freedom of heterodox affections. He enjoyed food and drink, and, as one would expect, sought them out with appe-tite and discernment. It was not for any specific defect that Greek tavernas brought out in him a certain reluctance, it was more the custom (which I like very much) of choosing one's meal by peering into the pans in the kitchen that worried him. ('Do go down and haruspicate.')

Asked how he had enjoyed the weekend at a hotel in Nauplia, he said:

> I had a little trouble with the people in the next room. They kept the wireless on at night, full blast, even when I banged on the wall. I saw there was nothing for it, so I gave them that noisy song of Scaramuccio and Truffaldino out of *Ariadne auf Naxos*, even louder. They turned their wretched machine up, so I sang louder still until the management imposed silence and I had a perfect night.

He also mentions dreams now and then in the diaries. One of them I find impossible to forget. He was in a house near Cambridge; Royston perhaps. Looking out of the window, he saw, coming up the drive, a steamroller on which four Edwardian gamekeepers were sit-ting in gaiters and deerstalkers, their hatchet faces staring fixed and unblinking to the front. Seized by fear, he dashed through the house and opened the back door, only to see the same steamroller and the identical expressionless gamekeepers advancing up the kitchen path, and woke up.

I assemble these scattered fragments, hoping they might counter-point the solemnity of the text with a lighter and more spontaneous side of Roger's character than we are usually allowed to see; but, looking back over the diaries, I think I was wrong – they are not solemn at all. But they are serious, even though the seriousness is leavened with enough wit and humour for the reader to get a pretty clear idea of what Roger was like. The thoughtful disquisitions scattered through the book played only a small part in everyday conversation, except, perhaps, with companions as erudite as he. But the range of knowledge which gave rise to them, the familiarity with everything beautiful in Europe, the command of several languages, and of their literature and poetry, the love of music, the absorption in every manifestation of painting and sculpture and architecture, the assiduous travel, the pilgrimages and observation and memory – all this gave a wide range and much stimulus and charm to his society. His passionate devotion to the world's rare and precious things and his awareness of their fragility filled him with justifiable dread for the future of civilization. He thought deeply on great problems, shunned fashionable signposts in the process, and arrived at his conclusions by arduous and solitary paths; and his seeming detachment while he did so was always a red rag to zealots. Most creditably, he left his written opinions as he set them down at the time.

It is true that his devotion to the arts, to literature, to travel and writing and study – indeed, to the sifting of his thoughts in these diaries – may have limited his contact with some pursuits which others prize. A fastidious shudder intervened; or so he maintained. He professed, for instance, not to care for the country; unadulterated nature meant little; it had to be a setting for some beautiful or famous building or associated with a painting, a figure or a passage of music which stirred him. Yet no one who has read his discourse on the trees of the different parts of Europe or the marvellous description of the fields and leaves and branches at Balleroy – even if there is a *château* at the heart of them – or wandered by proxy round other French castles all set about with 'that ghastly gravel that enters the very soul', can ever allow him the purely urban character he sometimes claims for himself; he tacitly confutes it, too, by preferring to all the rest of the story those descriptive passages of *À la recherche du temps perdu*, sometimes hurried through by the less percipient, where the plot is made to mark time for twenty or thirty pages while the detailed splendours of the sea and the landscape and the vegetation and the birds and the clouds are unfolded in such slow and magnificent pavanes. His own gift for description is discerning, exact, imaginative and often funny: inside Siena Cathedral 'one feels as if one were in the belly of a gigantic zebra'; and people, when he touches on them, are before us in a flash: '. . . Like all French poets, [he was] small, swarthy, restless and cross. He was dressed in uncompromising black and had a curious green stone in a narrow platinum setting on the little finger of his left hand. He kept nervously twiddling it round so much that one expected him to appear and disappear intermittently . . .' His self-imposed limitations, if such they were, cleared the decks for his elected pursuits. Above all, they left time and room for the other most important thing in his life, which was the company of his friends.

All this we know from his writings. But I shall have failed badly if I have not conveyed how strongly Roger's friendship and affection were returned and with what a feeling of loss his friends look back: not only to the achievements of scholarship and diligence and flair, but to the pessimism and prejudice and foreboding, and the inventiveness and fun and exhilaration that came so surprisingly to the rescue.

Iain Moncreiffe

from *Sir Iain Moncreiffe of that Ilk: An Informal Portrait*,
ed. John Jolliffe (Stourton Press, 1986)

Sir Iain Moncreiffe of that Ilk (1919–85) was interested in genealogy and history from a very early age. After the war, spent in the Scots Guards where he saw much active service, he joined the Court of Lord Lyon King of Arms (the Scottish equivalent of the Royal College of Heralds). He wrote several books on heraldry and the clans of Scotland.

I remember as though it were yesterday a drizzling November evening in 1939 in Codrington Block at the Guards Depot at Caterham. The Coldstream were taking on the training of thirty recruits who aspired to commissions in the five regiments of the Brigade and, one by one, in plain clothes for the last time, these lost figures mooched into the grim barrack-room out of the dusk, despondently drinking in that Caterham atmosphere of Potsdam, Dartmoor, and *I Carceri* of Piranesi, compound of carbolic, Brasso, bathbrick, Ronuk, pipeclay and Blanco which a distant whiff of drains touched like the hint of garlic in a perfect salad. The barked orders and the rhythmic stamping had died away outside and all was silent now except for bugle-calls. The last to arrive was a thin, dark-haired boy in a yellow waistcoat and the sparse beginnings of a moustache, Chatterton-pale in the twilight; and, in a few minutes, the mood had begun to change: he was talking about the Radziwills and the Colonna, and everyone started to cheer up. The windows of snowy castles seemed to come alight, banners unfurled, wolves pursued the sleighs of fur-clad magnates, Teutonic Knights sank spiralling through the ice; and then we found ourselves skirmishing with the Orsini across the Campagna or seated by proxy almost within earshot of Michelangelo's sonnets to great-aunt Vittoria under the ilex trees of Tusculum.

This was the first glimpse of Iain Moncreiffe. Considered a great innovation, the Brigade Squad we had joined was the first of its kind, a tough apprenticeship full of surprises for everyone; the new recruits must have seemed unusual and rather bewildering to the Depot staff, the squad sergeant and the trained soldier, and Iain was certainly the strangest. Slightly built, and not strong, I think he found the rigours of the course were more exacting to him than to the rest, and the guardsmen admired this, and he charmed them with his stories and his teasing. When we groaned about these months of Spartan initiation, his grumbles invariably took a comic turn; anyway, he would rather have been cut in pieces than miss going through the war with the regiment he had set his heart on.

The only things to enliven the barrack-room bleakness were the scarlet fire-buckets full of sand and adorned with the Coldstream battle-honours on painted scrolls – Talavera, Vittoria, Toulouse, Waterloo – a long muster of victories. The guardsmen knew them by heart as it was part of their training. But so did Iain, even the lesser known – Nivelles, say, or Fuentes de Onoro – together with the dates and the weather, the names of the commanders on both sides, that one had red hair, say, and the other a limp . . . The astonishment was general. This wasn't the result of special mugging up, but part of a wide-ranging concern in the things he cared about.

> And so for miles around the wonder grew
> That one small head could harbour all he knew.

A mixture of rum card and bloody marvel was the guardsmen's verdict.

Iain's grasp of history was wide and firmly based, and, as we know, in one or two branches unsurpassed. I knew he had been an only child and I had visions of him alone in a Scottish country-house library or under a tree in Kenya, reading feverishly and forgetting nothing. In one way his studies were as methodical as a university professor's, in another as romantic as Quixote's, and the two were sometimes at loggerheads, don against Don; but though he was a born romantic, the scholar kept Quixote under firm control and this struggle between facts and temperament made his search for historical fairness all the more creditable. His passion for continuity made him a lover of tradition, a legitimist, a stickler for ancient loyalties and an opponent of revolutionary notions, and his respect for the tribal evolution of law turned him into a tiger for the constitution. His genealogical studies were a by-product of his search for a particular aspect of historical authenticity, a feeling akin to the passion of all collectors; but where a more usual antiquary goes full tilt for Norman fonts, the specimens Iain pursued were flesh and blood rather than stone and dating as far back as documents could lead him, and if descendants still existed, they were live evidence of this continuity and, as it were, scored double. The epigoni might be rather battered or run to seed – 'Plenty of weeds like me,' Iain said, after a protracted clubland luncheon, years later – 'but not all. Look at that chap', and he pointed across the room at a tremendous grandee like a recumbent fragment of Stonehenge, faintly snoring: 'He'd be all right with a mace or a kirtle-axe.' He liked to think of the original rough begetters of tribes and dynasties, the mormaers, athelings, thanes, rhinegraves, voivodes, krals, kniazes, khans and kagans, and their ancient styles, not to mention later figures, comparable to Charlus as the Damoiseau de Montargis – who had issued from the barbarian half-darkness and scattered the re-emerging continents with their progeny. To these were added the paladins who jousted at Aspromont or Montalban and those who perished at Fontarabbia when Charlemain with all his peerage fell; and, with his eponymous ancestral hill in mind, he thought fondly of the first shaggy Moncreiffe looming out of the primordial bracken in this hoary forest of begetters.

But the range of his pursuits abolished all trace of parochialism; it carried him far beyond the Flodden Roll, clean across Europe and Christendom, the worlds of Islam and the Bible and a score of sham-anistic barbarian invasions, all the way to the Great Wall of China and beyond; and it simultaneously performed another task: as he would like to have carried his researches back to Adam and Eve – as, with the fallacious help of biblical family trees, it can be done – it meant that the entire world was related: they were all umpteenth cousins and fellow members of a cosmic clan; and this feeling, together with his rather old-fashioned good manners, may have been the half-subconscious root of his friendly address and his interest in people; it was a sort of classlessness that remained unchanged whoever he was with. It put him on level terms with everyone at the Depot and it explained, years later, a long discourse on Gillean of the Battle axe and Gregor of the Golden Bridles to the fascinated driver of the stationary cab which had brought him to White's, who switched off the engine half-way through and listened to the end.

Back to Caterham. Iain was deeply versed in symbols and emblems even then, and as I had had a sneaking craze for heraldry ever since *The Talisman* and *Ivanhoe*, this was a great bond. On the scrubbed table, or over mugs of cocoa in the Naafi, we had great fun covering sheets of foolscap with shields, helmets and mantelling. A fellow-recruit, finding us at it, teased us by quoting Chesterfield's comment on heralds – 'silly fellows who don't even know their own silly business', and Iain, looking up with his mandarin smile, said: 'Oh, but we *do*! Just look at these lovely tressures flory-counterflory! Anyway, it's better than teaching your son the morals of a whore and the manners of a dancing master.' Another link was Iain's interest in eastern Europe, particularly in Hungary, Transylvania, and the old Rumanian principalities of Moldavia and Wallachia. The hazards of travel had taken me exactly to these parts in the years before the war and, for the last two of them, I had been staying with a family in an old and rambling house on a broken-down estate in High Moldavia, and he couldn't hear enough about it and them.

This seems oddly prophetic now. He told me that, in spite of his passion for tracing descents, there was one quite recent one on his own distaff side that he couldn't follow for lack of documents: 'It might lead to a long line of mole-catchers or pickpockets or pew-openers for all I know.' Then one day, years later in clubland, I found him beaming. He took me aside with a drink, and the news that research had made a triumphant breakthrough; and across snatches of our neighbours' comments on death duties, cricket scores and wire, he unfolded how, *via* what he called a legitimacy hiccup and a Croatian serf, the lost line had been traced. It led straight back to all that was most resonant and august in Hungarian history, and, among others, to the great Transylvanian house of Báthory, which had reigned in Transylvania and Poland. 'And what's more,' Iain went on with a rapturous expression, 'we descend directly from Elizabeth Báthory, the Monster of Csejthe, sometimes known as "The Blood Countess"! This fiend of wickedness or folly,' he explained, 'was convicted in 1610 of the slow murder – in order that their blood might magically preserve her beauty – of more than six hundred girls. Her servant-accomplices were tortured to death and she perished in her grim castle after being four years immured in the dark.' Iain's eyes were sparkling as though he were leading in a Derby winner.

Anyone who knew Iain even slightly was aware of the warmth of his character and his deep kindness, and if he seemed to relish the deeds of monsters like the horrible countess, or of Vlad the Impaler (whom he insisted on calling Dracula), this was not due to any answering streak in his own nature. It was the survival into riper years of the sort of boyish gusto that revels in the rack in historical novels, the thumbscrew and the Scavenger's Daughter and the torments that Sioux and Hurons inflict on captured palefaces. Now and then, during Iain's stories, the fat boy in *The Pickwick Papers* seemed for a moment to climb into his lean frame uttering his famous words, 'I wants to make your flesh creep!'; and in his writing, these rare Pickwickian intrusions and an occasional mild facetiousness are the only literary foibles one could wish away. Otherwise, it is all fascination, originality, illuminating anecdote and strange lore. I never tired of listening to the results of his historical delving. But to the uninitiated, it may sometimes have been a little bewildering. I remember Iain sitting at luncheon in a club next to a tall, thickset and purple-faced stockbroking fellow-member who munched in silence while Iain unfolded to him an urgent dissertation on allodial fiefs, seizin, gavelkind and free-warren. During a digression on deviant usages in the Soke of Peterborough and a few wapentakes in the Danelaw, with parallels among the Salian and Ripuarian Franks driven home by snatches of Low Latin, Gaelic, Norman French, Old Norse and Frisian, his interlocutor's eyes began to project. Iain's voice was sinking to staunchless near-inaudibility while the other grasped fumbling at passing straws of meaning in the unfamiliar drift; and by the time Iain had moved on to soc, sac, scutage and infangthief, with outfang-thief looming and pit and gallows to follow, his companion's occasional grunts had fallen silent; a stunned fixity veiled his glance and his brow was dewed, as though he were about to dissolve or explode. Had Iain merely gone into overdrive, as he sometimes did, reversing full-tilt, and in the teeth of audience response, into the heart of the twelfth century? Or was he simply seeing how far he could go? I think it was mostly the former; but the flicker of eyebrow and a wicked Fu Manchu spark in the eye hinted, just hinted, that some of it might be the latter. It was this lure and the tempting glitter of thin ice which sometimes – and once in Rome, when we were together at the end of a dinner party of Judy Montagu's where much wine had flowed – inspired him, on the brink of disintegration, to murmur inventive and unorthodox suggestions into a hitherto unknown neighbour's ear, evoking great surprise. Next day oblivion had effaced all recollection: but, recalling it later, he would ruefully say: 'Ah yes! That was the night I behaved so well . . .'

Two years ago, and almost the last time I saw him, I was in Sister Agnes for twin operations on both big toes, which seemed to be turning to marble. ('Comes of living in Greece,' Iain said.) It was December and snowing heavily and Iain entered in an Inverness cape and a peaked travelling cap of the same challenging tweed as though he had bowled round from Baker Street in a growler. The passage of forty-five years had added a few creases and puckers, grizzled his hair and salted a moustache that pointed dejectedly down one side and musketeerishly up on the other like the Spanish sign that turns a canon into a canyon, but he was so unmistakably the same figure as the pale yellow-waistcoated recruit of half a century earlier that these additions might have been the illusory make-up of a guest in the last pages of *Le Temps retrouvé*. It was lamplighting time; the snow was muffling Beaumont Street in white; and suddenly, at the same moment, we remembered a similar evening many years earlier that neither of us had thought of since.

We had been allowed out of Caterham for short leave. It was a blank, bitter day and we went to earth in his aunt's house just north of the park. To make up for the abstinence of the Depot, we fell on her grog-tray as though we were dying of thirst, and, snug by the fire, Iain talked of clan customs; this led on to the pipes and to pibrochs, and he hummed a couple; I think they were called *MacCrimmon's Lament* and *Lochaber No More*. 'But the best of the lot,' he said, 'is the one they always play at Highland funerals, *The Flowers of the Forest*. Marvellous words too.'

'Do sing it.'

'I can't. It must never be sung or played indoors. It brings down a curse.'

'Let's go outside, then.'

We opened the front door; it had started snowing hard as we toped by the fire, so we struggled into our huge slate-grey greatcoats. 'I warn you,' Iain said, buttoning up his collar (a cross-saltire on his buttons, a crowned harp on mine), 'it always makes me cry.' In a minute we were on the doorstep. Iain sang the words and I joined in the refrain, croaking and quavering like carol singers with short back-and-sides under the whirling flakes:

'. . . But now they moaning on ilka green loaning,
The flowers of the forest are all wede awa . . .'

It was very moving. Back by the fire, I said that I thought that his eyes *were* a bit misty. 'I know,' Iain said, his face crumpling into a Pictish smile as he tipped the last of his aunt's decanter into our glasses. 'Highland Mist, I'm afraid.'

George Katsimbalis

from *The New Griffon*, n.s., no. III (Athens: Gennadius Library, 1998)

George Katsimbalis (1899–1978) dedicated his life and his private income to the advancement of Greek literature, and he has had an enormous influence on modern Greek letters. He created and financed Ta Nea Grammata, the most respected literary magazine of its day. He encouraged and supported many writers and poets, and he devoted himself to the study and bibliography of the Greek poet Kostes Palamas. He is the subject of Henry Miller's The Colossus of Maroussi, a book which celebrates his particularly Greek genius.

George Katsimbalis used to say that he looked like Raimu, the French film-actor, and a fleeting resemblance there certainly was; but the comparison was not wholly satisfactory: something was missing. Surely there was a closer likeness, vaguely remembered, somewhere? When I discovered it at last in the Uffizi Gallery in Florence, recognition was instantaneous: 'The Triumph of Federigo da Montefeltro Duke of Urbino (1422–82) by Piero della Francesca'. There is a commanding and incisive look about Federigo's triumphant profile that is lacking in the film-actor's. Here, too, are those keen eyes that can be either sharp or hooded or twinkling, and the full cheeks, the erect carriage of the head, the small firm mouth and the jutting chin; and when the years drove George's hair into retreat (he bewailed their flight), and turned the rearguard to silver, later portraits by Piero in Rome and Milan show Federigo at a similar stage and both men display the same bold shining hemispheres packed with energy, originality and brains. There, too, in the Duke's picture, is the nose like a bird's beak; a nose, indeed, that seemed at a second glance almost too fiercely aquiline . . . I learnt that the eagle-bend in the painted nose was caused by the point of a lance in a tournament; without it, the two men would have been identical. (An accident! How suitable! It calls to mind at once the bad leg which forced George, however fast he walked, always to carry a stick; or a broken lance one might say; or a magic wand . . .) The comic and dramatic part of George's idiosyncrasy, reflected by Raimu, is suddenly balanced and reinforced by the dash and the splendour of the great condottiere, who was simultaneously the most enlightened of the Renaissance tyrants, humorous, kind to everyone, hospitable and generous – and, above all, a great humanist, a lover and collector of books, a friend and protector of painters and writers and poets and a man who inspired affection in all who knew him.

Those memorable features first came my way in Athens, in the smoke and the noise of the Argentina night-club in the winter of 1940, where everyone went to watch La Bella Asmara dance. I was a lieutenant with a deceptively heroic-looking bandage round my head, and, because of it, the barman, and several others, had offered me drinks; then a tall and interesting-looking man in a Greek artillery captain's uniform turned up and did the same. Where had I been wounded, he asked. In Africa perhaps? When I told him that I had merely been overturned by a drunk driver in a truck of the British Military Mission, he laughed and said: 'Splendid! But don't tell anyone, or you'll get no more free drinks.' Friends at once, we sat up talking, working our way through that long procession of glasses till the place closed; and we forgot to exchange names. I left for Albania next day. *The Colossus of Maroussi* had not yet appeared, but I knew I had been listening to somebody extraordinary.

Meeting in Athens again in 1946, we recognized each other at once and it seems to me in retrospect that ever since, whenever I was in Athens, we saw each other almost every day: sometimes in Yannaki's but more frequently in the old Apotsos, before they both came to an end; at Saiti's and Xynou's and Zvinggos and Barba Zafiris; above all at Psara's, high as a bird's nest at the very top of the Anaphiotika steps; or lower down in the still virgin Plaka under the wide leaves of the Platanos taverna in summer or, in winter, upstairs under the interlocking whitewashed beams, often with Seferis, Rex Warner, Captain Antoniou or Niko Ghika, or all together; ending up, as often as not, among the billiard players and the nargilehs and the surrealist orders shouted by Babi the waiter, in the extinct Vyzantion. There were evenings in his house with Aspasia; and, most often, perhaps, with Joan (whom I later married) in a score of tavernas among the pines and the vineyards of Attica; and each one of these places became the *mise-en-scène* for an expanding golden cloud of wonderful stories.

A surprising lesser gift that went with his narrative genius, manifesting itself in sudden surprising outbursts, was his knack of improvised onomatopoeia: the rattle of machine-gun fire for instance, the cracking whips and the rumble of his battery of field-guns galloping with Theodore Stephanidis along the vile Macedonian roads; the hoofbeats of the stallion-drawn trams clattering up the steep and disreputable *mahalàs* above Smyrna; brief deluges of invented German, Bulgarian, Turkish or Arabic, the calls of muezzins, the rapid labial vernacular of a Senegalese fellow-student at Montpellier; massed ships' sirens; the cry of a large and mysterious black bird, which flew into his dining-room during a wartime visit of Palamas after curfew, perched on the lampshade, croaked ominously twice, and flew out into the dark . . . And Henry Miller and Lawrence Durrell have made his Acropolis reveille to the cocks of Attica ring all round the world.*

Sometimes a curious peripatetic meal, called a Cappadocian Feast, would change the usual pattern. It had three stages. Mussels and *kolios* with *tzatziki*, in the Asia Minor *ouzeria* in Santarosa Street, were followed by a stroll towards *döner kebabs* and perhaps *peinirli* in Omonia, continuing, after yet another walk, with *ekmek-kadaif me kaimaki* at the end of Emm. Benaki. The list of oriental cakes and sweets on the wall must have pressed a button in George's memory, for suddenly, as though in a trance, he began to murmur: «*Εἶνε τό ἄσπρο στῆθος σου ταζέδικο καϊμάκι/ τοῦ Ἀϊντίν-Ἰσάρ χαλβᾶς τό κάθε σου χεράκι/ μουχαλεμπί καί γκιούλ-σερμπέτ ὁ ἀναστεναγμός σου . . .*» He went through the whole length of the '*Καρά Σεβδαλῆς*' of Orphanides, growing a little less quiet with each line. The few late customers, all from Asia Minor, had fallen silent; and, at the end of the refrain – «*κι᾿ ἄν ἐγεννήθην σεβδαλῆς, ἀσίκης θ᾿ ἀποθάνω!*» – they broke into applause.

That prodigious literary memory, rooted in his lifelong passion for books – the Montefeltro side! – was another of his surprising gifts. He was expert in three languages and hardly a Greek, a French, or an

---

* See the letter from Lawrence Durrell, which forms the appendix to Henry Miller's *The Colossus of Maroussi*.

English-speaking poet seemed to have existed, however exotic or recondite, of which he couldn't recite, without a hesitation or a mistake, whole pages by heart. To many, including me, he was a miraculous mine of rare knowledge about Greece. If the answer was not immediate, kind and unerring research in the National or the Gennadius Library always unearthed it in the end. In spite of his narrative genius, he was no monologist; his stories sprang naturally out of the conversation; more often, they were dragged out of him by the rest of us; and they never emerged as set-pieces, in the sense of being frozen in a mould.

New facets would be revealed each time, because each time it was a live experience being drawn straight from a deep and fresh reservoir of memory. It was impossible to resist the temptation to lead him in the longed-for direction . . . Just for the asking, one could be plunged into the labyrinth of wicked and fascinating intrigues among professors in Provence, or join him in clasping Tombros's huge bronze Rupert Brooke memorial as it slid loose and lethal about the caique deck in a terrible storm off Skyros; or mingle in the low life of Montmartre and Montparnasse. Following his adventures in the great fire of Salonika in August 1917, one joined him by proxy when he and a fellow-artilleryman prudently filled their pockets among the tumbling debris of the Royal Serbian Bank, and waded into the bay to escape the conflagration; until, driven further out into deep water by flames and heat, they started to swim. Soon, compelled by the dangerous weight of the metal, they had to unload great cataracts of gold dinars into the Aegean mud and swim for their lives . . . It was in Paris that I heard this wonderful story. Purely by chance, we had bumped into each other at noon in the Rue des Canettes near Saint-Sulpice; and we were still together, after fifteen unbroken hours of conversation, gastronomy and noctambulism in the Pied de Cochon, by the now-vanished Halles, eating onion soup an hour or two before dawn. In George's narrative, too, it was nearly daybreak, but the dark city of Paris and the *forts des Halles* who were drinking all round us in their blood-smeared aprons, might not have existed. We were back half a century and up to our necks in the Aegean Sea: '. . . Looking back across the scarlet reflections of the water,' George was saying, 'we could see the whole town collapsing in sparks, yes, *millions of sparks*! And behind, high above the leaping flames, all along the sky-line, the tops of the minarets of all the mosques of old Salonika were burning like a forest of candles . . .'

So many places, for all his friends, were singled out by these kaleido-scopic sequences: in our case, all the halts of an unforgettable Peloponnesian journey in buses and trains: Patras, Olympia, Navarino, Methoni, Koroni, Kalamata, Tripoli and Nauplia, ending on the ter-race of Niko Ghika's house in Hydra – vanished too – each of them coloured by comic or remarkable events; for life, places and people, at his contact, always conducted themselves in an unusual way.

When his bad leg limited his radius of activity to Athens, his midday table at Zonar's became a magnet for Karandonis, Papanoutsos, Lorenzatos, Synadinos, me; and many more. Then time further short-ened that radius to his study in Alexander Soutsos Street, and, in my last memory – luncheon with our old friend two months before he died – there he is, surrounded by thousands of books, sitting in shirt sleeves at his desk with his Palamas documents pushed to one side to make room for the plates and bottles and glasses, recalling for our sake the racy, comic and extremely clever songs of Vincent Hyspa, the French *chansonnier* who had been such a favourite with George's gen-eration of students in the Paris of the 1920s. They still sounded hilar-ious and he sang them with such brio, carefully pointing out all the witty and scandalous word-play with his flourished forefinger, that our laughter soon reached the helplessness of tears.

Then he left us. The loss of a friend so brilliant and warm-hearted and beloved and so unlike anyone else, was shattering; but now, the very thought of George is a sure remedy against depression or sad-ness; for the gold cloud of reminiscence, comedy and personal myth that gathered all about him whenever he was at a table with two or three friends – a phenomenon so real that it was hard to think of it blowing away like smoke when the chairs under the leaves were empty again – was not a finite thing: the world that his sentences built was a real and a continuing mythology in which all his friends were enrolled willy-nilly and it still reverberates in our minds. It is this which makes it both difficult to speak of him in the past tense and impossible not to smile when he strides into our thoughts. Each time he does so – and it happens very often – he sets scores of live echoes ringing and the memory of strange and astonishing events springs up all round us like an emanation and a blessing. These pages are full of landmarks that have vanished, but George, in one special sense, is not one of them.

John Pendlebury

The Spectator, 20 October 2001

This article on the scholar and soldier John Pendlebury (1904–41) comes from a speech that Paddy gave at Knossos, Crete, in May 2001, as part of the commemoration of the sixtieth anniversary of the Battle of Crete.

John Pendlebury is an almost mythical figure now, and, in some ways, he always was. Everyone connected with ancient or modern Greece, and not only his fellow-archaeologists, knew all about him. He was born in 1904. In addition to his classical triumphs at Winchester and Cambridge, a dazzling athletic fame had sprung up. He broke a fifty-year record at the high jump by clearing the equivalent of his own height of six feet and flew over hurdles with the speed of a cheetah. His classical passion was humanized by a strong romantic bent; he revelled in novels about knights and castles and tournaments. And all suspicion of being a reclusive highbrow was scattered by his love of jokes and his enjoyment of conviviality. A strong vein of humour leavened all.

The British School of Archaeology was his Athens anchor and wide learning, flair and imagination led him to many finds. He dug for several Egyptian seasons at Tel-el-Amarna, but Crete became his dominating haunt. He was on excellent but independent terms with Sir Arthur Evans but, when he was away from Knossos and the Villa Ariadne, he was constantly on the move. He got to know the island inside out. No peak was too high or canyon too deep for him to claw his way up it or down. He spent days above the clouds and walked over 1,000 miles in a single archaeological season. His companions were shepherds and mountain villagers. His brand of toughness and style and humour was exactly right for these indestructible men. He knew all their dialects and rhyming couplets. Miki Akoumianakis, the son of Sir Arthur's overseer, told me he could drink everyone under the table and then stride across three mountain ranges without turning a hair.

Pendlebury's knowledge of the island was unique, and when, in the end, he managed to convince the sluggish military authorities, he was sent to England, trained as a cavalryman at Weedon, commissioned as a captain in a branch of military intelligence and then sent back to Crete as the British vice-consul in Heraklion. It was typical that he referred to his military role as 'trailing the puissant pike', like Pistol in *Henry V*. He didn't mind that his consular cover story in Heraklion fooled nobody. But his mountain life changed gear: he presciently saw that the Cretan veterans of the old wars against the Turks would be vital to the eventual defence of the island. These regional *kapetanios*, natural chiefs – like Satanas, Bandouvas and Petrakogiorgis, and many more with their sweeping moustaches and high boots – had many virtues and some, perhaps, a few faults, but they were all born leaders. They were all brave, they passionately loved their country and they recognized the same qualities in Pendlebury. They trusted his judgement when he began to organize a system of defence, arranging supply lines, pinpointing wells and springs, preparing rocks to encumber possible enemy landing places, storing sabotage gear, seeking out coves and inlets for smuggling arms and men, and permanently badgering the Cairo authorities for arms and ammunition.

When the Italians invaded Greece from Albania and were flung back by the Greek counter-attacks, the probable sequel became clear at once: Germany would come to the rescue of her halted ally. The whole Wehrmacht was available and so was Germany's vast Luftwaffe. The implications were plain. Pendlebury and the Cretans made guerrilla strikes on Kasos, the Dodecanesian island 25 miles from the easternmost cape, and there was a far-flung caique operation on Castellorizo, off the south coast of Turkey. Like all Crete, Pendlebury lamented the absence of the 5th Cretan division, which had covered itself with glory in Albania, only to be left behind on the mainland. With them, and the 10,000 rifles Pendlebury longed for, he felt that the island could be held for ever. But, to his exasperation, the arms only came in driblets. Even so, there was hope.

If the worst happened, Pendlebury was determined to stay and fight on with the guerrillas until Crete was free. His stronghold would have been the Nidha plateau, high on the slopes of Mount Ida. It was grazed by thousands of sheep, inaccessible by roads, riddled with caves – Zeus was born in one of them – and it could only be reached through the key village of Krousonas (the stronghold of Pendlebury's friend, Kapetan Satanas) and the great resistance village of Anoyeia (the eyrie of Kapetans Stephanoyanni Dramountanes and Mihali Xylouris). During all this time, the knowledge that the rest of Europe was either conquered or neutral and that England and Greece were the only two countries still fighting was a great bond.

We must skip fast over the German invasion of Greece. Most of the British forces, which had been taken from the battle in the Libyan desert to help the Greeks, got away from the mainland with the Royal Navy's help and the island was suddenly milling with soldiers who had made it to Crete. I was one. I was sent from Canea to Heraklion as a junior intelligence dogsbody at Brigadier Chappel's headquarters in a cave between the town and the aerodrome.

The daily bombings were systematic and sinister. Obviously, something was going to happen. It must have been during a lull in this racket that I saw Pendlebury for the first and only time. 'One man stood out from all the others that came to the cave,' I wrote later on. I was enormously impressed by that splendid figure, with a rifle slung like a Cretan mountaineer's, a cartridge belt round his middle, and armed with a leather-covered swordstick.

One of his eyes, lost as a child, had been replaced by a glass one. I heard later that, when out of his office, he used to leave it on his table to show that he would be back soon. He had come to see the Brigadier to find out how he and his friends could best contribute, and his presence, with his alternating seriousness and laughter, spread a feeling of optimism and spirit. It shed light in the dark cave and made everything seem possible. When he got up to go, someone (Hope-Morley?) said, 'Do show us your swordstick!' He smiled obligingly, drew it with comic drama and flashed it round with a twist of the wrist. Then he slotted it back and climbed up into the sunlight with a cheery wave. I can't remember a word he said, but one could understand why everyone trusted, revered and loved him.

We all know a lot about the battle: the heavy bombing every day, followed at last by the drone of hundreds of planes coming in over the sea in a darkening cloud, and the procession of troop-carriers flying so low over the ground they seemed almost at eye-level, suddenly shedding a many-coloured stream of parachutes. When the roar of our guns broke out many invaders were caught in the olive branches and many were killed as they fell; others dropped so close to headquarters that they were picked off at once.

Heraklion is a great walled Venetian city. The enemy forced an entry through the Canea Gate, and after fierce fighting they were driven out by the British and Greeks with very heavy losses. This was the first astonishing appearance of Cretan civilians, armed only with odds and ends – old men long retired and boys below military age, even women here and there – suddenly fighting by our side, all over the island. In Heraklion the swastika flag, which had briefly been run up over the harbour, was torn down again. The wall was manned by Greek and British riflemen, successful counter-attacks were launched and, apart from this one break-in, the town and the aerodrome remained firmly in our hands until the end.

After leaving the cave, Pendlebury and Satanas headed for the Kapetan's high village of Krousonas by different routes. They hoped to launch flank attacks on the steadily growing throng of dropped parachutists west of Heraklion. He got out of the car with a Cretan comrade and climbed a spur to look down on the German position. They were closer than he thought and opened fire. Pendlebury and his friend fired back. Here the fog of battle begins to cloud things. Pendlebury and a Greek platoon were still exchanging fire with the Germans when a new wave of Stukas came over and Pendlebury was wounded in the chest. He was carried into a cottage, which belonged to one of his followers, George Drossoulakis, who was fighting elsewhere and was killed that same day. But his wife Aristeia took him in and he was laid on a bed. The place was overrun with Germans; nevertheless, one of them, who was a doctor, cleaned and bandaged the wound. Another came in later and gave him an injection. He was chivalrously treated. The next morning he told the women of the house to leave him. They refused and were later led away as prisoners. A field gun was set up just outside . . . and a fresh party of parachutists was soon in the house. Here was an English soldier dressed in a Greek shirt and with no identification. A neighbour's wife saw them take him out and prop him against the wall. Three times they shouted a question at him, which she couldn't understand. Three times he answered 'No'. They ordered him to stand to attention and then opened fire. He fell dead, shot through the head and the body.

The battle raged on. Heraklion stood firm and we had similar tidings from the Australians and Greeks defending Rethymnon. After the lines of communication had been cut, we had no glimmer of the turn things were taking at Maleme over in the west. We thought we had won. The news became still more bitter later on, when we learnt that enemy casualties had been so heavy that for a time they had considered abandoning the campaign.

Much later we learnt what happened to Pendlebury. At first his body was buried near the spot where he fell. Later, the Germans moved him to half a mile outside the Canea Gate beside the Rethymnon road. I remember bicycling past his grave the following year dressed as a cattle-dealer. It was marked with a wooden cross with his name on it, followed by '*Britischer Hauptmann*'. There was a bunch of flowers, and new ones were put there every day until the enemy shifted the grave to somewhere less central. (He now lies in the British war cemetery at Souda Bay.)

Meanwhile legends were springing up. For the Cretans, it was the loss of an ally and a friend with a status close to that of Ares or Apollo. For the enemy, he was a baleful and sinister figure, a darker T. E. Lawrence, and perhaps he was still lurking in the dreaded mountains. Many bodies were exhumed until a skull with a glass eye was dug up and sent to Berlin – or so they said. According to island gossip, Hitler had been unable to sleep at night for fear of this terrible incubus, and kept the trophy on his desk. To the SOE officers who were sent to Crete to help the Resistance, he was an inspiration. His memory turned all his old companions into immediate allies. We were among friends, Pendebury – Pedeboor – Pembury – however it was pronounced, eyes kindled at the sound.

We must go back to 28 May 1941, seven days after Pendlebury's death and the night of the evacuation. The British troops were lining up to board the ships that were to carry us to Egypt. I was interpreter. Everyone felt downhearted at leaving the Greek friends who had fought beside us for the last eight days. The battered and silent town smelt of burning, explosions, smoke and fresh decay. All at once, an old Cretan materialized out of the shadows. He was a short, resolute man, obviously a distinguished *kapetan*, with a clear and cheerful glance, a white beard clipped under the chin like a Minoan and a rifle-butt embossed with wrought-silver plaques. He said he would like to talk to the 'General'. The Brigadier was a tall man and an excellent commander, tanned by a lifetime's soldiering in India. The *kapetan* reached up and put his hand on the Brigadier's shoulder and said, 'My child,' *'paidi mou'* in Greek 'we know you are leaving tonight; but you will soon be back. We will carry on the fight till you return. But we have only a few guns. Leave us all you can spare.' The Brigadier was deeply moved. Orders were given for the arms and a Black Watch lieutenant led away the *kapetan* and his retinue. As we made our farewells, he said, in a kind but serious voice, 'May God go with you, and come back soon.' Meanwhile, escorting destroyers from HMS *Orion* and HMS *Dido* were stealing towards the jetty.

It was only later, looking at photographs, that the old man was identified as Pendlebury's friend, Kapetan Satanas. He died the next year, after handing his gun to a descendant, saying, 'Don't dishonour it.'

Looking back, he represents the innermost spirit of Crete. Ever since, the two men have seemed to symbolize the brotherhood-in-arms that brought our two countries so close together and made us feel that this season of desolation would somehow, against all the odds, end in victory and the freedom they were all fighting for.

Books

Early Reading and Desert Island Books

from *The Pleasure of Reading,* ed. Antonia Fraser
(Bloomsbury, 1992)

'"TWANG." A clothyard-shaft struck the banqueting-board and stood quivering. A message was twisted round it, and, starting up, the Sheriff and the barons looked at each other aghast . . .' (It would be an insult to the reader to name the legendary tales this exclamation comes from, and most of the books mentioned later need no author's name. With less familiar books, especially foreign ones, I hope that the absent names, when they are unknown, will prove that exciting treasure-hunt and stimulus to curiosity which always lead us on to literary exploration and further delights.)

Pretending to read, I was really reciting by heart – I had followed the words often enough, after badgering people to go through that particular page aloud; for, though I was six, reading was still beyond me. I was ashamed that others could manage at four, the whole thing was a sham, I was unmasked when told to turn over and sighs of pity and boredom went up. It wasn't the first time.

Books, on one's own, still meant pictures. It had been all right earlier on. *Jemima Puddleduck* could do without the text, so could the contemptible *Chicks' Own* and *Little Folks* and the sophisticated 'Bruin Boys', and my hero *Little Black Sambo* too. (I gazed for hours at Henry Ford's illustrations in the *Coloured Fairy Books*; those wide-eyed kings' daughters, ice-maidens and water-sprites were exactly the sort of girls, later on, that I would pine for and pursue.) Luckily, there was a lot of maternal reading aloud: all Kipling's books for children, *Treasure Island, Black Beauty, The Heroes, Alice, Wet Magic, Three Men in a Boat, The Midnight Folk, The Forest Lovers*, Somerville and Ross, Surtees, scenes from Shakespeare and *Oliver Twist*. (Dulac and Rackham illustrations moved on to Phiz, Cruikshank, Tenniel and Du Maurier and then, downhill, to Shepard and Hugh Thomson.)

When the miracle of literacy happened at last, it turned an unlettered brute into a book-ridden lunatic. Till it was light enough to read, furious dawn-watches ushered in days flat on hearth-rugs or grass, in ricks or up trees, which ended in stifling torchlit hours under bedclothes. Book-ownership was the next step. To assuage a mania for Scott, I was given four Collins pocket Waverley novels every birthday and Christmas and my father sent sumptuous works about animals or botany from India, wrapped in palm-leaves and sewn with a thousand stitches by Thacker & Spink in Calcutta or Simla. When the Scott craze died, I tried Thackeray, loved *Vanity Fair* but failed with all the rest. Dickens became a lasting passion and there was no looking back with *Pride and Prejudice* and *Wuthering Heights*. Moments of illumination followed fast: falling scales and initiations – epiphanies unloosing journeys of discovery that rushed away and branched and meandered all through the years between six and eighteen.

Untimely ripped from school at sixteen and a half and sent to an Army crammer in London, I read more in the next two years than ever before or after: but, instead of Sandhurst, I suddenly longed for Constantinople, caught a boat to Holland and set off.

My literary state of play on departure is best approached through contemporary poetry. I knew nothing about Pound or Eliot, and of Yeats only 'Innisfree', one sonnet, and 'Down by the Sally Gardens' – which, anyway, belonged to singing – and nothing at all about younger poets now venerable. My favourites were Sacheverell, Edith and Osbert Sitwell and, in prose, Norman Douglas, Aldous Huxley and Evelyn Waugh. I judged earlier poets now by whether I knew anything they had written by heart that I could recite as I slogged along the roads of Swabia and Bavaria. At home and at school there had been much learning by rote, both compulsory and by choice. The young learn as quick as mynahs, at an age, luckily, when everything sticks: and the list starts with two or three Shakespeare sonnets, a few speeches and choruses from *Henry V*, some Marlowe ('Ah, Faustus . . .'), Milton (*Lycidas*), and Spenser's *Prothalamion* ('Sweet Thames! runne softly . . .'). Then came stretches of Tennyson, Browning and Coleridge, bits of Shelley's 'West Wind', most of Keats's odes (no Byron; Keats was still the yardstick), and fragments of Gray and Pope. Some of Scott's verse survived, with Rossetti as a medieval aftermath, though fading fast. Several border ballads were next, then 'The Burial of Sir John Moore at Corunna', patches of 'The Scholar Gypsy' and *Hound of Heaven*, 'Cynara', *The Dead at*

Clonmacnois from the Irish, a lot of Kipling, Hassan's serenade of Yasmin, plenty from *A Shropshire Lad*, and (part of a recent metaphysical addiction) passages of Donne, Ralegh, Wyatt and Marvell. Carroll and Lear abounded, but, for some reason, not Chesterton or Belloc. *Horatius* and most of the *Battle of Lake Regillus* were the longer pieces: *Granchester*, and, more or less in sequence, the *Rubaiyat of Omar Khayyam*. I loved French, but the entries are soon over: one poem of de Banville ('*Nous n'irons plus au bois*'), two of Baudelaire, a bit of Verlaine ('*Les sanglots longs des violons*'), Ronsard's original of the famous Yeats sonnet, and another by du Bellay ('*Heureux qui comme Ulysse...*' etc.), and finally, Villon, starting with the *Ballads of the Dead Ladies* and *the Hanged Men*; a recent and all-absorbing mania.

Moving back and changing step, tracts of Virgil, hammered into my head by countless impositions at school, now boomed out over the snow, a few odes of Horace and some Catullus, including a bit of the *Attis*, six lines of Petronius and Hadrian's five lines to his soul. Next, two Latin hymns, remnants of a spasmodic religious mania, and some recently learnt verses from the Archpoet and the *Carmina Burana*. I ended with snatches from Homer, two or three epitaphs of Simonides and two four-line moon-poems of Sappho.

Roughly speaking, the date of this giveaway rag-bag is the winter of 1933, when I was just short of nineteen. The general intake is approached through verse because the inevitably larger prose corollary, by a shadowy logic, automatically suggests itself. Now, with an unknown language and shifting scenery, something quite different was on the way. The language assault was through village talk and Schlegel and Tieck's *Hamlet, Prinz von Dänemark*; Austrian inns, Vienna, and a Schloss or two in Slovakia; German poets were turning into something more than names. It was a season of inklings; I was put on the track of Hölderlin, Rilke, Stefan George and Morgenstern; and by the time I got to Transylvania that summer, I could arduously and very slowly hack my way through *Tod in Venedig*. They were haymaking in Hungary, the dactylic canter of Magyar was mettlesome and stirring, yet little remained; but Rumanian, a Latin tongue with some of the vowels Slavonically fogged, seemed much easier and enough of it stuck to help with the poems of Eminescu and Goga later on. Across the Danube that autumn a Bulgarian smattering and a grapple with Cyrillic came and went with the speed of measles: and over the next border, the agglutinative harshness of the Turks, laced with genteel diaereses, sounded like drinking out of a foeman's skull with a raised little finger.

Suddenly it was winter again. Constantinople was already astern, snowflakes were falling fast, and I was landing in Mount Athos, impelled there by the books of Robert Byron. (I had met him, before setting out, in a nearly pitch-dark Soho night-club where everyone was clouded by strong drink.) I knew by instinct that Greece was going to mean much in the coming years; but, in Cretan caves during the war, it was *David Copperfield* – read and reread and falling to bits – which kept us going. The other resources – literature without letters – were complex Cretan mountain songs and their spontaneous fifteen-syllable rhyming couplets to the notes of the three-stringed rebeck. Sometimes, for strange smoky hours, as we lay round on brushwood under the stalactites, our old shepherd hosts intoned a few miles of the marvellous *Erotokritos* myth. It is longer than the *Odyssey* and, like iron age Dorians reciting Homer before the alphabet, they could neither read nor write. But there was never a falter.

These two years of wandering ended with a backward loop to Rumania. I settled there for a long time in a rambling country house where the dales of Moldavia sloped away to Bessarabia and the Ukraine. As in the Russia of Tolstoy and in pre-war Poland, some Rumanian families, often to their regret, spoke French more readily than their own language and so it was here.

An octagonal library held the whole of French literature; encyclopaedias and histories beckoned in vistas; and, during two winters with snow to the windowsills and miraculously cut off except for horses and sleighs, I tried to advance deeper into this transplanted French world than earlier steps had allowed. It was a dominant and – or so I felt – somehow a debarbarizing passion. Books were a paperchase. *Le Grand Meaulnes*, left invitingly open, led to haunting new regions where *Le Potomac* and *Le Bal du Comte d'Orgel* were landmarks, until, totally at random, I would find myself up to the neck in *Le Lutrin*, *Mademoiselle de Maupin*, *Bajazet* or *Illusions perdues* – or, indeed, in *Arsène Lupin*; or Giono or Panait Istrati: Charles d'Orléans, Hérédia, Mallarmé, Verhaeren, Apollinaire and Patrice de la Tour du

Pin followed, and many others, and thanks to the fluke of my where-abouts, Russian literature first impinged in French translations. Matila Ghyka, the author of *Le Nombre d'or*, often came to stay, bring-ing the latest issues of *transition*, *Minotaure* and *Verve*; also fascinating gossip about Valéry, Léon-Paul Fargue, Paul Morand, Saint-Exupéry, Eugène Jolas and his other friends in Paris: he pointed the way to *Là-Bas*, *Axel*, *Les Diaboliques* and *Sylvie* and let the names of Corbière and Laforgue hang in the air. *L'Aiglon* was read aloud and *Les Fourberies de Scapin*; and now and then, to change from *analogies* and *bouts rimés* after dinner, somebody would take down the literary parodies of *Reboux et Muller*; the glow of shaded petroleum lamps lit the faces of the readers and the listeners. The four chief English-language mile-stones of that time were D. H. Lawrence, Virginia Woolf (*Orlando*), Hemingway and Joyce. *Paludes* and *Les Caves du Vatican* were the break-in to Gide: very excitingly, many people in Rumania seemed to have been friends of Proust. Once I had begun, allegiance was immediate and for good.

This house, then, resembled a chaotic and abounding waterfall. I was there when war broke out in September 1939, so there was plenty to think about, at the Guards' Depot two months later over the but-tonsticks and the Brasso. (When I went back to Moldavia recently, the house had completely vanished. Some industrial buildings, already abandoned, had taken its place, and the trees had been cut down long ago.)

'The eleventh edition of the *Encyclopaedia Britannica*, Fowler, Brewer, Liddell and Scott, Dr Smith, Harrap, Larousse, Lemprière, Duden, the whole DNB, *Hobson-Jobson*, a battery of atlases, concordances, diction-aries, Loeb classics, *Pléiade* editions, Oxford Companions, Cambridge Histories, anthologies, and books on birds, beasts, plants and stars –' I was looking through a list made years ago, when planning a house on a remote headland of the Morea: 'If you are settling in the wilds, ten reference shelves are the minimum.'

All right for a house, perhaps, but not for a desert island. Not under the present rules. Curiosity is half the pleasure of reading, so what's to be done? As I brood, my lids begin to sink . . . and my faculties lose hold . . . If it were Prospero's island, a wave of the wand could float an illicit and watertight trunk ashore, enough to fill ten sand-proof shelves in the hut . . . but if that's the way things are, Danaë might emerge, holding Perseus . . . I shake myself. There will be no trunk, no Danaë, no Perseus, no Miranda, no Calypso, no Man Friday even, and no puff of smoke on the horizon.

We are allowed Shakespeare and the Bible as well as the choice of ten books; but how many actual *volumes*? I plan to start with Auden's five-volume, brilliantly chosen *Poets of the English Language*: it runs from Langland to Yeats. No Eliot, of course, and, indeed, no Auden: but Maurice Baring used to savage a dozen books to glue in reams of extra pages, and I shall do the same . . . In goes *The Decline and Fall of the Roman Empire*, all seven volumes, with Bury's notes, followed by Evelyn Waugh's *Decline and Fall*. (But what about *Vile Bodies, Black Mischief, Scoop* and *Put Out More Flags*? I've got to have them. Perhaps they could be microfilmed or stitched together. If this won't do, it will have to be the first on the list and the same applies to *Antic Hay, Crome Yellow* and *Those Barren Leaves*.) *Old Calabria* goes in without a shadow of doubt; it's a particular style and cast of mind here that one can't do without, so Cyril Connolly follows. Next comes the Temple Classics Dante, with its crib, [and] *Kim*, read about every two years; the habit is too old to break. *The Odyssey*, certainly (glued to the *Iliad*?). No good without a parallel text, alas, so I'll get them stapled to Robert Fitzgerald's translations, or Richard Lattimore's. *Ulysses* comes next, and lastly *À la recherche du temps perdu*. When I finish the last page, I can start all over again.

Later.

I stack them on the locker.

As it turns out, the crew are lenient about the definition of 'book', and indulgent about staples and glue, but they are inflexible about number: 'There are eleven here, I'm afraid, sir.' At this moment the siren goes and a voice shouts, 'Island in sight!' All eyes turn to the porthole and with a conjuror's speed a slim volume flies into my bush shirt pocket: *The Unquiet Grave* is safe! And all goes well at the recount. The books are tidily arranged in the portmanteau, zipped up, padlocked and carried on deck.

A desperate moment! What about Saki, *Bleak House*, Walpole's letters, Burckhardt, Sheridan, Horace, *Nightmare Abbey*, Raby's *Christian and Secular Latin*? I'll never learn about *Hisperica Famina* now; (For a second I think I catch the faraway, accusing, millionfold moo of the unread; then it fades . . .) Gerard Manley Hopkins, Browning, Pius II's *Memoirs*, *War and Peace*, Plutarch, la Rochefoucauld, *Les Fleurs du mal*, Chaucer, Donne and Montaigne – there they lie higgledy-piggledy on the bunk. ('Five minutes now'; I stroke *The Wings of the Dove* for the last time.) They remind me of St Augustine's lifelong sins on the eve of his conversion: they plucked at his garments and twittered: 'What! Are you leaving us now? All your old friends? And for ever?' ('Stand by.') *Tristram Shandy*? *Mr Sponge's Sporting Tour*? *Huckleberry Finn*? Boswell? *Torrents of Spring*? *Phineas Redux*? *Far from the Madding Crowd*? ('Steady there.') Lorca? *Uncle Fred in the Springtime*? *Urn Burial*? *Tintin* . . .?

'We'll have to look sharp, sir. They are putting the boat down now. Oh, thank you, sir!' (I shan't need it) 'and the best of good luck to you, sir.'

The Strange Case of the Swabian Poet

The Spectator, 28 September 1996

An image like a god's I gazed on as I slept,
Which a resplendent throne full richly did upraise,
While foolish multitudes, from need or pleasure, crept
To serve, or stand on guard there; and my gaze
Saw how, in the true God's despite, it did accept
Hungry, but never fill'd – vows, offerings and praise,
And how its lightest whim spared some, but others reaped,
And joy'd in punishment, revenge, and wickedness.
To smite this ingrate image down did Heaven oft-time
Assemble all its stars in many a sign and wonder,
Yet still this idol's voice rang out more loud than thunder,
Until at last, when pride did the high zenith climb,
A flash of lightning struck the shining form asunder
And all vainglory chang'd to worms and stink and slime.

Years ago, chancing on this sonnet in an anthology, I was fascinated by the metre – the extra foot at the end of each line – and
by the strange and ambiguous vision it conjured up. 'Dream: on the
D. of B.', it was called, or rather 'Traum: von dem H. von B.', for the
poem was in German, and a footnote explained that the initials
meant 'H(erzog) von B(uckingham)'. I made an immediate dash at
translating it, so the creaks, the faulty rhymes and the Wardour Street
syntax are not the poet's fault, but mine. (The poem in its original is
given at the end of these pages.)

Ever since reading *The Three Musketeers*, we have all been haunted
by the Duke of Buckingham; haunted and dazzled by the satin and
the diamonds and the strings of pearls, the starched lace zigzag ruff,
the preposterous splendour and the panache; and when we learnt
later on how this Phoebus Apollo had been stabbed to death at
Portsmouth with a tenpenny knife, the horror, eerily laced with
relish, was almost too much to take in.

And here, in the sonnet, was a contemporary foreign poet smitten by the same astonishment: 'G. R. Weckherlin,' the anthology said: '1584–1653'. I had never heard of him; nor had anyone else.

In the German-speaking world, I learnt, Georg Rudolph Weckherlin, from Swabia, was thought second only to Martin Opitz, 'the Father of German Poetry', and though some writers call him early Baroque, both of them really belong to a group of late Renaissance German poets akin to the Pléiade in France a couple of generations earlier, with Ronsard and Du Bellay as their brightest stars.

He was also a scholar, a diplomatist and a courtier at the Duke of Wurtemberg's palace at Stuttgart and travelled widely in France. Some time after 1602, he was three years at the Court of St James, and was sent on missions to central European states and the Empire. In England again in 1616, he must often have been under the same ceilings as Buckingham. He entered the royal service and accompanied Charles on his expedition against the Scots, and soon afterwards he married Miss Elizabeth Raworth, of Dover, and took root in England. He seems to have changed sides at the Commonwealth: he became Latin Secretary, then Secretary of Foreign Tongues, to the Joint Committee of the Two Kingdoms, and held both posts until he was replaced by Milton, perhaps because of ill health. Paradoxically, he often helped the older poet when his eyes began to fail; then he succumbed to his adopted country's distemper and died of gout.

He had been equally at home in German, Latin, French and English and almost certainly knew some Italian and some Greek. It was he who brought the sonnet and the sestina to Germany and he left a mass of poems, strongly influenced by his friend Samuel Daniel and his fellow-diplomatist, Sir Henry Wotton. (As I read about him a dignified figure began to take shape, with a kindly blue eye gleaming above a pale fog of beard and a wide collar fastened with tassels breaking over black broadcloth and silk: half-Van Dyck, half-Honthorst, lyrically wreathed, perhaps, in a chaplet of bays . . .)

Completely English by now, his daughter Elizabeth married Mr William Trumbull of Easthampstead in Berkshire, whose deer park was part of the King's Chase. He served in several diplomatic posts, most notably in the Low Countries; and his son, Sir William Trumbull, followed him in his career. Beginning as a youthful Fellow of All Souls, he made the Grand Tour with Christopher Wren, visited

Tangier with Pepys, sat in Parliament for a Cornish borough, became
Charles II's ambassador at Constantinople, then Principal Secretary
of State to William III, and retired at last to his Berkshire library and
the company of his friends. It was Sir William who first prompted
Dryden to translate Virgil, and he performed the same office for
Pope by suggesting Homer. Kneller painted him and Pope wrote the
verse epitaph on his fine tomb at Easthampstead, where he still
reclines in his full-bottomed wig.

I forgot all about them. But in *The Times* a few years ago, Miss
Sarah Jane Checkland announced, with infectious alarm, the imminent sale of 'the largest and most important collection of English
state papers to be offered at auction this century'. They were the
Trumbull Papers! The archive included letters from James I, Charles
I and II, Sir Francis Bacon, John Donne, Samuel Pepys, John Locke,
John Dryden and Alexander Pope, twenty-nine letters from Philip II
of Spain, secret correspondence about the Council of Trent and
much concerning the British colonies in the New World.

> Perhaps the most exciting of all [the column went on, to my growing
> emotion] is the hitherto unrecorded series of papers belonging to
> William Trumbull's relative, the German poet Georg Rudolph
> Weckherlin, Charles I's secretary from 1624 until the Civil War. These
> include letters, signed but not sent, from Charles to Louis XIII,
> Gustavus Adolphus and Marie de Medici, as well as many Royalist let-
> ters intercepted during the Commonwealth. Finally, there is a beauti-
> ful calligraphic manuscript of a still unpublished verse-translation of
> Book VI of the *Aeneid*, which Sir John Harington, Elizabeth's 'witty
> godson', prepared and presented to James I, in 1604, for the young
> Prince Henry.

(Harington was also the author of a racy disquisition on water-
closets that he punningly called *The Metamorphosis of Ajax*. When
cross with him, the Queen used to catch him by the belt, even when
he was grown up, and give him a good shake as she taxed him with
his misdeeds.)

What a haul! And what a tragedy if such an Aladdin's cave were to
be ransacked! The contents had come down in a direct line of a
dozen generations from Weckherlin and the Trumbulls to their

present-day descendant, the Marquis of Downshire. The heritage lobby was in despair. There had been talk of a private sale to the nation; now it seemed that the open sale was to go ahead. The total price predicted – two million pounds – sounded enormous, but it was very little more than the damages which had been awarded in the recent Cossack libel action. If – albeit ludicrously – ordinary people were thought to be capable of forking out sums like this, there ought to be some public fund or government organization to deal with such emergencies; but there isn't, and things looked black. 'In a few days' time,' the article had said, 'this unique and wonderful collection comes under the hammer at Sotheby's. Once split up, it will be scattered to the winds.'

At this point I was overcome, as though by an onslaught of heady gas, by dreams of grandeur. I would try to help save the Papers! After all, not every millionaire was an illiterate philistine. My mind's eye evoked a rich, unknown and hypothetical humanist, steeped in concern for the country's treasures. As he was only conjectural, the approach would have to be indirect.

Emulating Miss Checkland, I wrote two stirring pages and sent them to a famous weekly (this one, indeed) which I felt sure the unknown saviour was bound to see; on publication morning, kind fate and my wishful thoughts would waft him up the steps of clubland and lead him to the table where the weeklies were spread, and then guide his hand. Next, this not impossible he would be deep in an armchair with his glance halted at the right page. He would finish the piece with a pensive 'H'm'; and a few minutes later my mind's ear would detect a finger riffling through the telephone directory; then dialling: 'Lord Downshire? Good morning, this is – I'm so sorry to bother you. Could you spare me a few minutes, if I came round?'

It all ended happily, and fast, but not at all as it was planned. News suddenly came that the owner had solved the whole problem with impeccable generosity and public spirit, and all the treasures were safe. The piece, of course, never came out, the putative benefactor dissolved into the shadows and I suffered from a touch of the flatness Raleigh might have felt if the Queen had preferred a convenient plank. The anticlimax, bit by bit, gave way to exhilaration at the thought of the brimming deed-boxes, the crackling tiers of parchment, the faded pink tape, the hundreds of broken seals and all the mystery and the dust. The improper jokes of Harington cheered the air, and Buckingham's ruffling plumage, and the thought of classical tags bandied by candlelight round Sir William's table. I was buoyed up, above all, by adumbrations of Weckherlin, backed by youthful memories of the arcaded castles of bookish Stuttgart, and the vineyards and the ricks and the beetling oakwoods of Swabia: the landscape, after all, of the earliest sonnets and sestinas ever to be heard beyond the far bank of the Rhine and to the north of the Black Forest and the Danube.

Traum: von dem H. von B.

Ich sah in meinem Schlaf ein Bild gleich einem Gott,
Auf einem reichen Thron ganz prächtiglich erhaben,
Auf dessen Dienst und Schutz, zugleich aus Lust und Not,
Sich die törichte Leut stets haufenwies begaben.
Ich sah, wie dieses Bild, dem wahren Gott zu Spott,
Empfing – zwar niemals satt – Gelübd, Lob, Opfergaben,
Und gab auch wem es wollt das Leben und den Tod
Und pflag sich mit Rach, Straf und Bosheit zu erlaben.
Und ob der Himmel schon oftmal, des Bilds Undank
Zu strafen, seine Stern versammlete mit Wunder,
So war doch des Bilds Stimm noch lauter dann der Dunder,
Bis endlich, als sein Stoltz war in dem höchsten Schwang,
Da schlug ein schneller Blitz das schöne Bild herunder,
Verkehrend seinen Pracht in Kot, Würm und Gestank.

Under the Bim, Under the Bam

Review of Maurice Bowra, *Primitive Song* (Weidenfeld &
Nicolson, 1962), *The Spectator*, 6 July 1962

Saying what song the sirens sang is as hard as any of Donne's hypothetical tasks. But it seems almost easy compared to the question
Sir Maurice Bowra asks himself and then sets about answering. He
leads us back through airy millennia, far beyond the singing sirens on
their mythological rocks, to the earliest detectable traces of song, to
the conditions which made it likely and incubated its shaggy genesis.
Those sounds, slow to emerge and long silent now, were the first
harbingers of verse; and could we miraculously tune in and equally
miraculously understand them, or guess at their nature by analogy
or deduction, we would possess most precious knowledge of the
impulse and inspiration which lead to poetry and the pristine work-
ings of the human mind; knowledge, indeed, of urgent relevance to
the world's entire poetic achievement, which, in its most elevated,
sophisticated or recondite flowering, has been the author's lifelong
study. This new aspect of his theme, which is no less than a bold and
sustained assault on the primitive mysteries, gives special importance
to an absorbing and most unusual book.

We must picture Sir Maurice pondering the first hints of primitive
song – for, as he proves beyond reasonable doubt, where there is
sympathetic magic, mimicry of wish-fulfilment, ritual and dancing,
song always breaks out – on the silent cave-walls of Altamira,
Lascaux, Alpéra and Niaux. We see him turn from the leggy cavort-
ing bowmen, chasing their dream-bison, with his brow locked in conjecture, but not in despair. For the Late Stone Age doings painted in
these scattered grottoes, and those of Russia and the Arctic Circle –
indeed, wherever they emerge and however far apart – all display
similar data, closely related resulting phenomena and subconscious
cosmological inklings; related, not by descent from a common
source, but by the response of primitive man everywhere, regardless
of latitude, climate and date, to the problem of survival. Invariably,
too, up come the same rough-hewn metaphysics. What they all

possess in common is far more striking than their marginal variation or their wide stylistic differences. Broadly speaking, like *yin* evoked like *yang*, and even more interestingly, like Jung. The same, moreover, is discernible today in those scattered and shrinking rock-pools of mankind which, by a random dispensation of history, still live a late Palaeolithic life. One glance at the paintings of the aborigines, the Veddas, the Eskimos, and the Bushmen of the Drakensberg, tells all.

Here lies the secret and the Open Sesame: to guess at their nature by analogy or deduction . . . But in the new field which suddenly unfolds and the accompanying windfall of raw material for study, the need for guesswork goes. For here we have not only the paintings but, carefully recorded and classified, the songs themselves, and, in nearly every case, the singers; the contemporaries, in fact, in every way except the not very relevant dislocation of fifteen or thirty thousand years, of the cave-artists of Aquitania and the Pyrenees.

There are a number of these Stone Age societies. The most apt for Sir Maurice's purpose are the Gabon and Ituri Pygmies, the Bushmen and Dama of South-West Africa, the Semang of the Malayan jungle, the Veddas of Ceylon, the Andaman islanders, the many aboriginal groups of Australia, the Eskimos of the Arctic and the Selk'nam and Yamana of Tierra del Fuego. Some of these are perilously close to that deadline of extinction over which the Tasmanians preceded them, with a helping hand from us, in 1877. They live by hunting, fishing and gathering, sometimes in as humble a form as the search for molluscs, termites, edible grubs, roots, fruit and scaling cliffs for honeycombs. There is no cultivation or taming of animals except the keeping of dogs, which were already the familiars of Mesolithic huntsmen. Dependent, to keep alive, on the seasonal shifts of their animal and vegetable prey, they are of no fixed abode. Their social unit, sheltering in an igloo or a hut of leaves or skins, is the family. Some are so simple that, though they can keep a fire alight, they cannot kindle it. The taints of sophistication are slight and few. Here and there an iron arrowhead, obtained by barter, may replace the usual chipped stone; the Pygmies know how to buy iron and work it, but they are unable to smelt. The Semang have borrowed the blowpipe. Perhaps the most unsullied of all were the Kalang of Java, 'the most ape-like of men'; but they have gone the way of the Tasmanians.

As in the cave-paintings, the search for food dominates all. Pictures of the quarry and a simulacrum of its chase and capture, make success more likely: a pantomime involving dancing, shouts, cries and, in time, song; at first, perhaps, on the evidence of some groups, songs emancipated from any need for meaning. For instance, when two of the crew of HMS *Beagle* landed in Tierra del Fuego, the Yamana greeted them by seizing their hands and forcing them to jump up and down with them, a few inches a skip, singing, joyfully and interminably,

Ha ma la   ha ma la   ha ma la   ha ma la
O   la la la la   la la la la.

One can see how, once started, it might be difficult to stop; and the women still dance to the words:

ma-las-ta   xai-na-sa   ma-las-ta   xai-na-ta

which, repeated *ad infinitum*, are quite unburdened by sense. It remains their only kind of singing. Before dispelling a curse, a *xon*, or medicine-man of the Selk'nam, intones for a long time *wubwubwub-wubwubwub*; another *xon*, summoning a spirit, improvises with *lolololo . . . hoiyoiyoiyoi . . . yeiyeiyeiyei*. Though meaningless, these rhythmic cries with their cumulative iteration express a mood for the listeners as clearly as *willow-waly* or *derry-derry-down* in more sophisticated verse; or, for that matter, *tararaboomdeeay* and *vododeeodo*. Perhaps we may discern, at the other end of the poetical scale, a survival of the same need for spirited but, in the logical-positive sense, only partly meaningful utterance in T. S. Eliot's words (which, indeed, seem obscurely apposite to the entire theme we are discussing):

Under the bim
Under the bam
Under the bamboo tree.

Primitive song may have begun like this and the poor Fuegians, almost extinct now, have not moved on. But it is not so with the other groups. Articulacy, the yoking of sound to meaning, and its elaboration have been at work for a very long time. The author locates its

stimuli and traces its development from pure sound to actual state-
ment, on to repetition, parallelism and variation and a mixture of
both, to alliteration, intermittent and internal rhyme – both of them
unplanned, but eagerly exploited when they crop up – to planning
metre to fit music, the skilled use of onomatopoeia, the emergence
of the refrain and the marshalling into stanzas or couplets. A single
verse of a long hunting song of the Pygmies, a solo which the rest of
the company clinches with a refrain, carries us a long way from Cape
Horn:

> On the weeping forest, under the wing of the evening,
> The night, all black, has gone to rest happy;
> In the sky the stars have fled trembling,
> Fireflies which shine vaguely and put out their lights;
> On high the moon is dark, its white light is put out.
> The spirits are wandering.
> Elephant-hunter, take up your bow!
> *Elephant-hunter, take up your bow!*

During his analysis of the composition, performance and method of
primitive singers, and his scrutiny of their interpretation of nature
and the human cycle, of imagination and myth and symbol, the
author conducts us straight into their lives. It is an enthralling journey. We grasp the paramount status of the chase and of the supernatural apparatus that surrounds it, the evolution of gods, spirits,
ghosts, demons, ancestors and totems, the velleities of religion, the
often interchangeable roles of the shaman, the medicine-man, the
singer, the *xon*. Attitudes to birth, childhood, puberty, nubility, marriage, old age and death run on strikingly similar lines among these
groups, and give rise to songs which can readily be compared. We
know that there have been less backward societies which have failed
to put two and two together in the cases of coition and birth, old age
and death (e.g. the Caribs three hundred years ago). These primitives,
however, all seem abreast of these interdependences. Some of their
love-songs, of which there are not a lot, are deeply touching and their
dirges speak a language we can all understand.

Prayer for help in their various undertakings – frightened, cajol-
ing, imperative, comminatory – usurps a large part of their reper-

toire; magic, incantation and exorcism scarcely less. The supernatural world is so real, familiar and omnipresent, and so large a part in their lives is played by animals, birds, fishes, insects, trees, flowers, rivers and mountains that all these natural and supernatural elements mingle in song on equal and unquestioned terms with human beings. Sometimes they change places. Anthropomorphosis infects animals, humans become zoömorphic. Shamans tell in song how they have ravened as tigers and plunged as cormorants. Like Excalibur, Durandal and Notung in European myths, weapons assume names and personalities.

But rather surprisingly, heroic poetry is rarer. Primitive peoples have all been involved in conflicts over game and epic hunts have stuck in their memories and their songs; but avoidance of trouble, a Boojum-like disappearance, has been their usual stratagem at the approach of strangers; an understandable one considering the short shrift they have received at the hands of white settlers and missionaries. Telling evidence of this reflex subsists in the songs of certain Australian aborigines driven from their coastal habitat generations ago by white settlement. Hundreds of miles inland now in the dry khaki interior, they still sing of the lost ocean that none of them has ever seen or will see.

Nothing, the author warns us, could be farther from primitive songs, or from their forms of artistic expression, than art for art's sake. Every syllable is a means to an end; they want results: food, luck, health, supernatural backing, pardon. Words, especially rhythmic words, are implements to bring the unintelligible into one's power – to establish small areas of command in dark disorder. Even when their songs seem pure anodynes, they are tools for maintaining hope, without which the singers despair and die.

If Sir Maurice means that the extraordinary lines quoted on every page are to be read merely as illustrative points, his warning must fall on deaf ears. (Of course he does not.) They are all of them beautiful or extremely odd, a sort of Pitt-Rivers museum in verse. It is impossible, for a start, not to pause and marvel at the curious fauna, flora, gear, scenery and dramatis personae which crowd in on every side: ice-floes, apes, flying foxes, bullroarers, boomerangs, blow-pipes, opossums, wallabies, kangaroos, termites, fieldmice, garlands, monitor lizards, porcupines, badgers, harpoons, poisoned arrows, bamboo spears, lions, giraffes, caribous, dugongs, musk oxen, polar bears, whales, centipedes, snakes, thunder, string-bark trees, tomahawks, carved antlers, igloos, cabbage palms, chameleons, unspecified gallopers, skeletons with snapping teeth (Kra! Kra!), white forest ghosts, wreaths of tanyong flowers, yams, honeycombs, blubber, rainbows, clouds, ice-holes, waterfalls, anteaters, talking mynahs, kestrels, head-dresses of blossom, coolibahs, billabongs, catfish, prawns, frogs, lotuses, baboons, spinifex, falling stars, elephants and earth voles.

To bring him strength, an aboriginal woman beats her child with a bustard's wing; the Djapu of Arnhemland look on death as a wind full of maggots; ancestresses weep on far-off windy mountain tops; Kantijia, an Aranda ancestor and a god of thunder, lightning and rain, mourns under many waters; the Pygmy Khrum travels along the Milky Way 'gathering stars as women gather locusts'. The Andamanese cranes from his canoe to fling his harpoon after the twirling manatee; the white bear rushes across the ice at Orpingalik the Eskimo, innumerable degrees below zero . . .

It is hard, as the theme sweeps on, not to form favourites. The condemned Fuegians excite pity, and one feels sympathy for the aborigines in their forlorn and dusty lairs:

What is that? What is the cry?
Flying-foxes suspended there in the tree, comrade;

and gratitude to the Semang for their tropical Arcadia; and there is something engaging about the humility and innocence, laced with cunning, of the Veddas:

Ha ha ha
Ha ha
I am the one whom the lynx derides.

It is hard to feel the same towards the Eskimos, as reflected in their songs, in spite of their advanced poetic fluency; perhaps because their twilight world transmits a shiver, perhaps because the directness of their stance towards the seal, though unfaultably Stone Age in sentiment, strikes no answering spark.

When the broth-producer was going to rush up to me,
Beneath me, I could feel nothing else,

and

There was the big, blubbery seal on the ice
I struck smartly with my harpoon.

It is the same with the musk-ox and the caribou. These men lick their
lips as they stalk through the snow. How different from the Pygmies'
approach to the elephant! Admittedly, one song speaks of 'the meat
which walks like a hill'; but he is not only a meal. He is a god,
an ancestor, the lord of the forest, a destroyer and a protector.
This multiple apprehension of the divine, worthy of more evolved
religions, surely hints at a flexible cast of mind.

Perhaps I feel this bias because they are the only one of these
groups I have met. There they were, close to the Congo's banks in
the Ubangi-Shari, stamping and turning round a fire in the dark and
liana-looped forest, their primeval arms and tackle leaning against
the giant boles; a troop of tiny, cheerful Palaeolithics. They clapped
and sang in time to the drums and the twangling notes of graduated
metal prongs projecting from wooden blocks, the 'equatorial piano'.
Wrinkled and benign, they were a captivating community. The forest
had flowed over and befriended them. There was no conflict here;
in fact, they lived in the trees, and their intelligent little faces were
free of tension. (The difference from the delving and reaping
Negroes who lived on the forest's edge was compelling. They
seemed to be engaged in an unequal and never-ending boxing-
match with the great arboreal bruisers that sheltered the Pygmies;
forever reeling back with thick ears and flattened noses; huge,
groggy, baffled and sad.)

There is a chance that Pygmy dances (and perhaps Pygmy songs?)
are the oldest in existence. The young Pharaoh Pepi II captured one
in the twenty-fourth century BC, and prized him for dancing 'the
dances of the gods'. He was taken prisoner in Yam, south of the
Sudan, on the way to Ruanda, where they still exist. Nor, perhaps,
is their war with the cranes a mere Homeric myth: their remote

kinsmen, the Bushmen, still sing of the blue crane, and pursue it eagerly. Perhaps those dancers by the Congo . . .

There are a number of these alluring byways, and I wish there were more; but they must be resisted here. Much of Sir Maurice's task must have been exclusion. In a world of shadows, surmise and folk-memory he is right to seize the established data of recorded song by the scruff and then grill, screen, compare and deduce remorselessly. A softer technique, swaying to the seductions of every coincidence and historical chance-shot, would end in a fog where everything can be everything else, beyond which nonsense might loom. The author's scholarly rigour and controlled intuition gives us the reverse: unprecedented insight – has this task been attempted before? – into the birth of primeval poetry all over the world and the sources of its inspiration; and corollary surmises which are next door to facts – and how could they be more? – about the nature and thought of our earliest ancestors. It is an impressive achievement and one of lasting importance.

But, beside the main scope and findings, many lesser details fix themselves in the brain. Are they lodged there so firmly by the thought that this peculiar poetry must be akin to the metrical murmurings which our own earliest begetters accompanied on those bone flutes dug up in France? Or because some of the singers will soon be gone as irretrievably as the archaeopteryx and the pterodactyl which cast their slow shadows across the swamps and the giant mares'-tails of prehistory? Long after the book's argument has been absorbed into the intellectual bloodstream, unusual syllables linger and echo in the ear, scanned in imagination by claps and the dusty thump of calloused feet, by horns and twanging percussion; or failing this, and more austerely, delivered in the author's measured tones:

. . . For the lynx is the one who is cunning.
   Haggla haggla haggla
     Haggla haggla
   Heggle heggle heggle
     Heggli
   Heggli heggli heggli
     Hegli n!

Cold Sores

Review of *Literary Lifelines: The Richard Aldington–
Lawrence Durrell Correspondence*, ed. Ian S. Macniven and
Harry T. Moore (Faber & Faber, 1981), *The Spectator*,
26 September 1981

Aldington's share in this book came my way at a bad season.
Memories of the fine early novels had all been superseded and
effaced by the publication of *Pinorman* – if Aldington was a friend of
Norman Douglas, what need of foes? – and, finally, by *Lawrence of
Arabia*.*

Many had felt that Lawrence had piled it on a bit in the *Seven Pillars*.
Temporary *folie de grandeur* had touched him. He rashly claimed
Shereefian rank and rather vainly hinted at honours offered and
refused. He had the knack of retreat into the limelight; the Doughty-
biblical style, endemic to Arabists, ran riot; the doings at Dera'a were
uncorroborated; and his psychological make-up was complex and
unorthodox in the extreme. All deplorable, but allowing for a highly
strung nature, not to be judged harshly. His faults, after all, were
outweighed by his courage and flair for command, by a mass of
strange gifts and by a strong touch of genius. Then came Aldington's
book. Muckraking fit for *Le Crapouillot* and sneers like Peyrefitte at
his slimiest were combined with the monomania of a pack of
hounds. Hate and relish showed through the veil of sorrowing
impartiality and the ensuing revulsion against Aldington was not
caused, as he untiringly insists, by his success in felling an idol –
Lawrence was no longer quite that – but by the manner of the
onslaught. Perversely, all Lawrence's blemishes shrank overnight to
peccadillos and the axe, jumping in Aldington's hand as it often does
on jobs like this, gashed him to the bone. And the aftermath haunts
all these letters.

---

* Aldington's book on Lawrence of Arabia, which appeared in 1955, did his career a lot
of damage. From having been a respected author and poet, he suddenly found himself
shunned by critics, publishers and editors alike. Britain was not ready for such a vitriolic
attack on one of its national heroes.

A few months ago in Damascus I noticed a book in Arabic selling like hot cakes. The cover showed the famous features and the Bedouin headdress and I could just decipher the words *Laruns* and *Arabiya*. How appropriate for this capital which he had entered with Feisal in that victorious turmoil of neighing and *feu de joie*! But the book was not the *Seven Pillars* in translation – the bookseller had never heard of *Aamid al Hikme al Sabaa* – but the life, by a 'Mister Aldingtoun', of a wicked western spy: it was on sale all over Islam. Through the following days at Dera'a and Azrak, and Akaba, and Wadi Rum and at all the Lawrence landmarks, I felt, perhaps by reaction, that every word of the *Seven Pillars*, even the most questionable passages, rang true, and left with the conviction that the book was a great work of art and unique, and the opinion stands.

So I opened *Literary Lifelines* dark with prejudice and found most of it justified. Aldington never ascribes his neglect to waning powers or change of fashion: *camarillas* are to blame, and collusion and cliques; and there is always 'MacSpaunday', a four-man portmanteau not hard to unpack, blocking the way for older poets. 'The Pound-Eliot faction or coterie' – this is 1959 – 'practically blocks ALL literary means of expression except the Communist and the Fascist. Which is why I have taken up with Mosley's lot, not that I like them or approve, but nothing else will have me.' This is before his Lawrence book. Its publication welds 'the establishment poets, hacks, commies, sods and draught-dodgers' – 'the chairborne warriors of the knife-and-fork brigade' – into an alliance with Lawrence's other champions, 'the Edens and Vansittarts and Wingates and even the Churchills, all his close relations on the wrong side of the blanket . . .' This was roughly the state of play when the Aldington–Durrell correspondence began.

It really began – after a brief 1933 exchange – in 1957. Both of them were settled in different parts of France. Aldington at sixty-four was out of fashion after wide fame. Durrell at forty-five, though his poems and novels and his brilliant Greek island books were well known, was still on the brink of his great success and when it suddenly rose to a flood, we are faced by the situation of an old lion in decline and a young one in the ascendant; Henry James would have dealt with it very well. (Aldington would have hated this: his scorn of 'Henrietta' was intense.)

At last Aldington could let off steam to someone who did not mind the fixations and the rancour and Durrell comes shiningly out of the exchange; cheering Aldington up; encouraging him to write; tactfully hinting that the persecution and the conspiracy were both chimerical, trying in vain to arrange a comeback in a series of BBC interviews ('You'd have them cold') and then, jubilant but unspoilt, involving him in his own sudden good fortune. In real life, Larry Durrell himself is very lightly peppered with blind spots and perhaps this helped him to deal tolerantly with the cracked invective of Aldington's letters. His brimstone is hurled at random, some of it prompted by envy or disapproval ('Mr Evelyn Waugh is rather a baw; Mr Evelyn Wuff writes plenty of guff' etc), some of it painfully feeble. It is a relief when he switches to praise. He is unswervingly loyal to D. H. Lawrence (the right initials at last), to Roy Campbell (with an old sweat's proviso: did he actually fight in Spain?), and to his long-separated first wife and fellow-imagist poet, Hilda Doolittle: her death came as a heavy blow. There is nothing but unstinted rejoicing at Larry Durrell's ascending star. Durrell's buoyancy and encouragement and his fluent and vivifying zest must have utterly changed the last five years of Aldington's life, the period the letters cover. The parts that deal with the problems of writing are absorbing. Aldington, in spite of his repellent foibles, is revealed as learned and civilized, devoted to French literature and the classics and, with his discourse on food and wine and the records of their meetings and feasts and jokes, an unexpectedly warm and genial character begins to surface.

His life had a last ironic climax. The letters bristle with abhorrence of the Left. But the vogue for his books in Russia had never flagged, and, out of the blue, to honour and celebrate his seventieth birthday the Soviet Writers Union invited him to Moscow and he went.

He revelled in the interviews, the testimonials framed in blue leather, the silver plaques, the banquets and the tributes; but in the last letter before he set out, he ruefully quotes Tony Weller – 'I don't take no pride on it, Sammy' – and one suddenly likes him. He died a few days after he got back.

It is a remarkable collection, well worth publishing. The heart of one correspondent is firmly in the right place and the other not exactly in the wrong one, but askew.

The Art of Nonsense

Review of George Seferis, *Poiémata me Zographies se Mikra Paidia* (Athens: Hermes, 1976), *The Times Literary Supplement*, 28 January 1977

Pure nonsense is as rare among the arts as an equatorial snowdrop. It was understandably scarce in classical times, though Aristophanes, especially in composing *The Birds*, sometimes forgot his satirical duties for a moment, but the polysyllabic knockabout of Roman comedy had heavy axes to grind, and so had the Dark and Middle Ages. The wild scenes that run riot in wall-paintings, capitals and stained glass are lunacy only to the uninitiated: pagan survival, the apocryphal gospels, faulty translation, demon-lore and the bestiary, in collusion with the Thebaïd and the torments of anchorites, solve every riddle. Familiar broodings hatched out the eggshells of Bosch, identifiable furnaces stoked his rocketing and backfiring journeys and lit up the apocalyptic scenes; and the same impulses, reinforced by Spanish tyranny and the spectacle of folly, unloosed the skeleton onslaughts of Breughel; all his allegories and proverbs and parables, even the teeming amphibian chaos, have their explanations. Luckily prolific zest made Rabelais and, later on, his illustrator Doré, overshoot all their targets, and a kind of spellbound invention transported Goya beyond the *Disasters of War*, as though bats' wings had lifted him there, to the enigmatic regions of the *Caprichos*: 'his great merit' (according to Baudelaire) 'is the creation of plausible monsters. No one has gone further than he in the acceptable absurd.'

But all of them and the extravagances of Swift and Lautréamont and Jarry and the visual punning of Arcimboldo and Grandville, can be explained; a fierce warning underlies the apparent frivolity of Cocteau's illustrations in *Le Potomac*; even *The Naked Lunch* has a clear purpose – like *Portnoy's Complaint*, it is a seminal work – and the maze of *Ulysses*, once baffling, is plain as daylight and a clew has been unravelled for its sequel. The function of Augustan follies is tamely scrutable and Gaudí could expound his heterodoxy with almost Vitruvian logic. Perhaps the concavo-convex freaks of Bomarzo in the ilex woods of Upper Latium – hollow monsters, gaping ogres the size of houses, houses nightmarishly tilted to a drunken slant; all cut from the Etruscan tufa with wonderfully aimless exuberance by Turkish captives brought back by the Orsini as their spoils from Lepanto – are the closest approach to true three-dimensional folly in Europe. Dada and Surrealism, through self-conscious gravity and the diffuseness of their claims, loaded themselves with disqualifying fetters. Free, purposeless, spontaneously born and ideologically disengaged, the genuine article bombinates in a vacuum.

By nature France is stony ground for this sort of stuff but it may not always have been so. We know how significantly her poetry changed after Malherbe; as banefully, some thought, as her vineyards later on at the touch of phylloxera (an opening here: phylloxera = withered leaf = Malherbe), and the same critics might point to Descartes as his prose accomplice (*Cogito ergo sum*: the first six clockwork notes of a metronome that clicks all through the reign of the *philosophes* . . . Voltaire dismisses Shakespeare as *ces pièces visigothes*; flinty encyclopaedic smiles snap round us like nutcrackers for a century or two; finally, salutary but quelling, Valéry murmurs with a Cartesian sigh that 'la bêtise n'est pas mon fort'). In verse, the logical straitjacket was further stiffened by an inflexible prosody; vocabulary was pruned to the bone and *chênes séculaires*, roses, laurels, cypresses, myrtle, thyme and marjoram were allowed in the lyrical garden, but nothing else.

These obstacles turned French poems, when genius triumphed over the vetoes, into dazzling feats. But sometimes, to outwit the iron rigours, poets sought refuge in a kind of momentary nonsense – or verbal cheating, rather – which was innocent because confessed, even though the confessions were far from plain sailing. Mallarmé, at a loss in mid-sonnet for a rhyme for the river Styx, and having used up the Pnyx – there is no 'pyx' in French – invents one: '*ptyx*': a non-existent knicknack with which he saves the line, and then conjures deftly back into the Mallarméen shadows: 'nul ptyx, / Aboli bibelot d'inanité sonore . . .' The words implicitly admit the ptyx's lack of being. Similarly Victor Hugo, in *Booz Endormi*, stuck for a rhyme to the last syllable of '*demandait*', fabricates a biblical city, puts the inhabitants to sleep and sets it down without a blush beside a real one: 'Tout repo-sait dans Ur et dans Jérimadeth'. Here it is the invented word – 'J'ai rime à "dait"' – which whispers an excuse and an explanation. (He makes no apology for Ur, however. The Chaldean city was as far from the Judaean stubble-fields where Ruth and Boaz met as Southampton is from Barcelona. He had a wild way with details.)

These strictures offered a perverse intellectual challenge. During the last half of the nineteenth century and the first of the twentieth, scattered Frenchmen responded with a glittering display of acrobat-ics. Only one creaking palindrome surfaced – 'L'âme des uns jamais n'use de mal'; the language rebels against these amphisbaenas; but famous holorimes abounded – 'Gall, amant de la reine', 'O, bois du djinn', etc – and anagrams, spoonerisms, back-formations and artifi-cial malaprops: intricate *normalien* stunts unfolded like a glasshouse full of hybrids. About forty years ago, Eugène Jolas (under post-Joycean influence, I think) published verses in *transition* which relied entirely on improvised onomatopoeia. (One line has stuck, probably inaccurately. A tramp is ravishing somebody in a wood: 'Je la triffouille! Je la ziloche! Han! Et hanhan!') An ingenious galaxy of writers, examined by Matila Ghyka in his *Sortilège du verbe*, explored and deployed the secondary and tertiary functions of the language. Laforgue, Apollinaire and Tristan Derème spring to mind, and Léon-Paul Fargue. There is something engaging about his way of declar-ing an incident closed – '*L'inciclot est dent!*' – and his proposal of '*Ossitoyarmezin!*' as a new chorus for the Marseillaise. Finally, in novels and essays and triumphantly in his *Exercices de style*, there is Raymond Queneau – and scarcely are these words down before the sad news of his death reaches the Himalayan slope where these lines are being written.

But of all these artifices, the portmanteau-word is chief. Translators' brows are pensively knit over Mr Earwicker's horrorscup; and how can they make it clear, in Frankfurt and Angoulême, that he was not his bloater's kipper? We have recently seen the deep hermetic role of these devices in the poetry of Paul Cerdan and the exegetic strife they unloose. Queneau devoted a whole issue of a learned monthly to different translations of 'Jabberwocky'; for the fount and origin of portmanteaux has been done, among other tongues, into ancient Greek and Latin (*'Coesper erat'* = *coenum* + *vesper* = *brillig*, broiling time); into French, and into German: once where all the double-senses were scrupulously dovetailed and once where the sounds – *'Es brillig war, Die schlichte Töwen/Wirrten und wümmelten im Waben'* – were all right, more or less, but where the sense had to take care of itself. Of nonsense poetry away from its home ground, the best single practitioner is German; unexpectedly, perhaps. The short stanzas of Christian Morgenstern, a Bavarian who died just before the First World War, are touched (though he resembles neither) by the same unforced magic and poetical flair and above all by the inexplicable pathos that single out Carroll and Lear and make them memorable and perennially strange.

'Away from its home ground' – a giveaway phrase! But this does seem to be territory where England has unintentionally staked the leading claim; and the claim is ungrudgingly allowed. Brief symptoms of an illogical poetic bent erupted at scattered points in the past – in pomanders, baillies' bells, parrots and haycocks, a whiff, a peal or a squeak, Browning's runaway is caught grazing on strange grass-blades, and reason closes in again – but it was never a large field; the full-grown authentic blooms are only two, but the seeds have blown far. Even so, a modern translation of the whole of Edward Lear into Romanian – *Rime fără Noimă*, by Constantin Abaludă and Stefan Stoenescu, brought back by John Betjeman from a tour of Moldavian monasteries – is an exotic and marvellous surprise. Isolated, trend-free, unsponsored and a work of love, the task is magnificently carried out. The enforced juggling with place-names is wholly legitimate – 'properly', in Romanian, is no rhyme for Thermopylae – but all the other details emerge from their transformation intact and the remoteness and scarcity of the Jumbly regions lose none of their poignancy. Even though it only reaches us by chance, an offering so different from trade figures and travel folders, Eastern Europe's usual literary exports to the West, breathes a spontaneous and vivifying freshness into the air. These lone scholars deserve a salute from their country and from us.

In Greece, with its strong English links, the tie-up is more predictable. In his introduction to Paris Takopoulos's entertaining *Kenē Diathēkē*, Panayiotis Canellopoulos – by far the twentieth century's most erudite prime minister – makes the Lear–Carroll connection plain. *Poiémata me Zographies se Mikra Paidia,* verses George Seferis wrote and cheerfully illustrated from time to time for a small relation, will please the many other children for whom, in the title, they have been assembled and published. Seferis was devoted to Lear and these limericks are gratefully attributed to his inspiration. Like Lear's, they are a world-gazetteer of eccentric conduct, usually with the pristine reduplication of first and last rhymes which the flight of time now seems to touch with a dying fall. The recent elaboration of the limerick, the intricacy, the multiple interior rhyming (and in many cases, of course, the hair-raising impropriety of the brief plots) – all this, in the hands of unpublished virtuosos like the late Constant Lambert, has rather spoilt us for the original simplicity of the metre. (Ironically, the unpublished Greek limericks that Seferis sometimes enclosed in letters to friends – to George Katsimbalis, to Nico Ghika, whom Lear has also prompted to seize his pen like Ingres' violin, to Lawrence Durrell and once to me – would delight the most exacting judge.) The best pages are the translations of 'The Nutcracker and the Sugar-tongs' and 'Father William', and the thing which really shines forth is the goodness and kindness of the writer. But this everyone knew.

A brilliant translator as well as a poet of unparalleled gifts, Seferis was often thinking, and always rather sadly, about the ultimate incompatibility of tongues. Behind the deceptive equivalents in dictionaries the secret resonances are at war. Each word is the spearhead of an expanding phalanx of alien tribal ghosts and we can aspire no higher than the approximate. In Cairo during the Second World War Lawrence Durrell combined some of George's half-anaesthetized sayings, uttered as he came round after an operation – understandably incongruous ones – with some of his own imaginative flights in an amusing and affectionate poem called 'Mythologies', of which the last line is: 'Men of the Marmion class, sons of the free!' (Seferis had recently learnt – I hope the details are correct: there is no way of checking them under these deodars – that towards the end of his life, a friend of Hardy's had given him *The Waste Land* and asked his opinion, which was, a week later: 'Very interesting, but is it quite in the Marmion class?' The haunting phrase wove itself several times into George's crepuscular murmurs.) Later on, he translated the poem into Greek and 'Shatterblossom', an imaginary figure in the poem, became '*Anthospastes*', the exact and perfect Greek equivalent. 'But it's no *use*, my dear!' His soft and meditative voice began to conjure up the rival associations: shelves of anthologies and a fidgety procession of spastics receded into the distance on the Greek side, while the English grew dark with shattered hopes and Cherry Blossom Boot-Polish. He developed the comic polarity until his laughter – a slowly overmastering and infectious upheaval which set his head and shoulders soundlessly and helplessly rocking – brought his elaboration to a halt. But of course he was right, and buried somewhere in his theories lies the key to this theme.

It was with Maurice Bowra that we last heard Seferis speak of such matters, in the sea at the bottom of a steep and pine-fringed bay in Poros, a few summers ago. They were treading water with just enough exertion to keep their animated busts afloat. Ostrich-egg smooth, the head of Seferis caught the gleam of the westering sun; immersion had flattened Bowra's hair on a pink brow, and his energetic voice scanned the other's discourse with staccato laughs and interjections of cheer and assent. To a listener on the terrace above, his interlocutor's murmur could barely be heard, but now and then George's hand emerged with a forefinger raised in illustration of an inaudible point, then dropped back beneath the water, evoking a burst of comment and an answering splash in the twilight; for the outlines were beginning to grow faint. Soon they were silhouettes, like the torsos of seals in a fjord, each the centre of expanding and overlapping hoops which rippled and widened over the still pallor until they vanished beneath the woods of the Argolid. Sounding between air and water in these Saturn rings, their voices and the random plops of their gestures could still be heard when the dark had enfolded them. Men of the Marmion class! They only broke off when a call from above summoned them to land and up the pine-needle covered steps to where candles for dinner were being lit.

A Greek Gentleman in a Straw Hat

Review of Edmund Keeley, *Cavafy's Alexandria: Study of a Myth in Progress* (Harvard University Press, 1977), *The Times Literary Supplement*, 14 October 1977

The Alexandria of the Ptolemies, Seleucid Antioch, Commagene, Sidon, Cappadocia, Osroene, the declining Greek world that sprang up in Alexander's footprints, the shifts of doomed Byzantium, the arguments on prosody and particles of grammar while the Eastern hordes are fidgeting offstage – all this, on a preliminary ruffle through *Cavafy's Alexandria*, is far enough from the Greece of school studies for the reader to feel flattered at the author's implied assumption, however ill-founded, that his knowledge is shared. Respect for Edmund Keeley's previous work and his translations with Philip Sherard deepen the pleasure.

Sometimes the author explains the poet with the hushed respect of a family doctor, and his bedside manner can have the fleeting effect of a temple being walled in with opaque explanatory bricks. This single but recurring blemish is the more surprising by its contrast with the clarity of the translations – his own – which shine in quotation from every other page.

Apart from this puzzling foible, all is gain. Nobody is better equipped than the author for dovetailing the spiritual and physical worlds of Cavafy (for which Alexandria is both the reality and the symbol) and for unravelling the historical and geographic background of the poems. He conducts us first through the seedy modern township itself. Arab at last, it is only remotely akin to the blacked-out, jolly, rather wicked wartime port, scented with kebabs and drains and jasmine and soon to be doubled by *Justine*'s fantastic metropolis, which many of us remember. Closer in spirit to the Egypt of the Lagids than to Nasser's, it was still not very different from Cavafy's Judaeo-Hellenic Franco-Levantine city: a cosmopolitan, decadent, and marvellous hybrid, old in sin, steeped in history, warrened with intrigue, stuffed with cotton, flashing with cash, strident with cries for baksheesh, restless with conjuring tricks and, after sunset, murmurous with improper and complicated suggestions. The place is a palimpsest in reverse, where the earlier centuries are the clearest and by far the most interesting; and, by dividing it up into the literal city and the metaphoric, the sensual and the mythical, Mr Keeley traces the poet's relationship with all of them and demonstrates in detail Cavafy's spiritual immersion in the entire Hellenistic past.

How closely his attitude to beauty and letters and hedonism – and especially to erotic matters – tallied with theirs! The company of the Jupiens and the Morels of the Rue Rosette with their slim wrists and their wide Fayoum eyes, and his random café encounters in the Attarine quarter, were touched and transposed for him by all the charm of similar unions beside the Nile or the Orontes twenty centuries ago. Written with less skill, depicting, as some of them do, the homosexual equivalent of a *vieux marcheur* brooding over former embraces – pale brows of yesteryear, transports in hired rooms (though not the blue-chinned waterfront ambience of rough stuff, the dirty singlets, onions and crabs so deftly captured in Mr Hockney's drawings) – these particular poems might have ended in absurdity. A lesser hand could have turned his ancient world into Jean Bosschère's illustrations for Pierre Louÿs, with a dash of Art Déco and Lalique thrown in; it could have evoked waxwork Alma Tadema arrangements of goblets and petals and tired ephebes wilting along the marble; or, at its unluckiest, those tinted postcards of wreathed Taormina striplings taken at the turn of the century by a German baron and sought after still.

The metrical languors of Canopic youth, the lament in Antioch for spoilt and gifted favourites laid low by excess, Iasys dead and *defutatus* ere his prime – all this is beset with literary peril. Votaries bent only on this facet of the Cavafy polyhedron might have reduced his poems to sodality passwords and the literature of a clique.

How does he escape? 'Because he is a poet of the highest order?' This is true but unhelpful, suggesting, as it might, the masking of heterodoxy in elaborate stylistic cocoons – indeed, from the last paragraph, one might assume a wild proliferation of ornament. In a very complicated way it is the exact reverse. Auden wrote that no other poet used language more simply than Cavafy. It may appear so in translation, but the original, which perplexed his Greek contemporaries, is a unique and cunning alloy in which the fragments of legal diction and ancient Greek and inscriptions on tombs and old chronicles – one can almost hear the parchment creak and the flutter of papyrus – are closely haunted by the *Anthology* and the Septuagint; it is contained in a medium demotic perversely stiffened with mandarin and beaten at last into an instrument of expression which is austere and frugal in the extreme. (E. M. Forster thought that Cavafy's literary ancestor, if he had one, might have been his fellow-citizen Callimachus; but he is much closer to Simonides, to the terseness even of the Lacedaemonians, whom – writing under the guise of an Alexandrian in 200 BC – he affected to scorn.)

Against the rigorous background of his verse, his occasional use of repetition has a great cumulative force, and explicit emotion unfolds with the suddenness of a blossoming walking-stick; but, generally speaking, the scarce elaboration and adornment are always relevant and it is usually from the gaps between the words that the pomps and the garlands form in the air. Perhaps his singularity is best hit off by the attitude Forster used to detect when he ran into him between his office and his flat in the Rue Lepsius: 'a Greek gentleman in a straw hat, standing absolutely motionless at a slight angle to the Universe'.

A book like this should instruct, touch off new trains of thought, promote fruitful discord and, above all, send the reader back to the original. Mr Keeley does all this, and, as the spell of the original returns, a familiar and interlocking question takes shape as well: why, almost alone among Greeks, has Cavafy won his large following abroad? His verbal felicities, after all, and the strange fabric of his language evaporate perforce in translation; only the bare thoughts remain; and as it is chiefly through English that he has reached the Gentiles, these versions are very important.

There is never any doubt about meaning. It is a problem of ear more than scholarship. The clear prose crib which Constantine Trypanis appends to the poems in the *Penguin Book of Modern Greek Verse* will be a blessing for many. Of the metrical translations, all are good in their different ways. Naturally, there is plenty of metaphrastic swerve – dodging the ski-tracks of forerunners, that is – and each has its drawbacks. It is hard not to enjoy the versions of the poet's friend George Valassopoulos, all the more so as Cavafy, who spoke excellent English, must have vetted them. The late John Mavrogordato has a strong whiff of the same aura, though some terseness vanishes in his rigid following of the original metres and rhyme-schemes. The later ones are more free. Rae Devlen, otherwise excellent, jars ear and eye with an almost non-existent word for 'unlawful' – 'the so deviate sensuous delight', 'the deviate desire of the flesh', 'the beauty of deviate attraction'. More disturbingly, her notes speak of the absence of a Byzantine empress, in 1347, 'from Istanbul'. (Cavafy would have turned in his grave; she has literally jumped the gun by 106 years – the gigantic siegepiece, that is, which Mehmet II cast in Adrianople and lugged across Thrace to blow a hole in the Theodosian Walls for the Turks to pour through howling.)

Several problems plague the translator. Herakles triumphed over Hercules long ago; rightly; but the tendency of some translators to transliterate time-honoured Greek names into demotic forms – in the hopes of freshness, no doubt – must pucker many brows. Describing a young prince as 'almost a Selefkid' will give long enough pause to a non-modern Greek-speaker for early Charlie Chaplin films to spring more nimbly into the void than the royal line of the Seleucids; and if this young Selefkid is made to reign over a Cappadocia spelt Kappadokia, the gap between poet and reader grows wider still. After all, Anglo-Greek proper-name formations, already familiar in Chanticleer's learned discourse in *The Nun's Priest's Tale*, have been in the bloodstream of English bipeds for thirty or forty generations, and Selefkids are as worrying as München and Firenze in the mouths of returned holiday-makers and the capital of Hungary made to rhyme with 'enmeshed'.

Vexatiously for Anglo-Saxon translators, Greek – and even Cavafy's spare diction – has more syllables than English. His interpreters very properly stick to his thrift and often the English words are like small peas in a rather large pod – the line is over too quickly. There is no way out of this trouble, and it leads to a trap which augments it. Bent on demonstrating that Cavafy is a demotic poet, translators overdo the short forms of verbs – 'I'll', 'you've', 'he's', 'she'll', 'we've' – and this treads on the accelerator when a touch on the brake would have helped. Worse still, it sets a tone which is too affable and too breezy. With notable exceptions Cavafy's *propria persona* is ruminative and solemn. Better by far to sin through formality. The most dangerous are the poems where the speech is genuinely informal. Disguised as godsends, false equivalents in slang rush into translators' minds. Discrepant by their very nature in time and place and associative field, these dread sounds are not windfalls at all but grenades with the pins out, to be flung back before they can blow up the poems they land in.

The best of his modern translators are Kimon Friar, who manoeuvres deftly through hazards of pace and vocabulary, and the expert team of Mr Keeley himself and Philip Sherard. It is precisely the dark forces haunting the border between idiomatic and colloquial which are leagued against these daring partners; and if their sallies across it have left scars, their own surgery has effaced the most serious. In an earlier *Selected Verse*, a Byzantine noble, cursing his failure to change sides when John VI Cantacuzene seized power, blamed it on 'bogus information' and 'phoney talk'. There was no slang in the original and the injected raciness surrounded 'bogus' (for this reader) with visions from *Vile Bodies*, while 'phoney' impinged through a mashed cigar; and to describe the vain display of the Alexandrian kings as 'show business' seemed equally out of key. In their recent complete edition, however, these have all been set right. But others linger.

(And suddenly, setting all this nit-picking to rout – it is really an appeal for some more changes in the final canon – here comes Ezra Pound, bloodshot and furious, with a harem of dishevelled Muses waving Sophocles' *Women of Trachis* and rasping, hissing and spitting out his own translation like a lunatic and monomaniac sheriff:

What's that screwball? Jus'lis'en a bit . . . slug, grunt and groan . . . I let out a shriek and WHIZZ! . . . [*fifes, kettledrums, oboes*] . . . Arf a mo', Ma'am . . . Let's put him to bed on the Q.T. . . . THUNDER of God! By the black vale of Oeta, don't weasel to me . . . HELL's full of good talkers . . . Some local bloke? . . . Blast it! . . . Tune up, you there . . . [*flutes, clarinets, grosse caisse*] . . . Ezakly! Thazza good start. C'est très beau. Give! [*low 'cellos, contrabassi, muffled drums in gaps between the phrases*. . .]

Amazingly, it works, and leaves my case seriously battered. Best to chuck it and move on.)

The bare thoughts, then, remain. 'When it was a matter of wonder', records Landor, 'how Keats, who was ignorant of Greek, could have written his *Hyperion*, Shelley, whom envy never touched, gave as a reason "Because he *was* a Greek".' Of course this applies a fortiori to Cavafy, but it is not the truism it might seem. The leaf-fringed Flaxman-Lemprière world of Keats – the Titans, Saturn, the still citadels poised above the nymphs and the harvesters and day-break slanting across a landscape of Claude – was much farther from Cavafy's chosen field than the English poet's. He knew all about it, of course, and revered it, but the former Greek world of which he is an honorary citizen in the Landor sense is never Olympus or Arcady and seldom Troy or the shining classical noonday of the famous city states – except for Athens and Sparta, and then only when they are in trouble or decay, or longed-for from exile – but towns and cities where the Greek genius burst into more abstruse and opulent bloom; and it is there that Cavafy, flying back through time, slips disguised into the crowd and goes native.

The end of Athens at the battle of Chaeronea used to be the signal for Greek scholars to put back their books with a Milton quotation and a sigh. It was closing time. They forgot that Philip's dishonest victory opened another lustrous age across the water; of course, a more garish one, a shade second-rate and not to be mentioned in the same breath as the fled wonders. But when the victor's son, with all the East at heel, had led the defeated Greeks to Bactria and the Indies, who could blame their descendants for a certain vainglory? Alexander had founded cities as others throw coins; the language was universal; marble acanthus leaves opened in thousands above the dunes. Letters, poetry, all the arts and all the pleasures throve in the half-Oriental afternoon of the Ptolemies and the Seleucids. The gods of Olympus were joining hands with Osiris and Astarte and Baal. A flash, but only a flash, might reveal Apollo and Pan in the same cave as Krishna; and, for centuries, a Phidian twirl marked the Buddhas of Central Asia. No wonder the citizens of the new king-doms yielded to every temptation: they were irresistible, it seemed. Why, in Seleucia, even one of the Immortal Gods could be seen hastening through the arcades at nightfall, bound for those lawless delights. One might have guessed.

In an essay comparing T. S. Eliot and Cavafy in the manner of Plutarch, Seferis supplies precious clues to the stratagems of his recondite and retiring compatriot. Adroitly and explicitly, Eliot glides into the confidence of his *hypocrite lecteur* by installing insidious, half-mocking Baudelairean feelings of brotherhood and similarity inside his defences. Cavafy is more devious. We find ourselves, without knowing by what hidden process – unless the poet (spectacled, inscrutable and apparently 'absolutely motionless') has advanced on us between poems by unseen grandmother's steps – promoted from outsiders to accomplices. The tribal feelings which sustain great poets are complicated among Greeks by an immensely long history, by rueful pride in early glories and memories of disaster and eclipse. They haunted Cavafy; they had nothing to do with nationalism in any boastful shape; very often his poems unfold in settings of decline, humiliation and the threat of servitude.

But the blame is laid on no outside enemy; only on the victims themselves. 'No villain need be: passions spin the plot'; they are brought low by their own failings: arrogance, mockery, shallow cynicism, infirmity of purpose, spirit of faction; by the lack, when they were needed most, of mettle, wisdom and probity. What could be deeper in irony and dark humour than citizens aghast with consternation when the barbarians fail to invade them on cue? (A Gordian slash might solve all! Or could it be blunted with flattery?) Again and again, without warning, in retrospective Proteus-like avatars, Cavafy abandons his own meditative tone to whisper dread, or to bandy jeers, to speak in lamentation or in boastful, angry or suppliant voices, through solitary masks of the past. The hypocritical reader can no longer listen with detachment. Initiated now, and an accessory, he knows he might have succumbed to the very weaknesses the poet simultaneously censures and condones. *Semblable et frère*, he shares the guilt.

Cavafy had a bookworm's knack for discovering passages in old annals from which poems could germinate. One such find gave rise to a Simonides-like epigram by an Alexandrian 'in the seventh year of Ptolemy Lathyrus' which exempted from blame the fallen

Achaeans whom blundering generals had led to defeat by the Romans in 146 BC; he published it, significantly, in 1922. It was only on reading it for the umpteenth time that it burst on Seferis that the lines were not really meant for 149 BC at all. They were a veiled threnody for the terrible 1922 defeats, for the entire destruction of Hellenism in Asia Minor; they were a cry of protest against defective leadership, an act of piety, and an anodyne. This play with mirrors and time and camouflage, once understood, deepens his poetry with a grim new relevance. Perhaps a prescient appositeness to the flux and erosion of modern times may be one of the hidden reasons for his influence.

Not Chaeronea, then, at all, but Cynoscephalae and Magnesia and Pydna, the fields where the Hellenistic kingdoms were destroyed by the Romans, and above all, the internecine feuds of the Epigoni themselves, were the defeats which seemed fatal. Here is the end of Demetrius Poliorcetes, the brilliant hero of a score of pitched battles and famous sieges:

> When the Macedonians deserted him
> and showed they preferred Pyrrhos,
> noble King Dimitrios didn't behave
> – so it is said –
> at all like a king.
> He took off his golden robes,
> threw away his purple buskins,
> and quickly dressing himself
> in simple clothes, he slipped out –
> just like an actor who,
> the play over,
> changes his costume and goes away.

Admirably conveyed by Keeley and Sherard, this is the true Cavafy note. This is his atmosphere, and it follows him past all the land-marks of decline; until the Romans themselves, half in awe of their philosopher-subjects, half, like Juvenal, disdainful of the *graeculi esurientes*, began to crumble and fail. Christ outsoared Mithras in the zenith; Julian came and went; the desert pillars were nests for stylites now and zealots and heresiarchs wrangled in the streets. The oracles had long ago fallen silent. When, at last, the Goths destroyed the West, it is worthy of note that, through all the centuries of Byzantine splendour, Cavafy stays silent too. But when omens darken the sky over the City and the corridors fill up with desperate rumours, he finds his voice again. His times are of trouble.

Living in post-Khedivial Alexandria and born of half-Phanariot descent in Ottoman Constantinople, no one can better assess the blight of subjection to corrupt or barbarous powers or the fears and shifts that precede them. *Nourri dans le sérail, il en connaît les détours.* He may forgive the triviality and the subterfuge; he blames it too; but the survival of older virtue in the midst of indignity – the demeanour of a hostage queen when Sparta's glories have long since moulted, the symbolic content, surviving intact when a late emperor is crowned though coloured glass may have replaced all the gems – glimpses like these stir his tragic sense and his pity to their depths. 'The beds i' the East are soft'; indeed; many of the poems, through various voices, extol their softness. But suddenly an utterance in his own reveals a different set of values. An ostracized Athenian – surely Themistocles? – seeks refuge in enemy Persia, and Artaxerxes loads him with gifts. Stifling among satrapies and Oriental splendours, he pines for the frugal rewards of Athens:

> praise from the Demos, and the Sophists,
> that hard-won, that priceless acclaim –
> the Agora, the theatre and the crown of laurel

– they, not the cloying riches of the Levant, are the only wreaths worth running for. Thoughts like these keep breaking through: the waste of time which imprisons him – or his reader – like an inescapable city; the meaning of the jagged Ithaca at the long Odyssey's end; the immanent Ephialtes ready to sell the Thermopylae of the spirit. Issued without preamble from an atmosphere of earthly delights, these warnings sound as harsh, for a moment, as the words of Mercury after the songs of Apollo at the end of *Love's Labour's Lost.* His cast of mind is too diffident, too patrician and civilized for emphasis or apostrophe, but, detached in manner, by corollary almost, and as intermittently as the fragmentary sentences on his imaginary funeral slabs, a severe and didactic message coheres.

The wisdom and the sad austerity of the emerging figure is a surprising double to set beside the decadent hedonist which many seem to think his distinguishing image. And, as for the hedonism, even back among the Mareotic vapours and the trams and the minarets of the Egypt of Abbas Hilmi and Lord Cromer, his skill with time and myth and reality is such that there is no need to follow his inclinations in order to share their interpretation in poetry. He has the gift of making private memory, passion, loss and valediction, and even the most trivial frailties, seem noble, moving and universal and akin to the ancient grief for Adonis, but with no promise of return.

Interfering in Greece

Review of Kevin Andrews, *Athens Alive* (Athens:
Hermes, 1980), *The Times Literary Supplement*, 13 June 1980

The writings of Kevin Andrews stand completely on their own and they are neglected at peril by anyone concerned with contemporary Greece. His latest book, however, takes us many centuries back and a quick retrospective glance is needed before we follow him there.

Sprung from a Henry James-like background in the east of the United States, and at least half English, he was brought up mostly in England. Stoic by education and temperament at the end of schooldays which roughly overlapped with the war, he served in the United States Army and then took up a travelling fellowship awarded for a prize essay on Ancient Greece. 'I was the only entrant,' he typically informs us; and this eventually launched him on many recondite travels on foot in search of the great strongholds which the Byzantines, the Crusaders, the Venetians and the Turks have scattered about the Peloponnesian sierras. These travels gave birth to his first book, *The Castles of the Morea*, which remains a classic of scholarship.

He spent many months among the crenellations and the ravelins; they lengthened into years; and when he was not clambering about the wreckage, tape-measure in hand, he was wandering in the mountains, sleeping on brushwood and spooning up curds with his shepherd friends in caves and on high pastures. Thus classical Greek, thanks to a faultless ear, quickly slid into many varieties of rustic demotic. Airs on the flute, Klephtic songs, with all their modulations and semitones and the neumes of Byzantine plainsong, soon mounted up.

Cloaked and shaggy, he would suddenly appear in the capital, moving for a while among the Athenians like a blue-eyed scholar gypsy, taking wing again just as suddenly for the scorching Mani, 'a star one degree closer to the sun'; or for the goatfolds in the Geranian ranges of the Megarid, to which he was linked now by the bonds of godbrotherhood; or for one of the smaller Cyclades; or Mount Olympus.

This apprenticeship to the mountains coincided with a time of tragic upheaval, especially in the Morea. They were the years when the pendulum of bloodshed, unloosed by fierce doings during the Occupation and kept in motion as much by thirst for revenge as by any political impulse, was in full and pitiless swing. A hint of the ancient panic flickers about Greek scenery. It was not, however, the woodland god that stalked through the mountains now, but the grim giant of Goya's picture. The towns filled up with frightened villagers in flight from whichever side was prevailing. These bad times have only been depicted, by other writers, with journalists' sensationalism or blind bias; understandably so, perhaps; all thoughts to rive the heart were there, but not, in this particular case, all in vain . . . What was this young stranger doing in the middle of it all? Of course he was eyed with suspicion, but never for long: good humour, transparent innocence and pure chance made him friends in turn with some of the most ruthless of these mountain figures and with their victims. His notes began to describe more than ivied keeps; another book was taking shape. Hatred of injustice prevented him, in spite of the appalling deeds he records, from any rash placing of original blame; rightly, he wasn't there when the dragons' teeth were sown.

The book ends in America – exile, by now – with the author at pains to find out why so little United States aid reached the stricken regions to which, inevitably, he returned. Intuition, desperate concern, strong literary gifts, poetic flair, a marvellous knack for decanting the Greek vernacular into English – all these skilfully interwoven strands turn *The Flight of Ikaros* (Weidenfeld & Nicolson, 1959) into one of the great and lasting books about Greece, and it is high time that it was reprinted.

His next book – and the first about the capital – is dedicated to E. R. Dodds. Lurking on bookstalls in the sheep's clothing of a guidebook and aimed ostensibly at an American newcomer, *Athens* (Phoenix House, 1967) appeared after further years of assimilation. Slipping into disguise among the tourists who outnumber the inhabitants in summer – lost herds, unprepared alike for the hangover of the legend and the impact of the reality – he begins with a startling picture of the growing awfulness:

> City of Perikles, home of democracy, nurse of philosophy, birthplace of tragedy, cradle of culture, Boston of Europe, republic of

(wasn't it) Plato – clear or foggy, our conceptions of Athens are the very price-tags of our civilization. Yet what do we find in the place where it all began? A highly active boom-town, but with nothing (it would seem) volcanic either in the jellied relic of the past or in the anonymous concrete waffle solidifying round it as far as the eye can see. No schoolbooks ever prepared us for this sock in the jaw, though I believe it is just the rudeness of the blow that relates most to Athens in its heyday, which fought and ruled, enslaved and banished, enjoyed itself sometimes by horrendous means and told outsiders to advance at their own risk. A description of the place may reflect this aspect of it, so read on at your own risk and look out for falling masonry and rocketing assumptions.

And, of course, we do read on, identifying ourselves with these hypothetical tourists, while, up on the Parthenon, the stimulating near-misses crash past:

. . . the yawning entablatures, the long and slightly convex sweep of the architraves – what carries that high, grave, unbroken trajectory of stone . . . Under it in all weathers, by the thousands every day, you, I . . . blobs of coloured clothing, figures no higher than the second level of the drums, with not much in the way of eyeballs perhaps but with the best of viewfinders . . . pass flickering from carpets of unrolled shadow into avenues of light, oblivious to the tumult of the vertical: the great rude naked spiritual rock-borne urgency of all those Doric columns.

It is a bracing counterblast to the commercialization of the fifth century BC which plucks at the newcomer on every side and it promotes a salutary vacuum in which a truer inkling may take shape. But the pages stray down by ways of thought and history where no guide would ever lead. This brilliant iconoclastic feat disintegrates the past, the present, the tourists, the guides, the Greeks themselves and their history and reassembles them in a way that might fling a conventional reader into apoplexy.

But the reality of the ruins, re-cohering in cobalt and blood-red, studded with metal, gaudy with idols, shiny with spilt honey and blood and reeking with sacrificial smoke, will have replaced the tinted ivory artefacts that had stolen their place and the void between the cutting of the flutes on the columns and the laying of the tramlines begins to fill up with people and events. The reader learns to distrust the cleaned-up, Westernized version of Greece with which the authorities try to palm him off: official folk-dances, for instance, 'carefully resurrected, costumed in a way we shall never again see in a village, flawlessly executed and dead as mutton'; and, above all, the reduction of the actual Greeks, those ambulant cauldrons of flair, inferiority complex, megalomania, courage, energy, folly and improvisation, into evzone dolls. (Clearly, Kevin Andrews is not one of the settlers here whom love has made blind; shallow Philhellenism, as one might expect, gets it in the neck.) One of the springs of the book is the author's anger at this doctoring of the facts all for the benefit of gently nurtured and wholly imagined foreigners: 'We don't want them to think we're Mau Mau.' Translations of the book should be compulsory throughout the Secretariat of Tourism and on the tables of every town-planner, mayor, nomarch and civil engineer in the country; all those in fact, who will only be happy when Greece, from Sunium to the top of Olympus, is safely concreted over.

Between *Athens* and *Athens Alive* his most notable items have been a perceptive essay on his friend Louis MacNeice (mine too; perhaps this is the right moment to say that I have been Kevin Andrews's friend for over thirty years) and *First Will and Testament*. This moving poem of about *Waste Land* length, published as a book in Athens and possibly not well known outside, is written with great poetic force and metrical skill. Autobiographical and topical in an elliptic way, it is a kind of exorcism of anguish and private trouble; and, most importantly, an act of protest and defiance, necessarily veiled, against the Dictatorship, which is when it first saw the light. The author was passionately involved in opposition to this regime, and when it suddenly came to an end he relinquished his American citizenship. So this singular figure, seated at his desk among a turmoil of papers or up since dawn like Hephaistos beating out torques and armlets on the beak of his anvil – and, in spite of his linguistic virtuosity, unmistakably an offshoot of both Atlantic shores – is now legally Greek. As the flow of nationalization is all the other way, this gesture must be almost unique. It calls to mind Henry James becoming English when his adoptive country was in a tight spot. The author is a life-long votary of the Master.

This brings us to *Athens Alive* – not to be confused with *Athens* by itself: a fascinating assembly of texts, over 300 pages of them, by Greeks and foreigners. Each entry concerns a different aspect and period of the city and its inhabitants. It covers most of the last two millennia and ends in 1940. This is a book of the greatest interest; one which it would be folly to be without; if I have complaints they are minor ones, easily over-ridden, or, if justified, put right; and here they are. Kevin Andrews, the most assimilated and tribalized of writers on Greece – in Haggard or Conrad terms, many days' march upstream in the hinterland of Romiosyne – is kind to his readers as a rule, pointing out hazards and helping them over styles. But his attitude here becomes mysteriously quelling, even touched with asperity, and the book's alternative title – 'The Practical Tourist's Companion to the Fall of Man' – compounds the reader's disarray.

'May the book succeed as propaganda,' the foreword says:

> the collection is addressed to the general reader ... but it is also aimed, with malice aforethought, in the direction of those earnest functionaries in the world's more active government agencies and business corporations who occasionally read books, to supplement their knowledge of a place and its inhabitants, while pursuing their steely but always fatal purposes of geo-politics and geo-merchandise.

The gnomic irony and obliquity of address make the reader more fidgety still. Plainly, the author suspects him of associating with secret agents, even of being one himself: a sinister transatlantic figure, perhaps, with a snap-brim Stetson and a manilla envelope full of laundered bribes; or an Iron Curtain operator with tundra-face, catfish smile and mortal umbrella. (Rather the former, it emerges later on, though the latter seemed just as likely a candidate for terminal bogey.) 'In this connexion,' he concludes, 'the present volume, though spanning sixteen centuries, has a specific reference – for those with ears to hear – to the time and place of compilation. Athens 1967–1974.' This exactly covers the Colonels' rule. If the book had come out then, dark innuendos would have been the only safe tone for a writer living in Greece. But the regime ended six years ago, the tyrants are behind bars, protests against foreign interference fill headlines and are boldly sloshed over furlongs of wall, and, at the very moment of writing, pacifically escorted young men in tousled thousands are marching through the capital under a forest of banners, punching the air by numbers. Cheerleaders with electric megaphones beat time to scanned accusations of treachery launched at the very figure who was thought, when the Colonels fell, to have rescued the country from chaos. With freedom of speech in so healthy a state the author's manner is strangely cloaked and circumspect, almost as though he missed clandestine times.

The foreword promises a sequel embracing the period from the Second World War until the aftermath of the Dictatorship. This is excellent news. The scrupulous fairness of *The Flight of Ikaros* soared high above the prevalent bias and melodrama; Volume 2, when it appears, will have different virtues. As we see, recent years have filled the author with feelings which are hot and partisan, so the result is certain to be lively, stimulating, and avowedly *de parti pris*. But, for myself, the great point of this still unseen work is that it might act as a catharsis. Polemical writing, which many can do, may at last take a step to the rear and make way for the sort of book which none but Kevin can produce. I don't know what his political allegiances are; possibly none; but I think Orwell's touchstone of 'common decency' would not be far off the mark: *First Will and Testament* was full of a passionate intensity, and it was all the better for it; but in *Athens Alive*, I think it pulls the wrong way.

All through post-classical history, Greece has been interfered with and exploited by foreigners and it is time this stopped. This, in simple terms, is the book's dominating theme. The author points out that in times of stress, Greece has saved herself by her own efforts. He doesn't point out that occasionally foreign help was neither selfish nor ignoble. But his main contention is true; it is depressing; it applies to other countries, though not for so long, it is a good theme for an essay. But it is too limiting a selective principle for this wonderful array of historical texts. The vigour of his manner could get the message through the reader's skull in a couple of pages: the texts themselves would hammer it home. Choosing passages only to point up a story of injustice and hard luck would have excluded too much that was valuable, so it is very fortunate that he often strays.

Meanwhile, what has become of our kind companion of *Athens*? The shared jokes, the outrageous outbursts, the bitter draughts so skilfully administered? The characters of most of the authors quoted have an interest apart from their works; they are well worth a few lines of introduction and perhaps an anecdote or two; and how well our former companion would have done it, weaving the whole thing into a continuous and captivating whole!

Instead, in the grip of his new anti-reader drive, the author packs us off each time to the six stark pages of bibliographical data at the back of the book. (My mind flies to a similar work, brilliantly carried out, but dealing with the much shorter period of 1453 to 1821: *Fair Greece, Sad Relic*, by the late Terence Spencer.) Our old *Athens* mentor would have redressed the balance of the letterpress, for all the editorial comment is reduced to lower-case footnotes and these, by their very nature, are condemned to seem simultaneously cramped and inordinately long. Our absent friend would have loosened them up, expanded and promoted them and then have guided them into a single flow with the text, with both on equal terms. As it is the two are sometimes so unwieldily off balance that the page looks like capsizing. Their drift, however, is just as absorbing as, from this pen, we have a right to expect.

Athens Alive is a paperback printed in the city it describes; the contents are of much more than passing interest; it will be reprinted; and I foresee hardback editions in England and America with the editorial apparatus unmuffled and updated – no great labour; it is less than a tenth of the whole – and adorned with illustrations. Could its scope not be widened? Yes, but what about the book's message, the author might ask: the full dessertspoon every half-hour? Well, I think the bottle should be given a good shake and the dose drastically reduced. Or perhaps he might simply let it stand in the cupboard. After all, he's the patient.

The author defendably starts his sequence with the Roman conquest rather than the battle of Chaeronea, and his first entry is a passage from Ovid about the city's desolation followed, after a three centuries leap to early Byzantine times, by a Syrian Greek's riveting account of the near-kidnapping of unwary new students by rival teachers of rhetoric. (Between these two might be glimpsed the lines of Juvenal describing the needy little Athenian émigré, by turns grammarian, narrator, painter, tightrope-walker, etc., 'ready to fly to heaven if you tell him'; all the more aptly as he is identified with Daedalus – the author's parent, mythologically speaking.) By now the city is sinking to a little provincial town of the Eastern Empire, vainly clinging to faded shreds of greatness. But there is enjoyable bickering still among the sophists, students' high spirits and riots now and then; in spite of the official change of religion, the mysteries in Eleusis are winked at and the Neoplatonic threat to orthodoxy riddles the shrunken population with exciting discord. Sneered at by the saintly, Julian the Apostate invokes the briefly reinstated Athena; and, a few decades later, appearing all-armed on the walls, she saves her city from the Goths.

For the first time (in my case) we read the Theodosian edicts against sacrificing; then Justinian snuffs out the philosophy schools, breaking the city's last links with Plato and Aristotle. This had an unexpected result: the philosophers fled to Persia where they were welcomed by Chosroes and showered with honours; but they sickened for home just like Themistocles among the satraps at Susa a thousand years earlier. The Great King relinquished them with sorrow and he even managed to extort toleration for their heterodoxy when they got back. These recondite and enthralling details come as much from the small print of the author's notes as from the texts themselves. They are full of interesting and rare illuminations like this, also of penetrating and original thoughts. One, which would have pleased Dodds, is that a strange kind of manic madness rushes to the help of the Greeks when things are at their worst. Alaric's vision of Athene Promachos had been positively her last appearance. When, half a millennium later, Basil the Bulgar-Slayer flung himself down in the Parthenon before its reigning patroness, the halo of a newer Virgin had replaced the shining helmet and the great semi-circle of horsehair. How scarce are the annals now! And how sad it is, in 1182, when Archbishop Michael Akominatos – a Phrygian Greek from Constantinople – finds that the speech of his flock is barbarized almost beyond understanding!

All at once, the villainous Fourth Crusade fills the landscape with marauding knights and long passages of medieval Burgundian put everything into enthralled slow motion: 'En celle manière come vous aves oÿ, si fu faict l'acort et le pays dou seignor de la Roche au Prince Guillerme. Et puis que la pais fut faicte et complie li jone bachellier mennerent grant feste de joustes, de rompre lances a la quintaine, et de caroles' – it is as though the castle were being captured and the lances splintered at the bottom of a treacle-well. The Low Latin pages of Maroni's 1395 chronicle may not be hard – 'Civitas Acthenarum ut hostendis per antiqua hedeficia alias fuit magna civitas in ea fuerunt, prout vidimus multas columpnas' etc – but it might make the hypothetical CIA reader scratch his head a bit, and here he would not get much help from the footnote, for it is medicine time; the author is lashing himself into a rage about General Metaxas, the Truman doctrine and NATO, so hasten on to the 1436 narrative of Cyriac of Ancona . . .

Speaking of the plight of Athens in the Dark Ages, the author thinks that the latter-day Greeks may have been unjust in blaming all the desolation on the Turks, though they certainly helped. Rather unexpectedly the first account of the city, two centuries after its capture in 1453, is by a Moslem, and the style of Evliya Chelebi has a strong touch of the Arabian Nights about it. The picture that he and his Giaour successors conjure up – pillars, cupolas, cypress-trees, ruins full of owls, stork-harbouring minarets; janissaries with pipes as long as their muskets yawning among the tumbled capitals, idle or oppressive *disdars*; the downtrodden and clever Greeks, pliant notables, cylinder-hatted priests, turbaned hodjas, and the vertigo-proof dervishes of the Tower of the Winds gyrating and ululating in their dark octagon. These things set the pattern until the end of the Turkish incumbency.

Here is an unforgettable glimpse, out of Dodwell, of the Greek secretary of an oppressive *voivode*:

Galloping through the narrow streets of Athens and endangering the lives and limbs of the passengers, he was easily distinguished at a distance mounted on a white horse with its tail and mane dyed of an orange colour, and he was attended by other horsemen who played on the violin as he rode.

Lifting all the storks from their nests, a Venetian bomb wrecks the Parthenon in the middle of this lapse of time; towards the end, Lord Elgin makes off with everything but the columns. The shovel-hats of Jesuits and Capuchins, the wideawakes of architectural draughtsmen and the tricorns of dilettanti join the queer and varied headgear of the village; and soon, far away in the libraries of the West, handsomely got-up volumes begin to appear. (Nine pages of lively reminiscence and instructive but marvellously implausible conversation are quoted from Guillet de la Guilletière, who never set foot in Greece: a reference to 'his supposed visit' is not quite enough warning against this diverting old fraud.) A mass of documents mounts up as 1821 approaches, with Lord Byron, quite rightly, well in the lead; just as Makryannis, when the country finally bursts into flames, is unchallenged among the warlike chroniclers. Nobody catches the flavour so well or describes it more simply. At the grimmest moment of the siege of the Acropolis, in command of a desperate handful of defenders, suddenly, over supper, he makes it up with a brother-in-arms with whom he had long fallen out; and he sings an old mountain-song they both remember: '"Brother Makryannis", Gouras said, "May this song bode well for us." "I was in the mood," I said, "for we had not sung for so long." For formerly, in our camps, we were always singing and making merry . . .' But towards moonset, bullets began to fly . . . 'Gouras fired at the Turks, they shot back at the flash and hit him in the temple and he never spoke a word . . .' The survivor led the breakout through the Turkish trenches. He was slashed by yataghans and hit by bullets again and again. With his head laid open and several bones smashed by trampling, he was flung senseless across a saddle . . . who would have thought that Greece would have been free only three years later? Or that the old Klepht would learn to read and write just to set it all down for us?

This great landmark is only halfway through the book. The task of selection must have been enormously complicated by the nineteenth-century rush of material and the chaotic sequel to the War of Independence: the tension between the old and the new forces – Mani towers, mountain caves, the Phanar, the guaranteeing powers, the despotic Bavarian triumvirate that governed Greece under a Wittelsbach King, the struggle for a constitution, brigandage in league with authority, coups, changes of dynasty, spongebag trousers ousting the kilt – all this is minutely documented. There are famous names – Chateaubriand, Lamartine, Finlay, Aubrey de Vere, Flaubert, Gautier, Gobineau and – once again anathema in Athens except to a few perceptive eyes – Edmond About.

But these are outnumbered by names less known, or not known at all, and some of the texts have been unearthed and published here for the first time. The extraordinary rustic narrative (1905) of Eva Palmer is one of these. This eccentric New York millionairess friend of Isadora Duncan became the foundress of the revived Delphic Festivals and the wife of the flamboyant laureate Sikilianos. (In a revised version, there would be a swarm of outside suggestions, a plea, even, for the flippant and the transitory as well as the learned; E. F. Benson, perhaps, for smart life in Edwardian times, Compton Mackenzie for the Venizelist-Royalist intrigues of the Great War, Robert Byron on the late 1920s, Cyril Connolly for a *thé dansant* of businessmen at the Grande Bretagne Hotel during the 1935 revolt. At the other end of the scale, I would sigh for an excerpt or two from Renan's *Prière sur l'Acropole*: but, such are the revolutions of taste, he may be as much a bane to Kevin Andrews as Fallmerayer was to the Athenians of a few generations ago.) He is right to stretch his terms of reference to include Hemingway's reports; he filed them as a young war correspondent in Smyrna and eastern Thrace: they describe, unforgettably, the Asia Minor campaign and the catastrophe that followed, and no part of Greek history more damagingly bears out the author's theme or has had a longer influence on Athens today.

No review can adequately explore this Aladdin's cave. One can only hope, by darting about inside it, to give some idea of its richness and variety. A dark, brooding, rather perplexing mood weighs on the book as it nears its end, just as the author wished; pens may be decked with myrtle as well as the blades of tyrannicides but I can't help longing for this particular quill to be laid out with scores of others for the great symmetrical pinions to be stuck together again, feather to feather; and at last, for the author to take wing, high above the snow-covered mountain chains and the archipelagos, as of old.

I wonder whether he was assaulted on finishing by the same escapist urge that lays hold of the reader? The dash for the bookcase, the wish to be lifted by magic to an earlier city, before the fumes of today had driven the Caryatids from their plinth, after twenty-three hundred years? Before the book has started, even; before all the trouble began?

> From of old the children of Erechtheus are
> Splendid, the sons of blessed gods. They dwell
> In Athens' holy and unconquered land,
> Where famous wisdom feeds them, and they pass gaily
> Always through that most brilliant air, where once, they say
> That golden Harmony gave birth to nine
> Pure muses of Pieria.*

* Euripides, *Medea*, translated by Rex Warner.

Dragons and Windmills

Review of *Robert Byron: Letters Home*, ed. Lucy Butler
(John Murray, 1991), *The Spectator*, 20 April 1991

It was only in his twenties that Robert Byron thought much about the identity of his surname with the poet's. The precise link, several centuries back, was blurred by lack of records, but both sets of Byrons sprang from Lancashire; the affinity had always been taken for granted; they were similar in background and heraldically identical and the degree of probability is very high. It means nothing, of course, that both stars were marked by originality, precocity, extreme intelligence, combativeness, courage, humour and a strong literary gift; but, had the centuries been switched, his ghostly lordship would surely have rejoiced in the thought of a link with his namesake.

As a brilliant letter-writer himself, he would have enjoyed this collection. It is impossible not to. All the letters are written to Robert Byron's mother and the racy vigour, indiscretion and wit, and the feeling, even at school, of grown-up complicity, shadow forth, like the unheard half of a telephone conversation, an addressee of great intelligence, astringency, kindness and comic sense. He loved his parents and his two sisters, this collection has been made by one of them, and her editing, introduction and explanatory notes – apart from an unawareness of the meaning of 'protagonist' (a foible shared by her brother which would have evoked a groan from Fowler) – are impeccable.

The earliest letters are from Eton, which he enjoyed in spite of getting into trouble over the ritual opening of an umbrella on an Officers' Training Corps parade. He professed scorn for aestheticism, but went flat-out for Art and architecture and the company of fellow-addicts, and remained true to all of them for good. His closest friends were Henry Yorke, later the Henry Green of *Living, Party Going* and *Loving* – and Lord Clonmore, a charming, vague, Anglo-Irish Betjemanesque High Anglican. (Converts, Anglo-Catholics and Roman Catholics were among Robert's pretended abominations, but he had close friends among all three, cf., later on, Christopher Sykes.) When he was sixteen, he and Brian Howard lured Sir John Rothenstein down to talk to the Arts Society; transported, Robert poured his theories into letters.

> In the old days [he wrote] Artists were *given* their subjects. They painted to *order*, more or less – set subjects, crucifixions or battle-scenes ... The Renaissance broke away from this, but still set subjects were painted – portraits and classical legends; then the Pre-Raphaelites tried to break away from this again and to paint *what they saw*. But then *others*, breaking away even more, left entirely to themselves ever since the Renaissance, flew to light and abstract form – just as abstract philosophy never solidifies, so modern art, brought about by this process, is only to be regarded in the light of an interesting experiment ...

Similar pages, laced with anecdotes and amusing gossip, flew home to Savernake Forest in an unbroken stream. This house and forest, and the family, dogs, horses and trees, and the exciting friends his mother's hospitality assembled there, became the haven he pined for on his travels. (In some bug-ridden Asian khan, he would dream that his dog had climbed on his bed and flung her forelegs round his neck or that he was pelting across country on his hunter Aubrey. These longings often recur.)

The cast at Oxford – Harold Acton with megaphone and grey bowler in the lead and captured to a T by Evelyn Waugh – constitute one of the century's riddles. Corks popped round the chief actors for much of the day, they were tight every night, 'dressing up' for party after party – Robert's impersonation of Queen Victoria was famous – or hammering out jazz on the piano till dawn; hangovers left just time enough for buying a bowl of Victorian wax fruit next day or, in the case of David Talbot Rice, 'for soaring over fences with the Heythrop like a heron in flight'; London was less than an hour away with its Great Houses and their glamorous denizens still inside them, and fascinating night-clubs dark as Tartarus beckoned; how, in the long run, could this enjoyable chaos turn out such a constellation of brilliant successes? In the short run, many came temporarily to grief. Robert Byron dispelled the fumes long enough to deliver lectures on Turner and filled the *Cherwell* with notions and theories; he read scores of learned, abstruse and extracurricular books; but he came down with a third-class degree he never bothered to collect.

Foreign travel was suddenly vital. He had very little money; journalism was the Open Sesame; so, with no evidence of capacity but his compulsive vim, Monomarks and Coppers had to be talked round. For magic carpet, there were like-minded aesthete-hedonists with motor-cars and cash, and Europe was their oyster.

The adventures and mishaps of the earliest journey were an intellectual *Three Men in a Boat*. The encounters and incidents are illustrated by lively and comic sketches which are much better than the rather over-finished formal pictures that appear in some of his books. The jaunt culminated in Greece where, for Robert at any rate, the discovery of the amazing and unspoilt beauty of the country, backed by the electrifying effect of his name on the inhabitants, set the stage for a life-long love affair. Preliminary reading had laid the way, Ravenna was the first visual hint, then the monasteries of Mistra, Daphni, St Luke and finally, St Sophia itself confirmed it.

This in turn led on to a memorable examination of Mount Athos with David Talbot Rice and Mark Ogilvie-Grant and the results are concentrated and distilled in *The Station*. Packed with original insights and evocations of the history and treasures and, above all, with their journey and the strange life, and bursting with vitality and humour, the book came out when he was just twenty-three. (Its impact and effect on at any rate one reader remain vivid. When, ten years later, I was about to set off on European travels, the sudden discovery altered my whole itinerary and, one thing leading to another, perhaps the course of a lifetime.)

These letters are the untreated raw material of his literary achievement and it is fascinating to see that none of the original verve was lost in the marvellously written final shapes. It is easy to forget how little about Byzantium, outside archaeological circles, was known in the 1920s, at any rate in England. In his attacks on Ancient Greece, he hoped to lift the killing shadow into which the classical past, by comparison, plunged the Eastern Roman Empire; he was at war with many centuries of scholastic bias; Gibbon and Leckie and Fallmerayer were his enemies; and when, next year, *The Byzantine Achievement* appeared he was conducting us round a Byzantine Empire from which, he hoped, the classical incubus had been exorcized. More surprising than either of these, perhaps, was the vast illustrated tome he compiled with David Talbot Rice, *The Birth of Western Painting*. It traces the descent and the flowering of a tradition to which Byzantium gave birth and which, in the West, breathed its last in Spain with the death of El Greco. He was at grips, in fact, with a resurgence of his old classical enemy, this time in the stately new trappings of the Renaissance. I reacted to this book years later, by hotly exhorting a hesitant reader:

> You will follow and perhaps disagree with his arguments. They explain how the same (Cappadocian Byzantine) trends blossomed simultaneously in Florence and Siena; where, short-circuiting Constantinople and Athos, Byzantine influence had already been at work in the pictures of Giotto, Duccio, Cimabue, Lorenzetti and Barna da Siena. You will be following the prominence and eclipse of Byzantine Art and enjoying some of the most spirited uncircumspect and powerful English prose of this century. It resembles a mettled horse. You may smile at the brio with which he deals with obstacles and opposition. Instead of evading or dismantling them, he points out the target, as it were with a sabre, and then with dazzling bravura, clears it in a bold leap or gallops over it roughshod, slashes and kicks it to matchwood and rides on.

Obviously, I was under his spell; and, mutatis mutandis, still am; lost in admiration, anyway. 'That some of his dragons long since turned out to be no more than windmills,' writes Talbot Rice, 'has, perhaps, to some extent been due to the violence of Byron's attack.'

The same pace carried him next year all over India and, most adventurously, deep into Tibet and then all over Russia in search of northern Byzantine traditions in the Slav world and the painting of Rublev. (He hated the regime but was fascinated by the country. One of the surprises of this remarkable book is the fact that the bias and rage that sometimes smoke from the page are often contradicted flat a score of pages on. These are private letters. It is as it should be.) Persia and Afghanistan, in pursuit of Timurid pre-Mogul remains with Christopher Sykes, was a protracted, hair-raising and wonderful adventure, richly rewarded by Yezd, Kabus, Herat, Balkh and Ghazni. They were worth all the snow-bound halts, the scarce or uneatable food – Byron hated hardship for its own sake – the vermin and the arrests on suspicion of espionage. Another bonus was the marvellous, page-long hilarious sequences of conversation with Shir Ahmed, the Afghan ambassador; they are scored like an opera and noted *diminuendo*, *piano*, and *crescendo*, the *fortissimo* sometimes swelling into capitals; and they leave the reader feeling weak. The result, *The Road to Oxiana*, is his triumph. There was always something odd to notice: 'The Russian consul here is not so austere as some comrades. He dresses in loud tweeds like Bloomsbury in the country': and in one frightful Christmas in Meshed he thinks ruefully of his Sitwell fellow-guests at Polesden Lacey the year before: 'I would enjoy a few minutes conversation with Sachie and Georgia!' Crossing Siberia, he spent months alone to write in a friend's house in Peking – Peiping then, before its jingo avatar – and suffered a breakdown of health and worked his way home through Japan and the United States.

War overshadows the last few letters. ('Ran says Sandy Macpherson at the Wurlitzer organ on the BBC is definitely lowering the morale of the fleet.') After a long search, he found a slot in the conduct of the war where his knowledge of Asia could have been of tremendous secret use; but, heading for the Middle East, his ship was torpedoed by the *Scharnhorst* off the north coast of Scotland. It was 24 February 1941. He was thirty-six. He was never found; and we can never know how many brilliant unwritten sequels to *The Station* and *The Road to Oxiana* were also lost off Stornaway.

Flotsam

Gluttony

from *The Seven Deadly Sins* (Sunday Times Publications, 1962)

In 1962 the Sunday Times *commissioned a series of articles by well-known authors on the Seven Deadly Sins. Angus Wilson wrote on Envy, Edith Sitwell on Pride, and Paddy on Gluttony. Covetousness fell to Cyril Connolly. Evelyn Waugh tackled Sloth, Lust was by Christopher Sykes, and Anger by W. H. Auden. The articles were later gathered into a small book with an introduction by Raymond Mortimer.*

'Gluttony. Yes. Let me see.' Mr Vortigern paused in the pillared doorway to light a cigar, and his ruminative murmur was punctuated by puffs.

'*Voracitas* . . . Γαστριμαργία . . . *Gola* . . . *Gourmandise* . . . Yes . . .' His cigar properly alight, he sailed down the steps to the sunlit street in an aromatic cloud. No one would have thought this hale and elegant figure was seventy-five.

'I have been a martyr to it, in a mild way, all my life,' he resumed as we headed for St James's Palace. 'So its presence among the Seven Deadly Sins has always bothered me. I console myself with the thought that Ambrose and Augustine – or was it St Clement? – had monks in mind more than laymen when the Deadly Sins first emerged; and, of course, they needed some corrective to late Roman excesses and barbarian disorder.

'You only have to read about the *vomitoria* and Trimalchio's feast in Petronius to get the point. And what was the name of that senator who had slaves walking backwards in front of him to carry his paunch? And what about Pollio – Vedius, not Asinius – who lived in Naples in the time of Augustus? He used to punish his slaves by throwing them into the tank where he kept his fish because he thought that a diet of live humans improved the flavour. And barbarian banquets were filthy. Think of those raw slabs of meat the Huns used to strap between their saddle flaps and the flanks of their horses! Things had got out of hand.

'There's nothing against good living in itself. We have only to remember the Marriage at Cana. St Benedict allowed his monks a *hemina* of wine with their meals. And look at the distilling traditions of the monastic orders, and the description of the Abbot's meal in Phtochoprodromos, the Byzantine poet. There has always been a port-drinking Horace-quoting tradition in Anglican cathedral closes, and all those paintings of cardinals clinking glasses must be founded on something.'

Mr Vortigern's humorous agate eyes caught mine for a moment. 'Do you know the story the Romans are so fond of about a Pope – a fairly recent one too and a saintly man – at the gates of Paradise? You don't? Well, there is a tradition that St Peter stands aside, when a supreme Pontiff arrives, to allow his successor to let himself in with his own keys. This one, who was famous for his appreciation of wine, was embarrassed to find himself, after a lot of twisting and turning, still locked out.' Mr Vortigern laughed. 'He had brought the keys of the Vatican cellar by mistake . . .

'What are the five ways of sinning by gluttony . . . ? *Praepropere, laute, nimis, ardenter, studiose?*' Mr Vortigern ticked them off on his fingers. 'Too soon, too expensively, too much, too eagerly, and making too much of a fuss. I am guilty on all points, alas; but at least I can be acquitted of St John of the Cross's Spiritual Gluttony . . . Too much and too eagerly are the worst. I shudder to think of myself as a boy, reeling from the table stunned with toad-in-the-hole and sausages and mash and jelly and spotted dog, and steeped in sin. And the torments that followed! Hell on earth!

'Mercifully, a glimmer of moderation came with riper years. For, now that Science has disarmed Lust of its retaliatory powers, Gluttony is the only one of the Deadly Seven which is visited by physical retribution this side of the tomb.

'Its vengeance is far more convincing than Dante's penalty for gluttons – permanent hounding by Cerberus in a non-stop hail-storm. Spiritual sins may rack the conscience, fill us with misery, lay the soul waste, and turn our hearts to stone. Alas, they do! But at least they don't ruin our blood pressure or hobnail our livers. What are snarling and hailstones compared with the pangs of indigestion, palpitations, muck-sweats, heartburn, bilious attacks, d.t.s., real alcoholism, nicotine poisoning? The Fathers didn't reckon with this.' Mr Vortigern flourished his cigar. 'What torments can match the agony of a chainsmoker short of tobacco? Surely these earthly pains and humiliations should shorten our sentences later on? And what about obesity, bottle-noses, bleary eyes, grog-blossoms and breath like a blowlamp? It is the only sin which turns us into monsters. I have got off lightly so far.' Mr Vortigern glanced with satisfaction at his reflection in a gunsmith's window. 'At least *girth* control invites no anathema, if we can but practise it. Always remember that outside every thin man lurks a fat man trying to climb in.

'The Germans are the worst, for sheer bulk. What miles of liver sausage, what oceans of beer: the quagmires of those colossal bellies! How appalling they look from behind; the terrible creases of fat three deep across solid and shaven napes! Necks wreathed in smiles, the stigmata of damnation; and delusive smiles, for when they turn round there is nothing but a blank stare and a jigsaw of fencing scars. If you are ever losing an argument with such a one you can always win by telling him to wipe those smiles off the back of his neck . . .

'The outward effects of food are a sure guide. In England they are very noticeable. Prosperous Edwardians had an unmistakable ptarmigan sheen. There was beef and claret in the faces of the squirearchy, cabbage and strong Indian tea among Non-conformists, and limpid blue eyes in the Navy, due to Plymouth gin, and so on. Above all, a general look of low spirits that tells its own tale. Those puddings named after Crimean battles, that coffee that tastes like boiled horseshoes . . . !'

Mr Vortigern shuddered. 'Meals as joyless as a moth's dark banquet in a cupboard. Everything tastes like a substitute. I think the flight from reality must have begun when Norman names superseded the Saxon after the Conquest – mutton for sheep, beef for ox, and so on – breaking into a gallop later on by the use of French in eating-houses. It culminates in those Bohemian little "Continental" restaurants whose walls are festooned with papier mâché chickens, dummy mortadellas and cardboard hams, all too emblematic of the phantom food below. The English seek escape from this ghost world in sporting preoccupations and foreign enterprise and occasionally in poetry. It's the same with the Irish. Have you ever eaten an Irish meal? Their literature has nothing to do with oppression, religion or the twilight. It is flight from the cruel realities of the table.

'These are effects by reaction; direct results are still more striking. Curry induces instability of temper and fosters discord; hot Mexican food leads to cruelty, just as surely as blubber, the staple of the Eskimos, spells torpid indifference. And look at the Belgians, the supreme exemplars of high living and low thinking! The rancid oil they cook with in Spain tastes as though it was straight out of a sanctuary lamp; no wonder the country is prone to bigotry. Vodka turns Russian faces into steppes, featureless tundras with eyes like minute and uncharted Siberian lakes. And those extraordinary grey complexions of the Americans I attribute entirely to breakfast foods, jumbo steaks, soft drinks, milk shakes and ice-cream at all hours, washed down by conditioned air and crooning.'

Mr Vortigern's words had brought us to the Mall. We crossed into the park and he smoked thoughtfully for a minute. 'The most convincing example of the influence of food on national character is Italy. Look at Italian art. Pasta wrecked it! Some say it was imported from the Orient by Marco Polo. Others that an old woman discovered it in Naples in the time of Frederick II of Hohenstaufen, the *stupor mundi*. I favour the second theory. Cimabue and Giotto and Duccio lived on dried fish and polenta and beans and black bread and olives. And you can't picture Dante eating spaghetti, or Amico di Sandro wolfing ravioli down. They lived on hard tack from the Trecento to the Renaissance, you mark my words.

'Then *pasta asciutta* came. It must have taken a century or two to conquer Italy, spreading from the south like a clammy and many-tentacled monster, smothering Italy's genius on its northward journey, and strangling its artists like the serpents of Laocoön. Thousands of seething and dripping tongues of macaroni squirming and coiling up the Apennines, gathering volume every mile, engulfing towns and provinces and slowly subduing the whole peninsula. The North held out heroically for a while – there is no pasta in those banquets of Veronese – and the last stand was at Venice. The rest of the country lay inert under its warm and slippery bonds – slippery, perhaps, but still unbroken today – while Tiepolo held out, and Longhi and Guardi and Canaletto, the last lonely frontiersmen of a fallen Empire.

'But one day some treacherous dauber must have swallowed a streaming green yard or two of *tagliatelle* – the end of the enemy's foremost tentacle, you might say – and, hotfoot, the rest of the huge, victorious monster came coiling into the Veneto and reared itself for the kill. And then –' the end of Mr Vortigern's malacca cane, which had been describing faster and faster loops in the air, stopped in mid-sweep – 'and then, wallop! A billion boiling tons of pasta fell on the town, and the proud city, the sea's bride, with her towers and domes and bridges and monuments and canals, went under. The piazzas were a tragic squirming tangle of spaghetti and lasagne, the lagoon ran red with tomato sauce. Italy's genius was dead, laid low by her own gluttony . . . not only Italy's painting, but Italian thought and poetry and literature and rhetoric and even Italian architecture. Everything was turned into macaroni.'

Mr Vortigern fell silent. The world seemed locked for a while in an elegiac hush. 'But,' he resumed at last, 'it had its compensations. Baroque's debt to pasta has never been fully recognized. In fountain statuary its influence was supreme. Think of those beautiful fountains at the Villa d'Este and Bagnaia! Think of the Piazza Navona and the Piazza di Trevi! Where do you think they found the inspiration for all those bearded Tritons, those Neptunes and gushing river gods and sea beasts, those swirling beards and fish tails and manes, all ending in water weed? That feeling for tempestuous and tangled flow, of deliquescence, of solidity in flux, that brio and speed and sweep?

'Where but in those swirling ingurgitated forkloads, those wild mealtime furlongs that keep a Roman going? They are pure Bernini, an Italian dinner played backwards, Gorgon-struck in mid-swoop . . . Conversely, how eatable post-Renaissance Italian architecture looks – scagliola rock cakes, Carrara barley sugar, marzipan statuary, pasta in travertine, ceilings and cloudbursts straight out of an icing-gun! It is not for nothing that the Victor Emmanuel monument is called the Wedding Cake. Perhaps,' Mr Vortigern continued with a change of key, 'one should adopt a gastronomic approach to all architecture, like a cannibal's attitude towards his fellow mortals. The Taj Mahal would be delicious, especially on a hot day. Gothic horrible; too bony. And I would not care for a square meal of Corbusier, either. Too square by half and far too austere. The food might be concrete, I feel, and the drink abstract . . .

'Cannibalism is a problem. In many cases the practice is rooted in ritual and superstition rather than gastronomy, but not always. A French Dominican in the seventeenth century observed that the Caribs had most decided notions on the relative merits of their enemies. As one would expect, the French were delicious, by far the best. This is no surprise, even allowing for nationalism. The English came next, I'm glad to say. The Dutch were dull and stodgy and the Spaniards so stringy, they were hardly a meal at all, even boiled. All this sounds sadly like gluttony.

'France, you will agree, is the place where the instinct has been most successfully harnessed and exploited. But this pre-eminence exacts a cruel price. The liver! That is their Achilles heel! It is a national scourge, brought on by those delicious sauces, by all those truffles and chopped mushrooms peeping through the liquid beige. Every Frenchman over fifty writhes under its torments. He is a chained Prometheus, a victim of the tribal inventiveness. Only it's no vulture that pecks at the weak spot but the phantom and vengeful beaks of an army of geese from Strasbourg. Now the Chinese –'

Mr Vortigern broke off. A mild flurry of excitement and a scatter of clapping reached our ears across the flower beds. We caught a glimpse of a long motor-car with a flag on the bonnet, and a gloved hand in the window fluttering in gracious acknowledgement. Mr Vortigern gravely raised his hat.

'Diet and royalty,' he said as he replaced it, 'there's a rewarding theme! Not only in our fortunate kingdom but all over Europe. It is the supreme illustration of the importance of regular meals over long periods. There's no question here of that unsettling swing between unwilling frugality and neurotic stuffing which has been the lot of most commoners. It is a matter of excellent meals in unfaltering continuity.

'Think of a chart of royal quarterings, each coat representing an ancestor and the number doubling with each receding generation; two parents, four grandparents, eight great-grandparents – sixteen, thirty-two, sixty-four, a hundred and twenty-eight, doubling each time – you've got over a thousand in only ten generations, and by the fourteenth century, counting four generations a century, over eight million.

'Eight million splendidly fed forebears! Turn this upside-down' – the ferrule of his cane drew an isosceles, the ferrule swept from left to right in an airy hypotenuse – 'and it becomes the base of a steaming pyramid of regular and wonderful meals – quadrillions of them! – on the apex of which each royal person is seated. Of course there are one or two hungry strains – the Bonapartes, perhaps, the Karageorgevitches and the Montenegrins – mountain life, you know, and the hardships of a pastoral calling – but the rest seldom skipped a meal. A religious ascetic here and there, I dare say, and perhaps a vegetarian or two in the last hundred years, but otherwise, it is an imposing edifice of breakfasts and luncheons and teas and dinners and, no doubt, delicious late suppers. A fragrant and unfailing counterweight to the cares of State.

'*It was all good stuff*, that is the point! And what is the result of this magnificent continuity? A much rarer quality than mere looks or brains or brawn, a priceless adjunct to outward splendour and inward dedication: no less than majesty itself. An indefinable aura, at the same time gracious, affable, untroubled, august, Olympian and debonair, to which few commoners and no chance-fed dictators or hungry and fortuitously nourished heads of state, whether beefy or scrawny, can possibly aspire. I hope you won't think me a reactionary or a snob when I say that these random figureheads have neither the breeding nor the feeding.

'I see by your puzzled brow,' Mr Vortigern continued, 'that you have spotted the fallacy in my theory. How could each of us have eight million ancestors in the fourteenth century – for we all have the same number, however obscure and hungry – when the population of England after the Black Death was under a million? You conclude that most of them were the same. Rightly. They were pluralist progenitors. It narrows the triangle and inter-relates us all. Remember, too, that if we take up a fundamentalist position, this expanding fan must begin to taper at some point, finally dwindling to Adam and Eve: two pyramids stuck base to base forming a lozenge.

'Each of us is at the bottom of one of these huge human rhomboids.' He described one in the air with four malacca strokes. 'This means that sooner or later you are related to everyone in the island. A glorious and intimidating thought.' His stick, leaving the rhomboid in mid-air like an invisible hatchment, soared in ample sweeps, symbolizing universal kinship – and then fell static, aimed at a figure lying supine on the grass. A Herculean and bearded tramp, his boots removed and a stove-in bowler over his eyes, snored contentedly among the mandarin ducks and the sheldrakes. 'That grimy old boy is sure to be a relation of yours. And of mine too, of course. He looks as though he enjoys his food. I would dearly like to slip him a fiver. After all, blood is thicker than water . . .'

We paused on the Regent's bridge, the crook of his stick safe over his arm once more while he lit a new cigar.

'But I fear I digress,' he resumed. His words were scanned by thoughtful puffs. 'It is odd that *solid* gluttony has inspired so small a literature – outside cookery books I mean – compared to its liquid form. There is Rabelais, of course, and the "Eloge de la Gourmandise", and the amazing Norman guzzling in Flaubert, and there must be more. Des Esseintes' black banquet in Huysmans doesn't really count: it was aesthetic, not gastronomic. But there is no end to poems in praise of wine. Hundreds of them! And some of the best prose of our younger writers – Waugh and Connolly, for instance – is dedicated to it. Those beautiful similes! Wines that steal up to one like shy fawns, and other delightful comparisons! They are charming! Charming, but hopeless. These gifted writers face the same problem as mystics attempting to convey their experiences in the language of profane love.'

He watched a pelican preening its breast-feathers for a moment. 'What a pity the same device is so seldom used in a derogatory sense: Algerian that charges like a rhinoceros, port-types that draw alongside like charabancs, liqueurs that reek like a bombed scent factory! Yes, blame, as well as praise, should be codified. Michelin allots stars for merit, and rightly. We follow them across France like voracious Magi. Vortigern's Guide would have them, too, but also a scale of conventional signs to warn my readers. A bicarbonate pill first, then a basin, a stretcher, an ambulance and, finally, a tombstone.

'Or perhaps, in extreme cases, a skull and crossbones: robbery and extortion as well as poisoning. For these malefactors are the true sinners. They, and the criminal accomplices who swallow their wicked handiwork without a murmur. These accessories after the fact are guilty of a far greater sin than gluttony.' Mr Vortigern's voice had assumed a sepulchral note. 'I refer to Despair.

'Surely it is not casuistry to say that neglect of the fruits of the earth is doubting divine providence? Why do sturgeons swim in the Volga? Why do trout glitter and dart, what makes oysters assemble at Colchester and plovers lay their forbidden eggs? Why do turtles doze in the Seychelles and crustaceans change their carapaces and mushrooms rise from their dunghills and truffles lead sunless lives in Périgord and grouse dwell in the Pictish mists? Why do strawberries ripen and why do vine tendrils grow in those suggestive corkscrews? Why is the snail on the thorn? Is it to test us or is it a kindly providence at work? But the Fathers have spoken. It's no good trying to shift the blame or to say that sin lies only in excess. How can one eat caviar in moderation? There is another peculiar thing about gluttony: its physical penalties may be the heaviest, but it is the sin that leaves us with the lightest deposit of guilt. One feels like St Augustine – of Hippo, not Canterbury – postponing his reformation. "Give me frugality and sobriety, Oh Lord," one might paraphrase him, "but not yet." *Sed noli modo!* But it's no good. Cerberus and the hailstones are waiting.' Big Ben chimed its preliminary tune and began to toll the hour.

'There,' Mr Vortigern said, 'is the note of doom. I must go . . . The time for emendation of life grows shorter. And the time for further backsliding too . . . *Sed noli modo! Sed noli modo!*' His voice had regained its wonted buoyancy and his eyes were akindle. 'Are you free this evening? Capital. Come to me at eight o'clock. Don't be late. I won't tell you what we are going to have, but I think you will like it. The condemned men will eat a hearty dinner.'

Some Architectural Notes

The Spectator, 24 September 1994

1. THE GREEK STONES SPEAK

'Metope with anyone?'

'A mutule friend.'

'Arris? 'E's a regula guy! Won't admit him pediment.'

'He'll abacus up?'

'Well, he's echinus on.'

'Capital!'

(*entasis*) 'Your façade speaks volutes!'

'Yes, but she astragal with her dentils, boss!'

'Hollow moulding?'

(*pendentive*) 'What a cavetto!'

'Well, I'm not soffit, Adytum last night . . .'

'He scotia there!'

'My cornice something Ionic!'

'Tried pilasters? Or a pillar entablature used to? Triglyph for relief, annule see!'

'No! Don't palmette off on me!'

('He'scotus all wrong!

What a cella!!')

'*Pronaos, but antefix!*'

('*He's in antis!*'

'*He's all of a dado!*'

'*In a stylobate!*')

'Peristyle?'

'No *Hypo*style!'

Archi*trave*!'   (He torus apart)

'Doric . . .'

'What, Gable?'

'We'll frieze in this gutta!'

'Do you . . . caryatid . . . ?'

'Mm! But don't telamon!'

(*Intercolumniation*)

'Ah! I feel like a taenia old!'
'Don't come an acropolis! Stoa 'nother?'
'Yeth! Cyma 'gain, plinth! Your lapith lovely!'
'Centaur-mental!'
(*Necking*)
'This is parados!'
(*base fluting and tympanum*): 'O tholos mio!'

II. THE GOTHIC NORTH

'In transept?'
  '*¡Si, aumbry!*'
'Dancing steps?'
'Yes. Who's that ball-flower? Newel?'
'Rose Window, a module. Trumeau's dorter, by a dormer tie.'
'Romanesque! . . . Engaged column?'
'No, free-standing. No offspring or diaper-work. But she's finial!
Pyx, you've no credence!'
  'Shall I . . . ashlar?'
'Not a chancel a mullion, with those clustered piers!'
'Tester?'
  'Wish I hagioscope!'
'Why not triforium, tell a clerestory? Or play a mandorla just in
caisson?'
  '*O cladding voussoir lunette* –' (*coffers, getting cloister*). 'May I, a spire –'
(*no responds*)
  '*If you squinch, aisle screen!*'

'There! You've sedilia can!'
  'Where's that organ?'
  'Aisle in choir. . .'

(*'Cantoris win the bolection?'*
  '*How decani tell?*')

'Corbel!'
  'Arch?'
  'Guilloche's off! They're laying on stanchion.'
  ('Put those Saxon here, Norman!'
  'Got the basket, arch? Bell hamper?'
  'Open the chamfer! Nook shaft!')

'Fillets? Impost? Herringbone? Fresco buttress? Jamb? Scallops? Vessica piscis?'

'*Ogee!*'

'Or broach the string course? Hammer-beam?'

'I'm not perpendicular, Arch.'

'Haunch, or rib?'

'*The lattice!*'

'Span? Crockets? *Mould?*'

'Some more trefoil, please.'

(*pointed*)' You're putting on flèche.'

(*beams*) 'Why wear a truss?'

'Another bowtell, Arch?'

'Mm! Fillet up – don't joggle!'

(*stained glass*)

'*Scroll!*'

'*Scroll!*'

'Dog-tooth? One wing?'

(*Flushwork! In their cusps again! They gargoyle in it, ravelin barmkins!*)

'I've a niche, a pinnacle on my postern . . .'

'Your reredos? Let me lancet!' (*skew-back*) '*Don't arcuate!*' (*stoups*)

'*Misericorde!*'

'Turn it up, Arch! Are you a crypt, o choir!' (*Rood-loft her . . .*)

(*Arch groins*): 'Billet me on the dome!'

'A stretcher!'

'Call an ambulatory!'

'Have a squint, or he'll piscina minute!'

'Look what that dripstone!'

'Who canopied here? Who's coping?'

('*A bit steeple! Not crocket! A debased spandrel! Re vaulting! Give him a dozen flying buttresses up the apse! Rough strapwork! Pulvinate him!' etc*)

(*Springing, archivolts undercroft*)

'Arch is a slype now.'

'They're both sleepers.'

'Won't liern! . . .'

'No. *Arcades ambo.*'

'Overhung?'

'Per apse, when dais done . . .'

In Andalucia and Estremadura

from an undated letter to Diana Cooper

This letter to Diana Cooper tells of a holiday that Paddy and Joan spent in Spain in early 1975, with their friends Jaime and Janetta Parlade. They were joined by Xan Fielding, one of Paddy's brothers-in-arms in occupied Crete during the war, and Magouche Phillips. She and Xan were to marry in 1979.

Spain. This was all glory. We arrived there on Christmas Eve, met by Janetta at Malaga, driving a Range Rover that could knock a hole in the Bastille. The house, Tramores, is marvellous, built about a ruined Moorish tower in a high valley of the Sierra de Ronda, in an interlock of mountains forested with pine and cork-oak, where wild boar roam (I saw five), in a great sweep of land owned by Jaime's father. It's very comfortable; blazing fires, half-manor house, half-farm, where the life centres on a great beamed kitchen with flags underfoot, hanging hams, a green parrot, two dogs and a cat in the same basket, a brisk house-boy called Miguel, and Zara, a bulky and always smiling she-Moor from the Atlas. One lolls about hobnobbing and swigging while Janetta, (with the same ease as someone else absent-mindedly knitting), chops, grates, strains and bastes, imperceptibly wielding colanders, rolling-pins, bunches of herbs, etc. till she whisks something stupendous out of the oven. Everyone is suddenly round a table, with a crimson baize cloth falling to the ground to keep in the heat of the great brass brazier underneath, and our toes warm; candles twinkling, the parrot's music-hall interruptions quelled under green baize and red wine gurgling out of a fascinating involuted jug, like an alchemist's flagon. I love Janetta and Jaime. Different but congruent, they have some light and fine-boned quality in common. He's busy building, planting and decorating all day, while Janetta crunches across the valleys to the neighbouring towns in that tank of hers – assembling still more delicious things for us all to eat. Lovely walks through the woods, which are full of streams – so much water seemed a miracle to our parched Maniot eyes – that the tiered gardens thrive like a marvellous jungle under control; in the evening there is chat, music and the Dictionary Game into the small hours. The participants were the four of us, Robin Campbell, Frances Partridge, and for a few days, Xan and Magouche. Both are radiant. There were visits to and from Gerald Brenan and Bunny Garnett, those two hale Bloomsbury stags; and lots of cheerful Spaniards.

For the New Year we all travelled west along the coast, peering south at Gibraltar and the Moorish mountains beyond, stopping to swallow countless sherries and about 100,000 tiny elvers, netted on their way to the Sargasso Sea, in Tarifa, Europe's southernmost point, where the inhabitants of the flat-topped houses have been going mad from the east wind since the dawn of time. We looked down on Trafalgar; and saw the New Year in among the crowds in the Cathedral Square of Cadiz where we stayed two nights, gazing at Zurbaráns and mooning along the lanes of the oldest inhabited city of Europe; the eccentric tropical trees that tower above the roofs here were planted by conquistadors hot-keel from the Indies. At Sanlucar we ate many large prawns in booths overlooking the estuary of the Guadalquivir and inspected a harem of beautifully groomed dapple-greys owned by Mrs Terry, (a famous sherry-growing lady), each preening in its spotless loose-box with lashes lowered, like odalisques. An ocean-going liner slid upstream across the landscape on the invisible Guadalquivir, Seville-bound under racing clouds and gulls. Here we turned inland, and to the north, looking out at the rock-perched castle and church of Arcos de la Frontera, after stopping for sips in Jerez, and, led by a ghostly white Carthusian, explored the overgrown Gothic precincts of the Cartuja there. (Last time, we drew rein at the tremendous battlements of Arcos to feast with the very nice English Marquesa de Tamarón who reigns in it, but it was too late and we had to press on.) It was a dramatic landscape, with night falling fast. Next stop, Ronda – I bet you know this wonderful Roman-Moorish-Spanish town, lifted into the sky, complete with bullring and churches and palaces on tremendous cliffs sundered by a narrow chasm from top to bottom, right in the town's heart, so that one peers over the bridge and down through the layers of choughs, jackdaws, ravens, swallows and crows to a cascade that looks a mile below. In the hills outside, we stayed in a farmhouse of Jaime's father standing as amply as a rectory in a forest of cork-oak. Joan, Jaime and I went for long rides through the ilex-forested hills on near-Palominos with blonde tails and manes, Moorish saddles and box-stirrups. They have a marvellous gait of their own, silk-smooth and tireless. From the hills we looked down on the wide airy waves of country, symmetrically criss-crossed with olives, hill towns rising on cones here and there, with white houses like flocks of doves settling, each village with a domed church and a ruin: Visigothic or Moorish or Spanish. Enormous herds of sheep and champagne-coloured goats grazed in the steep cork-woods, raising clouds of golden dust as they were herded back to their folds against the sunset. The horizon was bounded by a score of sierras as jagged as cut-out paper. Joan and I stayed two nights in the olive-grove house the other side of Ronda that Magouche is turning into a beautiful nest, helped by Xan: lucky birds with twigs in their beaks.

After three weeks, frightened of overstaying but bidden to stay, J and J planned a marvellously slow and adventurous joint return to Madrid, whence we had to take wing. So we clanked off happily in Janetta's siege-engine across Andalucia, stopping to see a beautiful life-size Roman bronze of an ephebe at Antequera, then on through Osuna to Seville, where we stayed in an hotel almost in the orange-tree-shaded cloisters of the Cathedral; eating an early 11 p.m. dinner in a rowdy joint beyond the plateresque Ayuntamiento and Snake Street. The walls indoors were so thickly covered with azulejos that every syllable uttered by the hundred munchers within bounced from wall to wall resoundingly as a fives ball. Cowering among these massed reverberations and echoes, and rivalling them with our own output, we drank ourselves into a blissful and travel-worn stupor, which was only broken by the clanging bells of the Giralda next day. Morning passed in the Cathedral; then a stroll under the oranges of the Alba house, where J had to pick up or drop something (its lady was away); then we went to buy some boxes of sweets (for presents) from a convent of enclosed Carmelites, no, Augustinians, I think. They were delivered through one of those wooden turntables that totally hide one's interlocutrix but encourage hobnobbing. Ours was an old friend of Jaime's, so the transaction involved much banter and laughter with the cheery wimpled chatterbox in the nether shadows. We crossed the Guadalquivir and stopped to peer at the Roman theatre at Italica, and wonderful mosaic floors with game birds and pygmies waging war on cranes and crocodiles. (Scipio founded Italica and Trajan, Hadrian and Theodosius were all born there.) Thence into the wilds of Estremadura and the Sierra Morena. It rolled along in wavering hillls and mountains suitably windswept and bleak, forested with cork-oak under whose branches enormous herds of black pigs were swallowing acorns against time, under their benign drovers' gaze, and almost visibly expanding. We stopped at a wayside posada beyond the stricken hamlet where Zurbarán was born. Here, tented by a table-cloth from the thighs down and with our forty toes clustering close to the charcoal's glow, we ate a brew of lentils and chick peas with jugged hare to follow and then partridges, under the gaze of courteous swineherds.

The next night was very different. We got to the steep castled town of Trujillo at nightfall. The ledge-like plaza, surrounded by arcaded houses, a palace or two and a cathedral, was dominated by an enormous bronze equestrian knight in plate armour with tossing plumes and a long sword. It looked familiar . . . It was the cast of an identical statue in the Plaza de Armas in Lima, of Pizarro, the conqueror of Peru! He was born here, a poor nobleman – so poor, in fact, that Prescottt says he was suckled by a kind-hearted sow on the steps of his parish church; gathering strength for his subsequent looting of all the sheet-gold from the sun-temple of the Incas in Cuzco. Here we dossed down in a vast palace of the Mendoza-Chavez family, owned and visited fleetingly every year or so by its Whitney owners, but inhabited in between-whiles by a hospitable Portuguese friend of Jaime's. The state was tremendous. A troop of servants unloaded our shabby effects, giant cocktail-shakers rattled, black velvet armorial curtains stiff with gold wire closed behind us one after the other down groin-vaulted corridors; bath-oil-scented steam enclouded us in Poppaea-like bathrooms and we dined in a forest of candelabras, watched by portraits of the Catholic Kings, the Cardinal-Infant of the Netherlands, Joan the Mad and Pedro the Ceremonious of Aragon; retiring at last to four-posters that could have slept three infantas abreast in their farthingales, or seven in their shifts. (Have you noticed the strong resemblance between the Infantas of Velasquez and Evelyn?* Especially the younger ones. I was struck by it again, later on with Las Meninas in the Prado.) We explored castles and churches all morning, banqueted sumptuously in the palace; then crept on to Caceres. It's full of conquistadors' palaces, some with shields on them showing a great sun and said to mean descent from Montezuma. Early storks were already repairing last year's nests here, after their season further south, on belfries: much roomier than the minarets over the sea that they had just left. (I forgot to say that, the day before, we had halted in Merida, where we marvelled at a wonderful Roman theatre with a nearly complete proscenium of sixty or seventy Corinthian pillars; also marvellous mosaics in a temple of Mithras, in rather flashy colours; dawns, sunsets, winds, constellations, tempests, chariots and gambolling dolphins.) That night we slept at Placencia in a draughty hotel, where the only other guests in the dining room were two dignified, deafish and parrot-voiced crones, who had dined there every night for thirty-seven years. *We nearly took their table by mistake* . . . Our journey was becoming rather like a picaresque novel: (Chap. XXXIII: 'How our four friends reached the old city of Placencia, what befell them there and the company they found. The Innkeeper's story' etc.) We craned at Gothic vaulting in the Cathedral next day, at the clustered piers, the blaze of gilt on the retables and Madonnas dressed as Mary Stuart, their pincushion-hearts seven times transfixed. Carved wooden Vices and Virtues ran riot over the Burgundian choir stalls.

Our next halt, where the wild last stretch of Estremadura climbs into the Gredos range, was rare, memorable and seldom visited, perhaps because of its remoteness. A small abbey is peopled by a little community of white-habited Hieronymite monks. Damp and sequestered, it is lost among chestnuts, walnut and ilex woods. To the wall of the church a two-storeyed kind of shooting box clings like a limpet, with airy loggias, a garden running wild among the brambles below, and a clogged fish pool. It is Yuste, where the great Charles V retired after his abdication in favour of his son Philip II! The walls of the seven rooms inside are hung with black velvet in mourning for

* Waugh.

his beautiful Empress Isabella; all rather small, with crucifixes and four-posters; and, forestalling the Escurial, a wide squint pierces the wall, aimed at the high Altar so that the Emperor could see 'God made and eaten every day'* as he lay gout-ridden in bed. He didn't take Holy Orders; in fact, he kept an advisory hold on the Empire's affairs and wars. A copy of Titian's portrait of him hung over the velvet, the one with his hand on a languishing hound's pate. His small court and staff and guard were quartered in the glum hamlets round about, complaining bitterly. He was particularly fond of fish, so every stream, river and pool for miles was assiduously fished to keep him in trout, pike and eels, so our wan conducting Hieronymite murmured; then he pointed out in the crypt the trough his body reclined in for a decade (with his head under the high Altar) till Philip II, having finished the Escurial, whisked it away to entomb it in the state that became a Holy Roman Emperor. Don John of Austria was present at his deathbed, not knowing he was the Emperor's natural son; the kind wife of a chamberlain brought him up as hers in the next village, where they were billeted. He only learnt who he was when Charles's will was read; a hardy boy of thirteen. Then there was no stopping him till the Battle of Lepanto, a decade later, when he utterly destroyed the Turkish fleet. We left this strange place with pounding hearts.

On we rumbled, Janetta and Jaime taking turns at the wheel of the great vehicle; breaking bread at 3 p.m. in the scowling keep of Oropesa, which had been turned into a parador inside; on again, with the snowy peak of Almanzor ('El Mansur' Arabic for 'the Conqueror') floating high in the distance; through Talavera, thinking of Wellington's victory; until, late in the afternoon, TOLEDO soared . . .

Well, darling Diana, you know all about this . . . I was flung into a trance from which I've not quite come round, never having seen it before. We stayed just outside the town, looking across the Tagus from roughly the point where El Greco must have set up his easel. There was the Alcantara Bridge and its barbicans, there St Martin's,

---

* From Browning's 'The Bishop orders his Tomb', a great favourite of Duff's and Diana's.

and between them, the twisting river, the cliffs and the complex hill
with the rebuilt Alcazar, the cathedral, a score of monasteries and
palaces and churches; with wintry grass green all round it, and, as
though to oblige, the weather, which had been like summer in
Andalucia, windy in Estremadura, and splashing into occasional rain
after we had crossed into New Castile, turned into just the fidgety
grey and silver disturbance of cloud that my fellow-Cretan lets loose
over Toledo. (It was like – do you remember? – being suddenly confronted outside Florence by the background of Benozzo Gozzoli's
Coming of the Magi – on that tortoise-crawl from I Tatti with B.B.,*
ages ago?) We were particularly lucky next morning. Arriving at the
cathedral the moment it was opened, we joined a congregation of
two in a little side-chapel where Mass is still said or sung in the
Mozarabic Rite, which differs considerably from the ordinary
Tridentine Mass, but is nevertheless O.K. at Rome, because it is a survival of the Rite used by the Visigoths for the centuries they were
under the Moslem Emirs of Toledo; *and it is still in Latin*; which makes
me think that poor Auberon,† recoiling from the new vernacular
missal after Vatican II, might have found solace as a Mozarab, instead
of becoming a Ukrainian Uniat.

Replete with marvels (and also with delicious trout from the
Tagus, eaten in the corner of the Plaza Zocodover) we rumbled out
under the great eagle'd barbican, and I dozed off – 'forty winks' is
called 'a bishop's nap' in Spanish: una siesta de obispo, 'sicta de
obipo' in Andalucia. I was roused from mine by the car stopping in
front of a little convent in the plain which Jaime knew, where a white
Mercederian sister showed us into the church to contemplate the
marvellous El Greco picture of St Ildefonso (pc enclosed). By sundown we were storming into Madrid; we stayed at a vast old-
fashioned, station-like hotel called the Victoria, rather nice with
labyrinthine furlongs of passage where one always lost one's way, by
mistake bursting in on loving couples, clergymen reading their bre-
viaries, or solitary Negroes frying aubergines on a primus . . . Here
we haunted the Prado for every hour it stayed open, while the

* Bernard Berenson.
† Auberon Herbert.

evenings were given over to social glamour and late feastings; until, two days later, there were rainy farewells at the airport, and off we flew. Across my lap lay a reminder that it hadn't all been a wonderful dream; viz. an enormous ham from Estremadura (cured and smoked, I was told, in Salamanca), muslin-wrapped, with the trotter still projecting intact . . . the trotter won all hearts at the customs in Athens.

So here we are, back in the cold and wintry Mani, with nothing planned till March, when Robin Fedden and I canoe down two northern Greek rivers – the Aliacmon and the Acheloös. One's waist is laced into light skiffs, it seems, like the waists of those Infantas in their farthingales. Before rapids, one lands and trudges along the bank with the boats upside down on one's head, like those salmon-fishers in Marvell.* I'm scribbling in the studio with great olive-logs blazing. Through the window I can see Joan (who sends her love) summoning her troop of cats to dinner; massed miaows ascend, and their tails wave like the sea; while, over the wall, I can hear Lela (who sends her love too) scattering corn to the chickens . . .

Paddy.

* Andrew Marvell (1621–78), 'Upon Appleton House':

> But now the *salmon-fishers* moist
> Their leather boats begin to hoist;
> And, like *Antipodes* in shoes,
> Have shod their *heads* in their canoes.
> How *tortoise-like*, but not so slow,
> These rational *Amphibii* go!
> Let's in: for the dark hemisphere
> Does now like one of them appear.

Christmas Lines for Bernard of Morlaix

The Times Literary Supplement, 21 December 1979

Urbs Sion aurea, patria lactea, cive decora,
Omne cor obruis omnibus obstruis, et cor et ora
Nescio, nescio quae jubilatio lux tibi qualis
Quam socialia gaudia, gloria quam specialis, etc.

> – Bernard of Morlaix in the Pyrenees, Benedictine
> monk of Cluny, *fl. c.* 1230

O golden Zion and long-fabled lion, both legend and hearsay,
Murmur at neap-tide, warmer by sheep-side, hear what the deer say:
'Smooth shuttles flickering where threads are bickering, o loom of
    doomsday
– Who can forestall the theft of either warp or weft, what woof or
    tomb-stay?
Why are the gold bells spinning their cold spells on Christmas
    morning?
Better than frost in May, rime on our hosting day, born shorn, not
    scorning
Cowsheds and mangers and herdsmen and strangers, while the wild
    snow falls.
Blown by the weather one shiny feather from the black crow falls.
(Hay-rack and waggon-gloom, strake not a spoke too soon, whole
    hubs unfelloed,
– Can this brass jingle, can these battered swingletrees haul half a
    hay-load?)'
In the rank chamber of dark dank December the angels and Angles
Scatter bright nosegays that flatter white rose-bays with tinkles and
    spangles.
(See how this lighter loot settles on rind and root, unfangled
    mangolds!)
King's Lynn and Chichester link sin, the niches stir, saints faint with
    painting,
Tongues tintinnabulate, rotten rungs escalate, all saints are fainting.
(Rats in the belfries and bats are the small fry ginger-cats laid low.)

Congeners congregate, Gregory contemplates. (All hail his halo!)
'No one to whistle to under the mistletoe,' throbs, sobs the robin.
'Better to chew the cud out of the sleet and mud,' Snowball tells
    Dobbin.
Hark to the ding-dong bell! What does the sing-song spell? Hungers
    and angers?
Welcome the bright shade's glow, no deadly nightshade now
    endangers mangers.
(Handle creaks, cattlecake flies like a shuttlecock, rattles the pailful:
Sniff while the harm of death dies by the charm of breath, all bales
    unbaleful.)
Daisy and Buttercup on lazy fodder sup, what crunch of munching
Clover by candlelight! These drovers can turn night brighter by
    bunching
Sticks in a pyramid, fixing their beer amid midnight's mad shadows
While thunder rumbles on Wrekin and Dumbleton's sheds, steads
    and meadows.
Repining in mantled clime, pining for antler-time, drear deer lie
    fallow.
Bell in the splinter thin! Icy in winterspring, ringtime rings hollow.
(Cockcrows cut bray and boom, down cowpats drop-like doom, a
    crumplehorn fanfare
Sounds in the coughing smoke; let no dull coffin-stroke thump for
    an encore.)
Small hours are donkey-grey, solan-geese honk-away, farm barns are
    yawning –
– What franker frankincense, frankly, can rank in scents with fawn-
    born dawning?
Weak we in Christmas week, lifetime a shrieking streak – lend
    length and strengthen!
Poultice the harm away, charm the short solstice day! Send strength
    and lengthen!